**Scripting
for video and audiovisual media**

. . . a Joye forever!

Scripting
for video and audiovisual media

Dwight V. Swain

Focal Press, London & Boston

Focal Press
is an imprint of the Butterworth Group
which has principal offices in
London, Boston, Durban, Singapore, Sydney, Toronto, Wellington

First published 1981
   Reprinted 1983

British Library Cataloguing in Publication Data

Swain, Dwight V.
   Scripting for video and audiovisual media
   1. Audio-visual materials
   I. Title
   001.553   TK5859.06

   ISBN 0-240-51075-5

American Library of Congress Catalog No. 80–41401

Typeset by Tradespools Ltd, Frome, Somerset
Printed in Scotland by Thomson Litho Ltd, East Kilbride
Bound by Hunter & Foulis Ltd, Edinburgh

Contents

Foreword

The job is there to be done. Somehow or other, and for whatever reason, some sort of audiovisual presentation must come into being. It may be a filmstrip, or a three-dimensional display with sound, or a unit of programmed instruction. Or perhaps the medium has not yet even been determined.

What counts is that you are involved. Or would like to be.

And what a wonderful opportunity it is! Imagine the fun the men and women had who first conceived the delightful *Small World* show at Disneyland ... the brilliant displays at Paris' Musée de l'Homme ... the marvellous demonstrations in London's Natural History and Science Museums.

Or, recall Norman McLaren working out his unique, hand-painted, synchronised animation for *Fiddle De Dee* at the National Film Board of Canada ... the slide shows and filmstrips and variable-speed presentations in a hundred industrial and teaching sequences ... the history in still photographs at Amsterdam's Anne Frank House ... in-house video productions for schools and hospitals and businesses ... sound-and-light shows and chalk-talks and overhead projections without number.

The very thought of such is enough to send shivers through many of us. It is the sort of challenge that sparks anyone's creative streak.

The only trouble is, you are forced to admit that at this point you know little or nothing about how to tackle such a job: to script the material required.

That is where this book comes in. It is designed to give every teacher, every school administrator, every librarian, every museum staffer, every industrial and organisational and governmental and military PR and advertising man/woman the information and guidance he/she needs to take the first few steps.

Those steps are the most crucial in your career, really. Without them, you will never gain a foothold. And inept and fumbling though they be, you are the only one who can essay them. Grope your way through them; try, and fail, and try again, and experience will do the rest. In spite of all difficulties, all handicaps, you will become an AV writer.

I think you will find its challenges and rewards more than worth the effort.

In a field as broad as audiovisual, no one person has all the answers.

That is why I am so grateful to the many friends and associates who have contributed so generously from their experience to provide facts and insights on specialised areas, as well as freely granting permission for use of excerpts from AV scripts and script-related materials. (Needless to say, they are in no way responsible for, nor do they necessarily agree with, the views I express in this book.)

Specifically, I want to thank Ron Acree, Director, Tourism Promotion, Oklahoma Department of Tourism and Recreation; Art Arjibay, US Postal Service Training & Development Institute Technical Center, Norman, OK; Loyd G. Dorsett, President, Dorsett Educational Services, Inc., Norman, OK; Robert and Wanda Duncan, AV writers; Mark Elder, AV writer; Valerie Evans, proprietor, The Bookshop, San Jose, Costa Rica; Gloria Freeland, News Editor, San Jose (Costa Rica) *News*; William Fulton, Professor Emeritus of Education, University of Oklahoma; Andre Gazut, Swiss Romane TV, Geneva, Switzerland; Will Gibson, US Postal Service Training & Development Institute Technical Center, Norman, OK; Townsend Godsey, AV writer; Candace Greene, AV Coordinator, Stovall Museum, University of Oklahoma; Wesley H. Greene, President, International Film Bureau, Inc., Chicago; Chris Hewes, Television Assistant, Baptist Medical Center, Oklahoma City, OK; Bruce Hinson, Associate Professor of Journalism and Director of Broadcast News Sequence, University of Oklahoma; Charles N. Hockman, Professor of Journalism and Director of Motion Picture Production, University of Oklahoma; Russell F. Neale, Executive Vice President, Hastings House, Publishers, Inc., New York; Charles A. Palmer, Executive Producer, Parthenon Pictures, Los Angeles, CA; William E. Pryor, Producer/ Director, Wm. E. Pryor Creative Services, Kansas City, MO; Thom A. Renbarger, Dorsett Educational Services art staff, Norman, OK; Lester V. Roper, AV writer, Jay Smith, Associate Professor of Education, University of Oklahoma; Ida Sloan Snyder, former Director of Communications, National Board, Young Women's Christian Association; Leonard Snyder, former Director of Graphics/Publications, YMCA of Greater New York; Rachel Stevenson, Director of Filmstrips, International Film Bureau, Inc., Chicago. IL; Chris L. Steves, Television Production Supervisor, Baptist Medical Center, Oklahoma City, OK; Carl Steward, AV director/ producer, Tampa, FL; Richard L. Thorp, Supervisor, Media Productions, US Postal Service Training & Development Institute Technical Center, Norman, OK; David B. Warren, Dorsett Educational Services art staff,

Norman, OK; and Dick Weston, President, Rocket Pictures, Inc., Los Angeles, CA.

Warm appreciation goes also to those organisations granting permission to use script excerpts: Baptist Medical Center, Oklahoma City, OK; Dorsett Educational Services, Inc., Norman, OK; International Film Bureau, Inc., Chicago, IL; National Board, Young Women's Christian Association of the USA; Rocket Pictures, Inc.; US Postal Service Training & Development Institute Technical Center; and YMCA of Greater New York.

I also must extend special thanks to four people: to Paul Petzold, for suggesting that I write this book; to my wife, Joye Raechel Swain, who discussed, typed, and scratched my back and my mind; and to my daughters, Rocio and Antonia, who maintained their good humour and helped me to maintain mine—sometimes—during the months which I was scripting *Scripting*.

Finca Las Lluvias   D.V.S.
Alajuela, Costa Rica

Part I
The parts and the process

1   Ideas vs media

Time: 1969.

Place: Los Angeles, California.

I was preparing the screen treatment for a science fiction film which, as it turned out, never was produced—a not unusual state of affairs in Hollywood's never-never land.

In the process, however, I met a young man totally possessed by a Stunning Idea: he proposed to rent some acres of space on the old Paramount Ranch, tether a gigantic balloon hundreds of feet in the air in the centre of the tract, and then project avant-garde films on its under surface. His audience? Thousands of the period's hippies, whom he envisioned as lying on the greensward in their sleeping bags while they wallowed in assorted fleshpots and the film's psychedelics.

It was a lunatic notion, of course, and it never did get off the ground, either literally or figuratively. It does serve, however, as a springboard to our topic of the moment: the wide, wide range of audiovisual media and presentations.

The young man's dream was an *audiovisual* concept, ie one that is designed to be heard (audio) and seen (visual) at the same time. And while his approach seems far out, the day may come when someone not only puts it into practice, but is hailed as a genius for so doing. If you do not believe me, I can only cite a case from the opposite end of the spectrum. It centres on a vehicle called a 'drug-mobile' (of which more later) designed by a friend of mine for use in a campaign against narcotics addiction. Later adopted in modified form by the Department of Defense to carry its anti-dope message to troops in Vietnam, it featured twelve slide projectors and three film units, all coordinated and operating simultaneously in accordance with the patterns set by a digital programmer.

The virtues of AV

As noted above, audiovisual media (AV) are those which offer their message to an audience through both the eye and the ear—in most instances simultaneously. A wide range of studies indicate that AV is one of the most effective ways to convey information and/or put across ideas. Where students are concerned, a recent report says that AV helps them learn more, retain better and improve performance.

At the same time, AV is widely available and adaptable to an amazing range of circumstances and situations. Yet such generalities are just that: general. Only as you get down to specifics, individual cases, does the true impact of this unique amalgam of media hit home.

Item: Slides of life among Chihuahua's Tarahumara Indians, accompanied by an anthropologist/lecturer's continuing commentary.

Item: What is sometimes termed a 'sound-and-light show' in which lights are coordinated with music to create a virtually hypnotic effect on the audience.

Item: Instruction in use of a complicated electronic device, the oscilloscope, presented via a special variable-speed projector.

Item: An 'underwater treasure hunt' in a simulated diving bell that creates effects by means of shadowy passages, wobbly ladders, flashing signals; taped sound effects and verbal orders; jerks, bumps and vibrations to mimic the craft's descent and movement over a lake floor; film (seen through 'portholes') of swimming fish, sunken wrecks, half-buried 'treasure chests'.

Item: A class in changing fractions to decimals, presented as programmed instruction on individual teaching machines.

Item: A planetarium's tour of the summer heavens—the stars and planets moving through their courses while a commentator describes what is being seen.

Item: A college's in-house video program, showing the enrolment procedures step by step to incoming freshmen.

Item: A filmstrip featuring a new type of oilfield pumping unit. A taped sales talk, outlining the device's points of superiority, is synchronised to accompany the pictures.

Item: A museum's slide presentation on the age of dinosaurs.

Item: Tapes of psychodramatic role-playing situations, played back to stimulate discussion and analysis by workshop participants.

Item: Computerised war games, extrapolating the potential of each move/decision to the nth degree.

With all this versatility, audiovisual presentations also are, as mentioned, widely available. Tapes, slide shows and filmstrips can be produced by virtually anyone. Programmed instruction, in-house video, simulations and the like offer more (sometimes a great many more) complications but are being developed by an increasing number of creative packagers every day.

At the same time, however, this wide availability is to a degree a snare and a delusion. For while almost anyone can come up with some sort of AV program, to devise a *good* one is something else again. Quality demands that an additional factor be added.

That factor is a competent writer, even if you choose not to call him by that name. Yet here too confusion can develop. For when we talk of a writer in the audiovisual field what we really mean is less a wordsmith (though this aspect is of course important) than a 'conceptualiser', ie a person, male or female, skilled in conceiving, thinking through and organising a project. It goes without saying, too, that he/she should be thoroughly familiar with AV and its specialised problems.

Ever and always, the writer's work starts with an idea.

What *is* an idea?

In defining an idea, we reach a point where my stand is totally arbitrary and adamantly subjective: an idea is something that excites someone. Especially you.

As a point of departure in defending this position, take the case of my friend Robert Bloch, master horror writer and author of the book *Psycho*, from which Alfred Hitchcock's classic motion picture was adapted.

I scanned *Psycho* when it came out. It read well enough but I could see nothing in it to raise it above the level of any number of Bob's other tales. Indeed, there were several I would have rated higher. Then, along came Mr—pardon me, *Sir* Alfred—Hitchcock and the next thing I knew, *Psycho* was off, running and racking up multi-million dollar grosses.

What was the difference between me and Sir Alfred?

Where I was concerned, I enjoyed *Psycho* and that was about it. Sir Alfred? Clearly, *Psycho* as an idea excited him. That is, at some point or other it generated a sense of mounting, goal-orientated inner tension in him. It started creative juices flowing—juices that, channelled through Hitchcock's private genius, developed the said idea into one of the top-grossing films of all time.

On the other side of the fence, some years ago I wrote a short novel titled *The Transposed Man*. It was ordered and paid for in advance by a magazine that had bought nearly half a million words of copy from me and had never rejected a story. The editor decided to make an exception of *The Transposed Man*. It came back to me like a yo-yo on a string, with a letter six pages long that detailed its flaws and shortcomings and described revisions that would have made it a totally different story.

I still liked, that is was excited by, the original idea so I declined the request for revision, refunded the magazine's money and set about marketing the piece elsewhere.

To make a lengthy chronicle short, it sold: first, to an American magazine; then to a US paperback house; then as a British paperback; then in Germany and assorted other countries. Twice it almost was made into a film.

What lesson can we draw from all this?

An idea is only as good as your own reaction to it, your involvement with it. Where and how it originates is of no account. Sometimes an idea hits so hard it jolts you out of sleep in the middle of the night. On other occasions it may pop up as an off-the-top-of-the-head response to an unanticipated phone call or unforeseen assignment. It may be the product of routine brain-racking as you search for a theme for a new industrial fair display or a means of setting forth dull but essential data more vividly on the job. All that matters is that you scrabble through the farther reaches of your mind until you find that 'something-fresh-and-different' that in some indefinable way fits the situation at hand.

This is not to say that the said 'fresh-and-different' will always be all that fresh or that different: old ideas, refurbished, sometimes prove best of all. What counts is that, at whatever length and by whatever means, you track down an idea.

How do you know whether or not an idea is a *good* idea? You try it out on other people involved in the area of activity the idea affects to see if it excites them too. If it does not then it could be back to the old drawing-board for you, as the saying goes.

Here is a case in point. I had an absolutely smashing idea for a TV show episode. Off the top of his head, the story editor catalogued four previous occasions on which this idea had been the focal point of other shows.

Naturally, nothing like that ever will happen to you. Indeed, right now, you have an idea that turns you on. So, as per the suggestion above and in ad agency jargon, you run the idea up the flagpole and see if anyone salutes. If they do you are on your way with a good idea!

Before you start, however, and since it is an AV idea, ie one for sight/sound presentation, you need to ask yourself three questions:
1   Can this idea be communicated, effectively, by AV?
2   Do other AV materials already cover the ground?
3   Is anyone interested?

Anything can be communicated audiovisually: boolean algebra; relativity theory; gnostic philosophy; anything. Whether it can be communicated effectively is another question.

AV is best adapted to things you can see and hear. Yet if we apply that notion literally, it limits us to topics like carpentry, musical notation or real estate sales and we know that is not true.

The real issue, of course, is that every subject is potentially the basis of an effective audiovisual presentation—always providing that we can bring the imagination to bear on it in such a manner as to *make* it seen and heard. The issue really then becomes: have we worked up our idea in a manner calculated to fit it comfortably into audiovisual form? (We will take up *how* to do this in future chapters.)

What about those 'other AV materials' referred to in 2 above? If you are considering a filmstrip on the life cycle of the duck-billed platypus and you discover that three other explorations of the subject already exist, it stands to reason that yours must offer some distinctive plus if it is to sweep the field.

On the other hand, do not be too easily put off. A fair number of detective stories have seen print down through the years but that does not prevent a host of writers from producing new ones.

Point 3 was: is anyone interested (anyone with the money or muscle to do anything about the idea, that is)?

A friend of mine decided that a filmstrip to be titled *Poisonous Snakes of North America* would prove a sure-fire winner. A number of herpetologist acquaintances agreed it was a splendid subject. A major distributor refused to touch it, however. His comment was, 'I don't believe I'd sell six prints.' Others echoed his opinion.

Perhaps this is crass commercialism but you do have to take it into account.

Content and presentation

Assume, now, that you do have an idea that meets the requirements set forth above. Immediately you are faced with a new dilemma: precisely what do you want your module to say and how best can you say it?

In other words, the issue becomes one of content and presentation.

This can be more of a problem than meets the eye at first glance because, to coin a phrase, the exercise is one of different strokes for different folks. Your assumption that ulcers are psychogenetically induced or that the reality of flying saucers is universally accepted may not get the reaction you expect.

For that matter, even the basic information from which you are working may prove inaccurate.

Here is a case in point: my wife once was employed to script a programme intended to promote the work of a state's American Indian fashion designers. Attacking the project with enthusiasm, she soon discovered a fatal flaw in the thinking behind it: locating such designers was a major task. Few had telephones, no definite addresses were available for many and most fell into the category of cottage industry, producing only an occasional garment. Only three were geared to commercial standards.

It was hardly the programme the project's sponsors had envisioned. The piece ended up as a magazine article.

Similarly, where presentation is concerned, some of us like the light touch: others prefer profundity or its simulation. Straight chronological handling holds charms for many but there are those who are inclined towards a problem-solving or an inverted-pyramid mode of attack.

These are matters we will take up in much more detail later. For now, merely be forewarned that the issues do exist.

Selecting your best bet

'Everybody wants a multi-screen slide show. Talk them out of it if possible. Two projectors, a dissolver and a sync playback unit are as complex as they should get. Because all that other stuff isn't portable. I made $8000 converting a multi-screen slide show to 16mm film a couple of years ago because the guy who made the slide show never thought about how to transport eight projectors, etc, on a plane.'

So sayeth William E. Pryor, independent writer/producer. The point he raises is valid. Simplicity, the principle of parsimony, is the issue. Always search out the least involved approach unless, of course, flash and ostentation are important, as they indeed can be upon occasion.

As a matter of fact, even obscurantism has its uses as does stylisation, symbolism, satire and all sorts of things.

When so many factors are involved and when they are intertwined and counterbalanced to such a great degree, how *do* you pick the most effective approach?

In the last analysis it is a matter of becoming aware of variables and then weighing each against the others. In other words, painful as it may be, you have to make individual judgments. You may be wrong and being wrong can prove disastrous but that is the name of the game. If you cannot take the heat, stay out of the kitchen. (Even mixed metaphors sometimes do have their place!)

Right now, though, we need to consider certain vital matters . . .

2 Concepts, scripting—and you

Like everyone, I have my pleasures among which is visiting art galleries, large and small. In one gallery, a few years ago, I encountered a (to me, at least) unique presentation. On entering, I found myself in a garishly painted anteroom or foyer. A continuing mural showed a range of jungle vegetation—trees, ferns, orchids, strange plants and grasses and the like.

The dominant feature, however, was a wavy line, clearly defined and perhaps four inches wide, which wove in and out through the pictured landscape at a bit below the viewer's shoulder height (but on the ground in terms of the painting's perspective). It extended all the way round the room, its ends extending into an alcove that led to the gallery proper.

I was puzzled. After a few moments of trying, and failing, to make sense of it, I moved on into the alcove. Here the line ended. On the one side, it terminated in a fantastic serpent's head; on the other, in the serpent's tail. I laughed, of course, and then proceeded—a bit warily—to view the rest of the exhibit.

In the years since, however, I have come to wonder if what I saw offered a bit more than the visual joke I at first thought.

Specifically, the artist had developed a concept: a mental picture of a mode of presentation that might or should exist but did not. A meaningless line, given a head and a tail, became a snake and thus acquired meaning.

Please do not be offended when I tell you that this same principle, properly applied, is the ideational foundation stone of any AV project.

Concept, concept ...

Despite the dictionary, I view the word *concept* in a somewhat different light than that in which I view the word *idea*. For while both concepts and ideas spring from the mind, I see *concept* as tending to evidence somewhat more bones and meat.

To put it another way, the idea is an exciting trigger; the concept, to a greater or less degree, is the developed product of the shot the idea fired ... a mental picture of the 'mode of presentation that might/should exist but doesn't' mentioned above.

This is indeed the bedrock of any AV project: the foundation stone on which it is built.

How does a concept come into being? For me, at least, the process can be narrowed down to a fairly set procedure. First, of course, comes the idea but an idea about what?

Always, by its very nature, an idea centres on a subject, a topic.

Thus, your assignment is to devise a fresh new audiovisual programme for the natural history museum where you handle public relations. The topic is: parasites in man and animal.

Attacking this assignment, you scowl and scratch and pace the floor, hunting for some sort of angle a little less jaded than the familiar rats/fleas/lice approach.

Where did that reference to rats/fleas/lice come from? If you have an eye for your craft, it will have come from a list. Lists are one of the writer/conceptualiser's most useful tools. When you need an idea, do not bother agonising for the 'right' one. On the contrary, just make a list of all the notions you can think of, whether good, bad or indifferent. Before you know it, the right one will turn up.

So. Parasites in man and animal. Rats, fleas, lice. A dreary index. Yet what other possibilities are there, without sliding over into polysyllabic Latin exotica? Rats, fleas, lice, tapeworms—

Tapeworms!

Enter mounting, goal-oriented inner tension, that is, excitement. An idea has been born and so, quite possibly, have the makings of a key point.

A key point?

A key point is a clear, concise statement of the precise thesis (essential thought) you are trying to sell your audience. (Some call it a *core assertion*.)

Pointing up your point

Do you see the direction in which we are going?

First, we have a topic: a programme about parasites. Next, we have an idea: tapeworms as a possible vehicle. Then, we develop a key point, a precise thesis.

How do you get the key point? Taking your topic/idea (parasites/tapeworms) firmly in hand, you ask yourself a simple question: 'What about it?' The statement you get back in answer is, when properly refined, your key point.

'What about tapeworms?'

For no obvious reason, your mind replies 'Tapeworms are faithful friends.' This is a strange statement. Whether or not you can prove it remains to be seen. Meanwhile, however, you have acquired a spring-board: a point of departure that captures instant attention. You have something to work with, a concept to flesh out and develop.

Not all key points are as far out in left field as this one. Most are quite routine, for example 'Here's a widget that will save you money;' 'Mother's milk remains the best;' 'Play is children's work, a tool for growth'. Unless you search out and compress your project's message to some such sort of summarising statement, your presentation is unlikely to go in a properly straight line.

'Define the statement of the film in one sentence' commands Stan Hayward in his excellent list of rules for animation writers in John Halas's *Visual Scripting* and the advice applies equally well to every audiovisual form. If you cannot nail down your key point in one sentence, it follows that you do not have your concept clearly in mind.

Difficulty in this area may come from a variety of sources. The most common is that of trying to work with a mixed bag—bringing in extraneous issues, meandering instead of marching. Assuming you do have an idea and a clear, concise key point, it is time to move on, to learn how to put these elements in script form.

Why script it?

Am I being too obvious when I suggest that, to become truly meaningful, a concept must be taken out of your head and communicated to others? Indeed, failing to do so, how can you hope to interest them in it? Faced with new thoughts and unfamiliar ideas, we all need some sort of detailing or description to appraise and ponder.

Such a description, in audiovisual terms, is called a script. It sets forth your proposal in written form so that your associates may share/admire your brilliance. In the course of this, your work becomes subject to discussion. Confusions are cleared up, obscurities eliminated and points of difference resolved.

Even if you are going to produce your project yourself, write a script. The process of putting your thoughts on paper will sharpen your presentation immeasurably. Reflection, study, analysis, debate—whether with yourself or others—cannot help but improve your work.

Beyond this, a script will bring other benefits to you and your colleagues—eminently practical benefits. For one thing, a script simplifies production. The producer/director sees what settings/actors/action are specified and so can plan accordingly. If scheduling is involved, it can be more easily arranged. If impossibilities/impracticalities are called for, they can be pinpointed so that other more feasible elements may be substituted. If contradictions or errors have crept in, they can be cut out.

In addition, a script cuts costs. Improvisation almost always proves expensive. Through pre-planning at the script stage, production time—which is money—is saved. Low-budget elements can be substituted for high. Duplications can be spotted and short-cuts devised.

What kind of script?

Scripts come in all shapes and sizes, as you will see when you reach *Putting Principles to Work* in Part II of this book. Meanwhile, I will only observe that I have seen perfectly adequate scripts scribbled on the backs of envelopes and others that ran to hundreds of pages of typescript. (The old *Laugh-In* TV show, a programme frequently featuring wild audiovisuals, was particularly notable for its long, involved scripts.)

AV constitutes a unique and quite specialised area. Writing for it is very different from other types of writing although there are similarities. It calls for an orientation all its own that allows the writer considerably more leeway in choosing the pattern into which he will cast his work than do most channels of communication.

Thus, sometimes, a simple present-tense narrative presentation is perfectly acceptable. In other cases—multimedia, especially—the instrumentality is so new and the techniques so complicated that no standard script pattern has yet been developed.

In most instances, however, scripts start from some sort of outline—a proposal, a treatment. The next step may be a production script, in either one- or two-column format. Finally, you may want what is known as a storyboard: a graphic summary of the material in drawings or photographs, which may be prepared before or after the shooting script.

Each of these ways of handling material will be discussed in the chapters ahead. For the nonce, it is sufficient to know that they exist.

All this may seem to be making mountains out of molehills as you contemplate the slide show you propose to put together about your vacation trip to the Poconos. I agree. Bear in mind, however, that it is not only a writer's prerogative but his duty to match script to project and the big issue is detail.

A scriptwriter always sets down his words for at least five publics:

1 Himself—to clarify his own thinking.
2 The sponsor—to nail down the message to be conveyed and the handling selected to convey it.
3 The producer/director—to spell out the presentation the writer plans.

4   The technical crew—to establish precisely what is to appear on the film or tape.
5   The ultimate audience—to create the effect the writer/sponsor seeks.

In planning your self-sponsored Pocono slide show, which you will also produce yourself, the odds are that you seek only to set up an effective working order for the 35mm shots you took last summer. No producer, director or technical crew need be considered. The ultimate audience will be a handful of friends and neighbours with whom you wish merely to share a pleasant interlude. You have no heartfelt message to convey, no product to sell. For this situation back-of-envelope notations will perform script functions well.

Imagine, however, that you are preparing an environmental/ecological presentation on the subject of strip mining. Slides and film footage will be shot in at least a dozen locales, by personnel most of whom will never meet each other. Extensive research must go into the project. Some sort of consensus has to be negotiated between the members of a large steering committee, several of whose members hold almost diametrically opposed views.

Then, the results of all this must be shaped into a finished project which will influence heterogeneous audiences across the country to take decisive political action in the face of strong, well-financed opposition.

The script problem becomes a little more complicated than that faced in our Poconos idyll. What can—and should—the writer do about it?

Getting started

Long acquaintance with a wide variety of writers leads me to assume that you are human. Which is to say, you come equipped with human attributes: the strengths and weaknesses, virtues and deficiencies of your kind.

On the positive side, this means that in all likelihood and in varying degree you possess creativity, imagination, initiative, insight, passion, patience, perseverance, sensibility and a host of other characteristics.

On the negative side you also offer an amalgam of components, ranging from small pettinesses to a capacity for murder. Of all these, we need give heed to only one: self-doubt. Other names for this are used: laziness, uncertainty, insecurity, vacillation, procrastination and even perfectionism.

They all come down to one thing. You can see it at any swimming pool when someone hangs back, not quite nerved up to braving the water's chill. In audiovisual, the water is any new project. And the thing that makes the writer hang back is self-doubt: the fear of laying an unsure ego on the line.

To put it in other terms, we all want to be right every time. We want success and admiration, the plaudits that come with genius.

Sometimes, we recognise that we cannot be sure of winning these. Especially in new situations or faced with unfamiliar problems, we can be wrong; we can fail; we can look like absolute asses to our associates and to the world.

One way of avoiding such catastrophes is to dodge the issue ... stall and put off and find excuses for not taking action. That works, of course. The only problem is, it also condemns us to failure by default. By refusing to play the game, we never can win the championship.

Speaking from experience there is only one cure: you have to take the problem in both hands and fight the job through—win, lose, or draw. Otherwise experience, that dear teacher, can never tutor you for success. If you hesitate, all is lost.

On the other hand, as an ex-cryptanalyst I can tell you that you will sometimes obtain amazing results just by plunging into whatever morass confronts you and threshing around till something gives. In other words, you *must* act—even if what you do is wrong. The worst that can happen to you is that, missing your target, you will check off one blind alley, one dead end.

3   Developing your idea

Through the years when I was operating within an academic framework, I had a succession of student secretaries—young women cashing in on their office skills to earn further education.

Working with these ladies, I soon discovered that their most paralysing fears centred on the writing of term papers. The envy they expressed at the apparent ease with which I did my own writing was flattering to say the least. When I suggested that term papers were not really all that difficult and offered to show them a simple procedure for dealing with such, their gratitude was heart-warming to see—especially when they tried out the procedure and found it really did work.

So, how do you write a term paper the easy way?

1 You know your subject. You attend classes, study your text and carry out any additional research that seems to be called for.
2 You pick your topic or, if one is arbitrarily assigned you, you work it up with proper care.
3 You write down everything you know about the subject, paragraphing at the end of each sentence.
4 You cut these one-sentence paragraphs apart and group like with like, in terms of similarity, contrast or contiguity.
5 You arrange these sentence-packets as logically as you can, going from problem to solution, familiar to unfamiliar, cause to effect, or any of the other patterns that you will find in any book on logic. You end with appropriate conclusions.
6 You rewrite and polish as necessary in order to give the final product unity, progression, proportion and continuity.

These principles are equally useful in developing ideas for your work in the audiovisual media. Indeed, this whole chapter centres on showing you easier ways to evolve effective scripts.

Building your background

It is hard to write about nothing and yet, perversely, that is what many beginners try to do. May I suggest that, instead, you *a* recognise your need for information on your topic and *b* set about acquiring it in a reasonably systematic manner?

Our case study this time will be my wife's work in writing an AV programme on the use of the oscilloscope. She started from scratch: she literally did not know what an oscilloscope was, despite the fact that she had a better-than-average scientific background.

Her first stop was *The American Heritage Dictionary of the English Language*, where she found at least a basic definition 'oscilloscope, n. An electronic instrument that produces a visual display on the screen of a cathode-ray tube corresponding to some external signal.'

The next stop was the technical manual for the particular model her script was to deal with. Having read it, she understood at once why an AV programme was needed. The manual, like so many of its kind, was totally beyond a lay person's understanding, including hers.

Fortunately, help was close at hand. A specialist had been instructing the sponsor's personnel in the mysteries of the oscilloscope. Not only was he immediately available, he was eager to assist. Indeed, the main reason for putting the instruction in AV form was that the work load had grown too heavy for him to handle.

Happily, the expert explained all to my wife: he spelled out oscilloscope theory and practice to her in painstaking detail and submitted himself to hours of cross-examination by her.

Even then my wife still could not grasp the finer points, despite more hours of study of technical books and manuals. Finally, in desperation, she taped the entire series of lectures that the expert gave to trainees and asked the sponsor to assign her an oscilloscope with which to experiment so that she could clarify her confusions by trial and error.

It soon became clear that the difficulty was—as is often the case in such situations—that the expert was *too* expert. Years of experience led him to take all sorts of things for granted, to perform a host of steps automatically, jumping from short cut to short cut, unaware that in so doing he was bewildering students.

Further, the oscilloscope involved was a highly sophisticated model, with a baffling variety of special controls. When my wife asked the operators what function some of these performed, too often the answer came back 'Beats me. I steer clear of that one.'

My wife, a persevering type, persevered. The day came when the programme not only was finished but hailed by all and sundry, including the expert, as the clearest presentation of the subject they had ever seen.

The point of this story, however, is less my wife's triumph and more the procedure by which she carried through the job. She began with the dictionary and the manual, ie *print research*. The next step was probing the expert's knowledge, ie *interview research*. Further study of printed matter followed, plus work with the oscilloscope itself, ie *field research*: the information acquired earlier was applied to the actual manipulation of the instrument.

Only then did she get around to what non-writers would term writing: the preparation of her script.

You might bear this in mind when you tackle your next job. A superior script is almost always built on a sound basis of background study.

Although no set pattern for doing such investigation can be spelled out, certain broad guidelines do exist. Thus, it generally helps to start with a quick look at what has been published on your subject. Do not study it in too much detail since the print tends to age quickly and much of what you find may be outdated.

The next stage is sifting through the experience of others—quite possibly experts and technical advisors. Properly handled, such conversations may fill you in on all sorts of odd details not easily obtainable elsewhere.

If necessary you should then return to the published data. Finally, you should go out into the field to gain first hand knowledge of radar, rodents, palmistry, pressure cooking or whatever your topic may be.

This is not always the way you go about constructing a script. Sometimes you may be lucky and find yourself assigned an expert so eager and brimming with his/her field of expertise that he/she gives you everything you need. A word of warning is necessary here: be sure your specialist is as much a mastermind as he makes out; a couple of times I have been led down the primrose path by smooth talkers whose insights left something to be desired.

Alternatively, you may find all you need in a clipping file, as I did once for a film on ulcers, or the examination of a widget, waffle or windmill may provide you with more than sufficient information.

However you handle the script, though, be sure you do not get in too big a rush. Indeed, where any writing is concerned, it is wise to go slowly.

Make haste slowly

A major reason I prefer freelancing to steady employment is that it saves you having to try to explain the strange ways of writers to employers.

One of the strangest of these ways, to the non-writer, is the writer's insistence that he is working when it is clear to all and sundry that he is just staring out the window. I well remember the difficulties I had convincing one of my erstwhile chiefs that he was getting his money's worth when I was sitting in a dark corner of a bar across the street from the plant with a glass of beer in my hand.

The issue is that the human brain seldom works in neatly ordered patterns, especially where creative matters are concerned. Just as it takes time for trodden grapes to ferment, so the raw material for a script, the ideas and research, must stew and seethe for a while before they effervesce and sort themselves into meaningful form. Repeatedly, I have been willing to swear that I have explored every byway of a concept and only later, sometimes much later, suddenly experienced the thrill and exhilaration of having exactly the right touch flash without warning into my mind.

In consequence, as every experienced writer knows, it does not pay to push too hard or to try to hurry things too much. More often than not, incubation time is an essential when you are trying to shape jumbled thoughts into a script. Sleeping on problems helps. I still prefer to shave with brush, lather and razor simply because so many issues resolve themselves in those mindless minutes. A fellow-writer walks his dog an hour each morning before he starts to put words down on paper. Allegedly, it is for the exercise but actually that period is when he gets his best ideas. If he fails to provide for it, his thoughts become increasingly mechanical and routine.

On the other hand, do not fall into the trap of using creative brooding as an excuse for loafing which, believe me, is easily done. You *must* keep it clearly in mind that you have a job to do, a script to write.

It helps, I think, to treat your brain as if it were a sort of cistern. As you take ideas, ie copy, from it, it is essential that you pour in research, which is the raw material of creativity, and let it churn awhile. (For a brilliant study of this process, as applied to the poetry of Samuel Coleridge, see *The Road to Xanadu*, by John Livingston Lowe.)

Often, the infusion of research materials is enough to start this fermentation. Ideas applicable to your script come bubbling up instantly, with little or no effort on your part.

When that does not happen, give your mind an opportunity to seethe unshackled. Forget the job. Take off and have that beer, see a film, or walk around the park. Then, go back to your desk. Make a date with yourself to do so: 'I'll knock off till noon (or three, or after supper, or whatever) and then I'll hit it.'

When the time comes, keep your promise. Sit down with pad and pencil, typewriter or recorder and get busy. The odds are that the jigsaw puzzle pieces will fall into place. (We will take up what to do if they do not shortly, when we discuss continuing elaboration.)

Nailing down objectives

Have you ever been lost in the Paris Metro system? The management has built in an audiovisual solution to help you find your way. It takes the form of big wall maps strategically sited in major stations. Each line is marked on it in a different colour and there is a button for each station. You push the button for the station to which you want to go. Promptly, a row of lights flash on, indicating the route you should take. All you have to do is get on one of the trains of that line, transfer at the point the map-lights indicate and, before you know it, you are at your proper stop.

What we have here is a crystal clear example of the importance of objectives in AV work and how said objectives may be established.

Each project on which you will work starts from an existing situation, a state of affairs, the way a particular segment of the world exists at the moment. Into this walks the sponsor. He views the situation darkly and believes it needs changing in some way or other. So, he sets out to help make the said change via an AV programme.

Such proposed changes take many forms: 'Children don't know enough about X. We want to give them information concerning it.' 'This piece of land is lying idle. We want to persuade people to buy pieces of it for homes.' 'These flowers are lovely. We want to show people how to grow them.' In the case of the Paris Metro, the problem was 'People are getting lost in our subway system. We want a fool-proof way to get them to their destinations.'

Your problem, too, must have a sharply focused objective if it is to prove effective. How do you go about nailing the said objective down?

First, you make very sure that you know what your sponsor finds wrong with the existing situation.

Second, you ask the sponsor (and yourself) precisely what changes he wants to make to the situation. This is not quite the same as the 'key point' principle we discussed in Chapter 2. A key point is a general statement of an attitude towards a subject, ie a point of view. An objective is a goal. It describes a new and different state of affairs you want to bring about. Thus 'Tapeworms are faithful friends' is a perfectly accurate and acceptable declaration of a key point, presented with a wry, tongue-in-cheek touch.

Your objective needs to be more specific and goal-oriented in terms of the change you hope to accomplish via your AV presentation. To that end, I recapitulate, you must check out the present state of affairs, ascertain what the sponsor finds wrong with it, and then spell out the change or changes that will make him happy.

In our example, the sponsor holds to the view that a parasite is a life form that lives in or on or at the expense of another creature. His objective is to convince viewers that parasites can be annoying, damaging, dangerous and hard to get rid of; therefore the viewers should do their best not to let such organisms move in with them.

The tapeworm then becomes a hook, a lead-in or a vehicle to help convey this message. Its importance is in no wise diminished but the key point that features it is not the same as an objective; it can be an unhappy mistake to confuse the two.

We will enlarge upon this point in later chapters. For now, though, it is time to move on to another aid to creativity.

Continuing elaboration

A major weakness of many novice scriptwriters—and occasionally professionals—is their tendency to the delusion that a script springs into being fullblown. They could not be more wrong. A script is built a step at a time. I use the word 'built' rather than 'grows' because ordinarily a very real effort goes into the process.

At the same time, that effort can be made a bit less painful by applying the process that I call continuing elaboration. The phrase means just what it says: you get something down on paper and then elaborate on it, ie develop it more fully.

It helps if you go about this in a half-way systematic manner. An approach that has worked well for me involves combining notes and typescript.

Thus, at the idea stage, I tend to scribble notes. These take in every aspect of my project that comes to mind, jotted down as they come with no effort at order.

Eventually, however, I get bogged down or the jumble begins to pall on me. Or I may just get tired and go away for a while. When I return I take my place at the typewriter and cast the whole mess/mass of my notes into typescript. While I still make no attempt to organise the tangle, a certain amount of structure does creep in. Words and phrases become sentences. Sentences expand to paragraphs. Relationships of a sort appear. Pieces are juggled from one point to another.

The thing still makes no sense; it remains a mishmash, a conglomeration. It is, however, a longer, more detailed and somewhat more coherent mishmash than it was before.

Again, in all probability, I will take a break. This one ends with me sitting down with the typescript and a pencil; I cross out, insert and change words, add margin notes and expand.

The time comes when the typescript is so marked up as to be almost unreadable. That calls for a return to the machine to produce clean copy.

Again, the copy changes in the process of retyping. Notions that seemed brilliant last night have now gone cold. New phrases pop up to replace old. Minor points take on new import. Major issues lose their stress or fall by the wayside.

You ride this seesaw until you achieve a satisfactory—which is to say, satisfying to you—product. This may not take as long as you imagine, for at some mysterious point your thinking synthesises. Bored with groping, your subconscious suddenly shuffles bits and pieces into place. Pictures sharpen.

A tight-knit pattern of organisation appears. The page that was hash an hour ago now marches neatly and precisely.

If you want a case study of how this can work out, take this book as an example. Its original plan was developed by this process, and so was each individual chapter and section.

While the continuing elaboration system may not offer instant acclaim or pure perfection, it does bounce you off dead centre with minimum waste motion and help you to move forward.

How much detail?

Some writers write lean, sparse scripts. Others tend to fat, loose ones. A third group favours what I call the blank verse school: prose poems in script form. All have their proponents; all are in some degree successful.

My own feeling is that too fat a script, one developed in too much detail, tends to grow boring and so to sacrifice attention. (I say this on the basis of having been known to write too fulsomely myself; I have then had to watch sponsors/producers/crews shuffle through my pages, trying to find the end to see if anything ever happened.)

Too sparse scripts, in turn, may on occasion prove ineffective simply because they do not get across a point or feeling. (Few of us read an outline or plot synopsis with the same enthusiasm with which we immerse ourselves in the original novel.)

Nowhere will you find a better field for poetic scripts than in AV. 'Mood' presentations may prove ideal for art, music, dance and the like—anything where communication of emotion is the issue: a room bathed in deep blue light; a glowing orb of iridescent colour against total black; the pulse of jungle drums while a deep voice recites Vachel Lindsay's 'The Congo' as a substitute for narration; sparkling Caribbean rhythms or Jean-Michel Jarre's futuristic music; puffs of scented air ranging from the fragrance of roses to the acrid bite of ammonia or pungent lemon; ribbons of nylon net afloat in eddying air currents to caress the cheeks; velvet's smoothness or the rasp of bristles—the sky is the limit! All you have to do is conceive it and get it down on paper in whatever form. The right client will love it. (I recall a bank in Mexico that paid one of our artist friends a fantastic sum to create a gigantic 'soft sculpture' hanging to complement mood music in its lobby.)

At the same time, remember that the *wrong* client will hate this sort of approach. Too imaginative excursions seldom offer sufficient form to please sponsors who want tightly structured teaching programmes or the equivalent.

Beyond all this, my own tendency is to try to capture the tone of a concept in copy, ie the feeling and flavour you want the finished program to carry. When Cap Palmer's narration speaks of teenage Galsworthy Gulley 'easing the pains of homework with the musical accompaniment of Malice Glooper and his All-Electric Aggravators,' he is making my point; and so, equally, is the anonymous author of an industrial accident script who reports 'Harry catches his hand between the handle and the metal door sill with such force that he sustains severe abrasions to the skin and bruises the tendons and muscles. The injury is painful and Harry experiences difficulty in moving his fingers freely.' Cap's goal is to maintain the light touch implicit in his approach to his material. The anonymous author strikes a more serious note but, again, one quite in keeping with his subject.

Finally, there is the matter of clarity. For shot instructions, especially, the crew needs to know what you are talking about; say what you mean, so that there is no possibility of misunderstanding.

Whatever you do, do it in as few words as possible and as many as are necessary. You should realise in advance that experience will teach you a great deal more on the subject than anything I may write, especially, that is, if you give proper heed to the audience.

4   The issue of audience

Some day you should read the autobiography of my friend Frederik Pohl, the science fiction writer. Titled *The Way The Future Was*, it is a vastly entertaining memoir. From time to time it also incorporates titbits of thought-provoking information. One of these is the story Pohl tells of how, as an advertising man, he found himself assigned to devise a way to sell 50 000 copies of an oversize volume which, it seemed clear, virtually no one wanted to buy.

Fred tried all sorts of ideas. In varying degree, each failed until he launched a campaign whose obviously ridiculous copy capsule shouted these words:

HAVE YOU GOT A BIG BOOKCASE?
Because if you have, we have a BIG BOOK for you ...

It sold out the edition.

The message here is, I trust, clear: you never know who is going to buy until you try, whether the product is a widgit or an idea. This is especially true where audiovisual presentations are concerned.

The complex world of audiences

Audience, as I use the word here, is another term for *special interest group*, ie the particular collection of people towards whom a programme is slanted. Indeed, every programme is, or should be, so pitched. Nothing is more surely doomed to failure than the presentation which presumes to appeal to the whole world. Even entertainment films (of which more shortly) try to call their shots in terms of specific groups: horror fans, bikers, family fare, the youth market, action buffs, sexploitation etc. Only a handful of blockbusters succeed in casting their shadows over true mass audiences; in most instances even they are more advertising/promotion achievements than they are cinematic colossi.

Projecting this principle into that segment of the audiovisual field with which we are dealing here, it may safely be said that a script is far more likely to prove successful if, abandoning the 'general public' approach, you write to/for a specific audience, for example hospital patients, basketball players, third grade pupils, librarians or what have you.

The first question then becomes how do you determine your audience? (This is by no means as simple a matter as it seems.)

The second question is what is the said audience's interests—the precise appeal that will yield the results your sponsor seeks?

What makes such questions complicated is the fact that, despite the fantastic amount of time and thought expended, no one has yet perfected a formula that works every time. Indeed, there is not even agreement as to the best procedure to follow. Thus, some experts in the field swear by scholarly studies, surveys, polls, demographics, statistical analysis, and the like. Others ridicule such, on grounds that they are hopelessly academic and can never give proper weight to the many variables which are bound to crop up.

A friend of mine who is a public relations man with a reputation second to none preferred what he called the 'hat trick'. When in doubt as to audience or audience attitudes, he would head out into the market-place, ie the area in which his chosen audience type of the moment was prone to congregate, and drift about, chatting and asking questions. Most of the time, he got excellent results but there were occasions when this sample proved too narrow and he missed the boat totally.

Another approach spotlights intuition—which is to say, you fly by the seat of your pants. Certainly that has to be the key where Fred Pohl's successful book-selling campaign was concerned. He simply racked his brain for a winning copy appeal until he hit the jackpot. (Phrasing it that way is in no wise intended to put down Fred. It takes talent to come up with a jackpot angle, especially one as offbeat as his. Most of us could try a million years and still not hit it.)

For my part, I recall a major, and expensive, effort made at the behest of a sponsor group to determine the attitudes towards science and scientists of junior high school boys and girls. It was set up complete with a top sociologist to prepare questionnaires and supervise a cross-country survey.

The results indicated that most of the youngsters considered scientists to be bearded old men in white coats who had no social life and were never home because they spent all their time trying to devise ways to blow up the world. The girls did not see them as at all desirable matrimonial material.

The results may have been accurate enough but I am not at all sure that an afternoon or two spent talking to teachers or drinking Cokes in student hangouts would not have given as valid a picture.

Which audience?

I once wrote a slide show heralding the glories of a new set of college dormitories—residence halls, they called them. Those of us involved sat through the approval showing. The lights came on. The Dean of Students, in charge of the project, turned to me, and said 'Good job. But one shot's got to go.'

My face must have mirrored my bafflement, because he laughed. 'Here. I'll show you.'

Seconds later, we were looking at a lounge scene, a colour shot, crisp and well composed. The lounge itself was a model of attractive decor. Clean-cut students here and there added touches of life and captured the social activity to be expected. For the life of me, I could not see anything wrong with it.

The dean stepped up to the screen and pointed. 'See?'

I saw, all right, but the dean's reaction still did not make sense to me. The four boys and girls, seated at a table and playing bridge, remained totally innocuous in my eyes.

'It's the cards,' the dean explained. 'This show's going to be viewed by parents, not just kids. Small-town parents, lots of them, and this is the Bible belt. They'll see those playing cards as the devil's picture book, with their sons and daughters on the road to ruin. So that slide comes out.'

For more than 30 years now, even though times have changed, that scene has stuck in my mind because it helped to teach me that what you think of as your audience may not be, after all.

Another example is a narcotics conference in Los Angeles' San Fernando Valley and a film designed to turn young people off drugs. Again, the lights came on. A probation officer spoke.

'No good,' he said. 'This stuff's slanted to adults, not juveniles. It's phoney. The kids know junkies and potheads. They'll laugh it off the screen.'

These examples are obvious, of course, in order to help me make my point but the same problem exists on subtler planes. When someone says that he would like an educational AV programme, what audience does he want to reach? Students? Teachers? Administrators? Parents? Legislators?

For example, is a travel show aimed at anthropologists, armchair adventurers, grant-givers or voyeurs who delight in bare breasts and naked bottoms? Is the state fair display intended for the passersby or the boss? Is the in-house TV show for line workers, management or public relations?

These are vital questions for the writer. In large measure they determine his approach, his point of attack and his line of script development. Somewhere along the line he will need to ask a lot of his own questions, and not just of one person, either.

He should also raise the additional issue of purpose.

Whose purpose?

As an information/education man in the army I showed a lot of films and other AV presentations. It did not take me long to learn that purposes of the viewer and producer often differed. A high proportion of men in the ranks, I discovered, saw any AV programme as a golden opportunity to either sleep or kill time and thus avoid distasteful duties.

Similarly, in a school situation, students may view AV as a respite from lessons. Teachers may call for a film because they are tired or bored with teaching. Administrators have been known to institute major programmes in order to impress colleagues/superiors with their school's or system's progressive approach.

Again, it is important for the writer to take heed of these different audience motives and plan his scripts accordingly. He must view the sponsor's desire to change a given aspect of the state of affairs within the context of the existing audience situation and attitudes.

Consider, for example, whether the audience is voluntary or captive.

The voluntary audience is one that comes of its own free will. By and large, it is present because it is interested in the subject and what the sponsor has to say about it. Consequently, the voluntary audience probably will accept the sponsor's purpose with a reasonably open mind. Its members will give honest consideration to the advantages of joining the country club, building a home in the new subdivision or learning how a limestone cave is formed.

The involuntary audience, in contrast, may prove a bit less tractable. More or less dragged in bodily, it may view the programme resentfully or, at best, as time out from normal life. As mentioned earlier, sleep is one possible response. In a classroom, horseplay may vie with the sort of boy-girl diversion known as playing footsie. Worker groups may indulge in under-the-breath humour.

How can one override these private purposes and render the sponsor's product more palatable?

The entertainment factor

What most people think of as the film industry, ie the cinema palace entertainment aspect of the business, is based on a firm foundation of offering the public emotional stimuli so much more vibrant than the realities of everyday life that vast numbers of people will pay good money for the privilege of experiencing assorted chills and thrills vicariously.

In contrast, the main function of audiovisual presentations is to prove information designed to change audience attitudes in the manner we discussed in 'Nailing down objectives' (p.25).

There is no reason why the emotional-stimulation techniques of the entertainment film cannot be applied to the information-providing, attitude-changing aspects of the AV programme, especially if you have skilled AV writers.

Certainly every writer should be prepared to at least make the attempt. At the same time, however, he needs to be aware of some of the problems and perplexities involved.

The big issue with the entertainment approach is that, apart from its function of providing emotional stimulation, it concentrates on filling time rather than setting forth information. In the eyes of many this means it *wastes* time and AV resources that they feel might better be devoted to getting across ideas.

Such a view is not totally true, of course. Often, emotional appeals and amusing bits are the very best way to make a point. The fact that some audiences consider the fun factor as a waste of time, however, should be considered.

Particularly where technical material is concerned, sponsors and viewers alike may frown on the introduction of anything that is not strictly a flat, factual presentation. I recall an instance where I devoted considerable time and energy to incorporating humorous touches in a training programme which had a reputation for putting its viewers to sleep. When the firm's superintendent saw the script, he promptly ordered me to remove all the laugh-lines, and no amount of arguing would dissuade him. He wanted facts and operational details only. (Interestingly enough, he himself did have a sense of humour, and he did guffaw unrestrainedly at some of my efforts. I never could figure out why he objected so strenuously to letting trainees have a chuckle also. All he would say was that light touches would 'distract' them—a statement with which I still disagree heartily.)

On the other hand, there also are audiences which will pay no attention whatever to your presentation unless they are given a dollop of entertainment with it. In general, these are the involuntary groups, the conclaves dragged in at the end of a rope. They have no prior interest in your subject; in effect, they challenge you to create one.

Although not always possible, interest can often be created. On occasion, a story line can be built into even a 100-frame filmstrip (see *Candles on the Cake*, p.141) or a tongue-in-cheek note added to a museum display (see 'Tapeworms Are Faithful Friends' in Chapter 2). It never hurts to try to incorporate interesting objects or action into your visuals to stimulate the imagination. For example, a unique artifact in an archaeological presentation, a rifle-scope's crosshairs centred on a lovely girl, a highly magnified bacterium shown on a slide with dramatic narration about the threat it offers may all prove effective in the right place. The most important point is that you *must* know your audience, which is not always the easiest thing in the world to manage because of the number of variables.

Variables, variables

A brilliant young scientist I knew was having a terrible time over an experiment on which his whole future quite possibly depended. When he performed the experiment in his own laboratory, he always got the same result: other people in their laboratories did not.

For a scientist this can be a crucial matter. If his results are not totally duplicable by others anywhere in the world, it means that something is wrong with his thinking and/or his procedure. Eyebrows are raised.

The scientist tried again, checking each and every step. The result was perfect. Colleagues tried again, but still had divergent results.

Seething with frustration, the scientist attempted to duplicate his results in a colleague's laboratory. The results were disparate.

Brilliant young scientists can go up the wall when something like that happens. If they are brilliant enough, however, they realise that somewhere, somehow, an unrecognised variable is throwing things out of kilter.

On that basis, the scientist settled down to checking all the details of the experiment. When at last he pin-pointed the significant factor, he discovered it to be, of all things, the test tubes he was using. Trace elements in the glass were affecting the validity of his work. New test tubes and a change in method resolved the problem.

As a scriptwriter you may, on occasion, encounter similar kinds of things. Thus, a mining company in Illinois once asked a writer I knew to prepare an AV presentation on certain safety problems. Happily, he agreed.

Only at the last moment did he learn, from a Miners' Union organiser, that the company had not thought to mention one vital item to him: the overwhelming majority of his audience would be men whose native language was Lithuanian. For most of them, English ran a very poor second.

As a corollary, the miners' attitudes and outlook were sufficiently different from those he had anticipated as to force him to revise his script almost completely.

This is the kind of thing that can give almost any of us headaches. The only solution is to check, check and check again on all the possible variables. Are your viewers to include religious groups with dietary taboos you never thought of? How should alcohol be dealt with? Is national/regional pride or prejudice a factor? Have your audience experienced snow, sea or modern farm machinery? What is their reaction to credit, car ownership, or extended families?

Then, as if the above were not enough, you must consider additional complicating elements.

5   Subject specialists and others

I once worked on a hospital picture with a very talented director. Everything went beautifully until he called me in to look at the rough cut.

The film was supposed to be a public relations film for the hospital but what showed up on the screen was a twentieth century chamber of horrors.

I screamed loudly. The director made appropriate excuses, apologies and placatory gestures and we went back to work, scrabbling up pieces of film from the cutting room floor. Anything that showed a smile or sunlight found a place. Eventually, the picture was completed and accepted.

Years passed and I found myself sitting down for an afternoon drink with the director's former wife. Somehow, the conversation turned to the near-disastrous hospital job. I found myself describing my bafflement at what had happened in the rough cut.

The ex-wife downed half her drink at a gulp. 'You know' she said 'I almost talked to you about that at the time. But Eddy (not his real name) and I were still married then, and I felt as if it would be disloyal.

'What you didn't know was that Eddy was walking a tightrope those days. His health—well, he kept thinking he might have cancer. So what he shot were his own fears, even though he probably didn't realise it.'

The lesson here is that, as a writer, first, last and all the time, you work with people. Each person has his own quirks and foibles and you need to be really aware of it before you touch pencil or pen or typewriter key to paper.

Who's paying?

You have no doubt heard the old line about 'He who pays the piper calls the tune,' and this is doubly true for the man who lays out cash for a script. Too frequently, he sees the pen that signs the cheque as also flowing with literary genius. Consequently, more often than not, he will not hesitate to explain your script's shortcomings to you, as well as to offer suggestions as to items to be inserted or excised.

Criticism is fine. We all can use it. An AV scriptwriter, however, is supposed to be, in his way, a sort of expert—a master or at least journeyman where this particular field of communication is concerned. It is assumed he does what he does for reason.

It follows that when, against your advice, Mr Moneybags decides to deck out earth elements as brownies or delegate the narration to his harelipped sister-in-law, it may have some slight effect on the total impact of the package.

What can the writer do about this? Often very little, I regret to say, unless you count biting the bullet as constructive action.

Actually, your sharpest weapon may be the fact that Mr Moneybags has money. The odds are that he did not get it by being a fool. If you point out that he stands to lose or minimise profit on a sizable investment, then quite possibly he will see things your way. This is especially true if your arguments are logical and well presented.

You may also find it helpful to listen with an open mind to what your patron has to say. Assuming he is knowledgeable regarding your subject, it is possible that he can make a useful contribution.

It is worth noting, too, that many individuals financing AV programmes have only the most perfunctory interest in scripting or production. Where they are concerned, delegation of authority is the rule. And that brings us to yet another question.

Who's got the muscle?

Like it or not, script decisions must be made where any AV project is concerned. The question is, who is going to make them? Will that person, having made them, stick by them?

These are terribly important questions. If the wrong man, ie one not authorised, lays down the law to you or if the right man proves too weak or easily influenced, you may have trouble for a workmate for the rest of the job.

What specific types of people are we talking about? We can divide them into three groups: the power-hungries; the indecisives; and, the impossibles.

The power-hungries are men such as the vice president of a firm for which I did a consulting job. He had gained his rank by marrying the daughter of the chairman of the board. Now he wanted to prove his merit in action. The company president, in turn, took a dim view of the situation. So far as he was concerned, the vice president was an upstart and a phoney.

My project became a bone of contention between them. Each wanted to run the show, determine its content and presentation. Anything one would approve, the other would veto. The completed job was a botched-up mess, of course. It could have had no other outcome.

This is not to say that someone seizing power cannot also be a good thing. Several times, I have watched projects floundering, only to have them saved by some individual who, taking command, insisted that all work meet his personal approval.

The indecisives offer a different problem. They are the boys who cannot make up their minds. Often, the reason is that they are afraid of being wrong. You can find them in droves in government and occasionally in major corporations; they are living examples of the old saw that responsibility is assigned, authority seized. Presented with a script, they will neither accept nor reject it but pass it on to someone else to make the (to them) peril-fraught decision.

You might define the impossibles as those individuals who lack the strength or drive to seize power and yet are still determined to have their own way with those beneath them, ie the innocent scriptwriter who strays into their web. Demanding endless changes for change's sake, they make it impossible to complete a programme satisfactorily. Nor do they particularly care. Ego-inflation is really all they are after. My own pet example of the genus was an academician of great prestige who had a large foundation grant to finance a series of presentations. The result was that we would end each meeting with me sent forth to work up a concept. By the time I returned for the next appointment, however, the academician would have come up with a new and (allegedly) more brilliant approach. Nor could he understand why I should find this both discomfiting and (since time is money) financially disastrous.

After three times I withdrew from the project. So did the next couple of writers he hired. I do not know if the job ever was completed.

Just in case you feel, after this recital, that I am too negative, let me throw in a few happier examples.

One involved a little cockney Englishman who was aide to the president of a national trade association for which I was assigned to script a major project. The president was pompous, the aide anything but. Every time the president started to throw barriers in my path, the aide would skilfully skate around them. I never had a job go with less friction. When it was all over, the president was convinced he had been in charge; the aide and I knew better.

Again, a large company's media branch, that is its AV section, became embroiled in a row with its public relations department. A clever executive's solution was to hire me to 'script' the project over which the fight had arisen—even though the scripting involved little more than changing commas. As my name drew screen credit, each contending side could, by devious reasoning, claim it had won the victory.

What all this adds up to is that—to reiterate—there will be decisions to be made on any project. As the writer you should be keenly aware of this and insist that *one* individual—the technical advisor is a good bet, since you will be working closely with him—have the power to call the shots.

This will have two beneficial effects. First, it is remotely possible (though you should not count on it) that the sponsor will stick by his word and *let* the chosen individual make the decisions. Secondly, the number of people with whom you have to deal in the preliminary stages will be reduced.

Who's doing the job?

Remember the director I described at the opening of this chapter? He has a lot of relatives. As before, let us divide the category into four divisions: the artistes, the egomaniacs, the incompetents and the procrastinators.

Artistes, for one thing, are artistic although their definition of their talents might differ a bit from yours or mine. Thus, the view of 'dramatic irony' taken by one man on a feature film I scripted almost brought us to blows over his insistence that the plane bearing the two young lovers into the sunset at the conclusion crash in flames.

There is not really an answer to this kind of thing. Certainly it does not warrant barring such people from the trade. Frequently the people who are the most difficult to work with come up with extremely clever approaches which a more practical mind might never have considered, let alone conceived.

The best advice, probably, is for you to grip your own sanity tightly and then take full advantage of any coruscating concepts an artiste may have to offer, while at the same time calming his more egregious excesses.

The egomaniac rates as much the same as the artiste, save that he has no artistic pretensions. He just wants to do everything his way, on whim and without forethought. Of course it is right because it is his idea.

The catch with this is that the sponsor rates a little consideration too. He has paid you to come up with an idea, a concept, an objective, a script. You have thought them through, worked them out, honed them down till they mesh like watch-gears. For the producer or director or anyone else to throw all that out on the chance that his own slap-dash notion will satisfy the sponsor better is neither intelligent nor fair.

What can you do about this? One nasty gambit I have come up with is to insist that I, the writer, have a separate contract—one which states explicitly that I am in no way responsible for the finished project. Failure to follow the approved script thus becomes the producer's headache, not mine. Indeed, I may find him hesitant to deviate from the script in any way without an OK from on high—which of course does not necessarily mean me but at least leads to an exercise of reasonable restraint. In addition, sponsors seem to like the idea. If things go wrong, it tells them whose back should bear the monkey.

Much the same situation obtains where the occasional incompetent producer or director is concerned. One such, for example, apparently was afraid of close-ups. He simply would not fill the frame with image, no matter how loudly it was called for. The result was that key shots lost impact and a potentially strong filmstrip turned to milk and water.

Another example is an ex-portrait photographer who could light faces beautifully. All his shots, however, came through as what sometimes are termed 'talking heads.' He could not seem to compose a visual to make a point or frame an idea.

The procrastinators are those workers who, otherwise competent, simply put off and put off and put off. When the pressure eventually erupts, these dawdlers' scruples too often fly out the window. In at least one case I lost a valued client because a producer whom I thought was my friend in my absence glibly blamed delays on me.

Again, the solution in most cases is to stand firm for separate contracts.

You also should think twice before you agree to front for a producer you do not know. Just because someone telephones to tell you they would like you to work with them on a project does not mean that you necessarily want your reputation linked with theirs.

I probably should conclude this section with an across-the-board apology to all the fine producers and directors with whom I have worked. *Truly, friends, I have no intention of slandering you. You are good, solid, conscientious and creative. None of my remarks in regard to artistes, egomaniacs, incompetents, or procrastinators are aimed at you. I fully recognise that just as no producer/director could get very far without a script, so no writer's script would mean much without you to translate it into sound and visuals.*

Writing is work—the writer's work. To survive, he has to face the dark side as well as the bright. He has to treat it as a business as we will discuss in even more detail in Chapter 12.

Talking to technical advisors

I wish I had a dollar for every time my neck has been saved by a technical advisor. Whether you term them subject specialists, information experts or project consultants, they remain pearls beyond price where we writers are concerned.

A technical advisor is the man/woman who keeps you on the straight and narrow track in relation to the subject matter of your script. If you are writing about Black Angus cattle, he is the one who can tell you off the top of his head that they are natural polls. If the topic is electrical symbols, he knows which sign designates a power source and which a resistor.

The key fact to bear in mind in regard to such specialists is that their work with you quite possibly will take a lot of time. Both your advisor and the person who assigns him needs to know this on the deepest possible level. A boss who thinks his chief aide can be both on the job and helping you is almost sure to end up irked if not bellicose. An advisor who does not realise that you are going to preempt the hours he intended to spend working on the budget may not accept it cheerfully. If you expect succour and do not get it, you are not likely to end up in the best frame of mind either.

Be sure that you have a competent technical advisor and that he will be available to you when you need him.

It does not hurt either to feel out how your personality meshes with that of your advisor. Sourpusses are seldom fun. Neither are strong, silent types who communicate in monosyllables and stand convinced that only a dolt could ask the questions you do.

Which brings up the matter of how to ask the questions. In general, your problems here will centre on either the individual who talks too little or the one who talks too much.

Where the man who talks too little is concerned, the section in Chapter 3 on research offers a sound approach. What you need to ask are the right questions.

The 'right' questions reveal a certain amount of intelligence and background where your topic's concerned, while at the same time dredging up the data you need. The reason you strive for this combination is that most experts or subject specialists are more prone to help someone who seems to have the potential to benefit by the said help than they are the individual who is apparently incapable of grasping any information.

At the same time, this does not mean that you yourself must be an expert in order to ask questions. A reasonable command of basics, such as you can obtain from rudimentary print research, is enough. You certainly should not hold back from poking into those aspects of your subject on which you need enlightenment. Indeed, as I have pointed out elsewhere (*Techniques of the Selling Writer*, pp 277–8), your greatest asset in this area can be a willingness to be thought a blithering idiot. An unwillingess to let your inadequacies stand revealed in the cold light of day can cut off your flow of data.

The other side of the coin, the man who talks too much, can prove an equal frustration. Bubbling over with his subject, hung up on trivia, he may babble on and on until you are ready to scream.

A combination of flattery and advance planning may prove to be your salvation: 'Man, you *really* know flippenroods, don't you? Right now, though—well, we'll get back to them after you've cleared up the hassenpfeffer principle for me.' You *must* retain some semblance of control if you do not want a week's work, or a month's, to be dragged out to a year.

While we are talking about technical advisors and such, it might be wise to point out that not all necessarily will be subject specialists in the usual sense of the term. Some of the most useful and, indeed, essential will come from the ranks of your production crew—your visuals people.

A good example may be found in the oscilloscope project mentioned earlier. One of my wife's biggest problems on it was the fact that a vital element in the AV programme was a 'trace'—a point of light (often seen as a line) which moves across the oscilloscope's screen. To film the trace involved major complications because coordinating the camera speed with the trace speed was fantastically difficult. If the synchronisation was not precise, the trace speed might be distorted or some portion of the light point's line of transit shortened, lengthened or placed in the wrong relationship on the screen. (You will see a less complex example of this kind of situation in western movies when the wheels of the stagecoach appear to move backwards because of the different speeds of the camera and wheels.)

The problem of synchronisation created a writing problem. Was it possible to describe the oscilloscope trace as behaving in a particular way and anticipate that it would so appear on the screen in the programme? Or must the problem be written around and, if so, how could the programme instruct students accurately and effectively in oscilloscope operation?

The solution came from a technical advisor not from the oscilloscope side but from the production team. His combination of mechanical and mathematical skills enabled him to work out a functionally effective procedure for filming.

There remains another aspect of working with people. This time it centres on you.

Mirror, mirror

All through this chapter, we have focused on how you best can cope with your colleagues. Is it possible that these colleagues may have just a little difficulty sometimes coping with you?

Let me cite two incidents that may make my point. In the first, in Los Angeles, I was discussing a possible script job with two local producers, and they were hesitating. Obviously something was not quite right.

Finally, after a cryptic exchange of glances, one asked 'How do you feel about style?'

I groped. 'Well ... I guess I never thought too much about it.'

As one, the producers heaved a sigh of relief. 'Thank God!' one said. 'The last writer we had screamed bloody murder about us ruining his style every time we changed a comma.'

I still recall thinking how idiotic that writer must have been.

For the second incident the scene was Dallas. It was a government agency's AV planning conference. Out of a clear blue sky, a woman executive cracked a joke.

Everyone laughed—except me. For, as I realised with a start, I was the reason for, not the subject of, the humour. Somewhere along the line, I had lost my sense of proportion. My voice had risen angrily. Whereupon the woman executive had deftly poured oil on the troubled waters with her wisecrack.

I wish I could claim that that was the only time when I have been difficult. Unfortunately, it would not be true, but at least it does not happen as often now as it did when I was younger.

The reason, I hope, is because I have begun to see such situations a little more clearly and to have worked out more satisfactory ways of resolving them.

In the first and most basic place, I now recognise that AV scripting is, by and large, a cooperative venture. People other than the writer of necessity get into the act.

I have also come to see that the world is not going to end if I do not have my own way on everything. Not everyone will necessarily agree with even the most brilliant of script ideas. Indeed, no mode of attack is the *only* way to tackle a project. It is important that the writer realise this.

There is also the matter of the script itself. Have you worked it out with all possible care or have you, conceivably, written too fast, skimped research or been a trifle slack on planning? Writers have been known to upon occasion and you are only human.

In fact, being human, is it conceivable this is not one of your best days? Has a cold, a headache or a disappointment put you in a bad mood and rendered you difficult to deal with?

These are only questions, not statements but they are worth at least a moment's consideration before we move on to our next topic.

6   **Getting it across**

He was a professor of archaeology who wanted an in-house video presentation of his latest dig. It sounded like an ideal subject. It ended in disaster.

Why? Because the professor, despite all protests, insisted on introducing lengthy discussion of the religious beliefs of his long-dead subject people.

Now a popular lecturer, skilled at playing to his audience, possibly could have gotten away with this. The professor, however, was *not* a popular lecturer and the points he sought to make were both abstract and hypothetical to say the least. Indeed, what he apparently hoped to do was to substitute an hour's video time for the total anthropological/archaeological literature on his subject.

Believe me, approaches like this do not work. Anything you can do to convince your clients that this is true will constitute a star in your crown.

As we observed earlier, audiovisual combines the heard and the seen. At its best, it offers an overview of a broad subject or a detailed analysis of an extremely limited one. Whatever you seek to get across with it, it operates most successfully, most effectively, when it adheres within a reasonable degree to certain rules of thumb which are standard in the field, in the same way a carpenter tends to use a hammer to pound or a saw to cut, rather than attempting to mitre corners with a brace and bit.

This is where you, the writer, come in. You are the one who helps the client to frame his message within the limits of the media.

What items need to be considered?

An eye for visuals

How do you present a smell on film or paper? How can the word *creativity* be translated into audiovisual terms? Can you devise a way to *show* me the atonality of Berg's or Krenek's music? Is it possible to taste thick cream or chilli peppers with your eyes?

It can be done; do not say it cannot. After all, someone has recorded his interpretation of a sneeze in animation.

The point is, to become an AV scriptwriter, you must of necessity develop an eye for visuals—images that in and of themselves catch interest and tell stories. The more acute this eye, the higher your rating as a writer.

Further, developing such an eye quite possibly may force you to expand your consciousness and stretch your imagination a good bit beyond your previous conceptions. Particularly, your thinking is likely to require readjustment if it is to shatter the confines of the film frame and proscenium arch.

Thus, to most of us, most of the time, a visual is a picture, but suppose your assignment is to create a walk-through exhibit encompassing five or ten rooms?

At this point, 'visual' may switch from graphic representation to mean light and colour—all-engulfing, wholly or partially non-representational, continually changing, and geared to set one or more moods. Perhaps there is also audience participation. Visitors push buttons, pull levers, step up or down or through light beams, peer into mirrors or through viewscopes, put on ear phones, feel textures.

The goal may be to make the world of phobias, unreasoning dreads, real to those passing through. One room presents claustrophobia, fear of confined spaces; another, agrophobia, fear of open spaces; another, xenophobia, fear of strangers; another, nyctophobia, fear of darkness, and so on.

To achieve this happy end, a certain amount of construction may be necessary, for example movable walls, which may too, in their way, constitute a visual. Indeed, such a programme may even introduce you to a different kind of technical advisor, one who tells you whether or not the effect you seek is practical or within the confines of the budget.

You should now begin to see why I say that a writer, in audiovisual, may be more a conceptualiser than a wordsmith.

Your tools, on a job like this one, will be, first, unfettered imagination and, second, a taste for variety. It will also do no harm if you are to some degree familiar with the artist's instruments—light, colour, mass, line, form, proportion, contrast, rhythm, perspective, composition—as applied on levels ranging from realism to surrealism, actuality to abstraction.

You do not need necessarily to be an artist yourself but an awareness of art and graphics certainly helps. An excellent starting point is to study other artist's work, both in AV and elsewhere. Stay alert to all the things that visuals can do—the flood of ideas and information (and sometimes *mis*information) you can transmit through the eye. Dali has lessons for you and so do M. S. Escher, Boris Vallejo, Frazetta, and maybe even Calder and Jackson Pollock.

Reading, too, has its place. You could do worse than begin with Chapter

13 ('Your Illusions Are Showing') of Magnus Pyke's *Butter Side Up!*
Another top-flight stimulant is John Halas's *Visual Scripting*, particularly
in such articles as Samuel Magdoff's 'The Advertising Message,' Ernest
and Giselle Ansorge's 'Painter and the Moving Picture,' Eino Ruutsalo's
'Typography in Motion,' Roger Macdougall's 'Writing Dialogue for
Animation,' and the Norman McLaren/Saul Bass piece, 'The Experimen-
tal Film Maker and Designer.' Roger Madsen's *Animated Film* is also
worth consulting for technical details on assorted procedures.

Beyond all such, however, the important thing to bear in mind is that
audiovisual offers perhaps the greatest opportunity for free expression of
any means of communication open to the writer. Many of your most
frustrating limits, you will discover, are self-imposed. The key lies in your
own thinking. You can, on the one hand, restrict yourself to the flatly
representational and pedestrian, walling yourself in with your own rules
both in concepts and visuals. On the other hand, you can search for the
new, the fresh, the unfettered, and find yourself bounding through an
exciting fairyland, a fantasia that delights you as much as it does your
fascinated clients.

This holds true whether you are scripting slide shows or in-house video,
multimedia or dioramas. There will always be those clients who insist on
the dreary, the plodding, the programme devoid of colour or imagination.
To make a living, you are likely to have to do things their way sometimes.

There will be other types of sponsor also, sponsors who seek something
new and different. For them, the touchstone will be verve, originality, the
far-out vision. For their sake, and for yours, you dare not allow yourself to
fall into moods of dullness, apathy, inertia. Imagination is what paves the
road to a reputation and a future.

Audiovisual presentations can take a hundred different forms. At the
bedrock level, they are every single one the same. Once you learn the basic
principles on which they rest, you can use any and all with adequate facility
and master virtually any approach with minimal pain.

That is why I devote so little attention here to specific media. It simply is
not necessary. What you are after is visual interest, no matter what format
it is cast in. That visuals should also convey appropriate ideas and
information in intriguing fashion goes without saying.

An ear for language

More writers would script first-class AV programmes if they learned to
listen to good story-tellers with both ears.

My reasoning for this dates from the 1930s, when the National Maritime
Union was hard at it organising Great Lakes shipping. To that end, they
sent a host of deep-sea sailors drifting into Lake ports, allegedly looking
for work but actually carrying the union banner.

Among these wanderers was a squat, foolish-looking Danish A.B. whose English was so thickly accented as to make you groan to see him get up to speak at the union hall. You only groaned the first time, though. From then on you could not wait to hear him.

The Dane was a natural-born story-teller and a funny one, at that. When he spoke, from the first stumblingly hilarious anecdote, he was 'Seafarer, Incarnate' and every man in the hall was with him. The facts he had to offer were nothing special but when it came to life, spirit and drama—there he had them!

Would it be treason to suggest that the narration in a good many audiovisual presentations would benefit from an infusion of life, spirit and drama? Or, to put it in slightly different terms, straight telling too often does not tell much.

Life, says my dictionary, is 'animation; vivacity; vigor.' Spirit equals 'inspiring principle; dominant influence.' The dramatic is 'intensely interesting; eventful.'

Those all are qualities valuable to narration.

The Dane's language, in turn, was in keeping with his audience. Long words, by and large, were out as were difficult words, complex words, obscure words. Active verbs, pictorial nouns and shared experience were his stock in speech.

This should come as no surprise to any writer, for example if you are writing for farmers, you use farm terms and farm situations.

Too often, however, we let the element of life slip out. Somehow an invisible pedagogue takes over and the spirit, drama and colour fade away. Thus, the narration for a teaching filmstrip need not always begin with, for example, 'This one-celled animal is an amoeba.' The class may pay more attention to 'This creature is his own ancestor—and that makes him the oldest animal in the world!' Similarly, the introduction 'You're not even breakfast size for a tyrannosaurus!' has its own potential in a natural history display and 'Who do you hate most?' lifts the voodoo doll out of anthropology and into life.

Your goal in audiovisual is as much or more to influence and inspire as it is to inform. Remember that changing attitudes is the issue. Indeed, that being the case, are you sure that narration is always necessary?

A sting of sound, a strain of music

Might not our tyrannosaurus, above, be more effectively presented via a button for museum visitors to press? Tyrannosaurus promptly gives forth with a 'realistic' roar. Attention thus captured, anything you have to say about him can be set forth on a placard or narrated later.

How about recording the sounds one hears within a Leopard tank?

Couple this with appropriate jouncing movement and footage filmed through a gunport and an audiovisual illusion is complete.

Speaking of sound, do you recall the paralysing fright created by Stuka dive-bombers in early World War 2 German propaganda films and newsreels? The air of implacable juggernaut menace that massed kettle-drums brought to Nazi rallies?

For that matter, where would *Star Wars* or *Battlestar Galactica* have been without their sound effects?

The same possibilities exist for your own work. The rattling of a rattlesnake, the ticking of a bomb, the hiss of air escaping from a tyre, the slam of a door and the pop of a champagne cork are all available for use when you need them. The radio sound effects men of the Thirties and Forties have charted the way for you in their amazing feats of mood and atmosphere creation, tension manipulation.

Music can be important too. *Casablanca* tightened the throats of millions with the 'Marseillaise,' 'Colonel Bogie's March' carried much of *The Bridge on the River Kwai* and the theme for 'The Third Man' gave the zither a new lease of life. The strongest element in Douglas MacArthur's try for the US presidency was his use of 'Old Soldiers Never Die' as a campaign song. 'Lili Marlene' set a mood for seduction of girls in untold numbers. The Beatles shaped a generation with 'Strawberry Fields Forever,' 'Lucy in the Sky with Diamonds,' and 'A Hard Day's Night.' Depths of sensation first explored in Bartok's 'Concerto for Orchestra' moved into the far future as Jean-Michel Jarre probed through the world of synthesisers.

It would hardly be amiss to say that, to achieve its goal, a successful AV programme often must go beyond what is normally thought of as its proper sphere and create an environment, a separate experiential world.

Words alone cannot do that; sounds and music are necessary too.

The art of analogy

Too often, under pressure, we writers fall prey to pedestrian thinking, taking refuge in a dreary literalism when we should be ranging high, wide and handsome through the imagination's farthest reaches.

One happy gate into these realms is that of analogy, metaphor: the drawing of parallels, actual or implied comparisons. Through such, we can bring the abstract/complex/general down to earth and translate them into concrete terms. Walt Disney's *Fantasia* offers a delightful case in point; music is translated into the frolics of animals and imaginary creatures. How better can you convey the concept that great music can be fun? Yet not one word on the subject has been spoken.

It goes without saying that this kind of approach is not limited to Walt

Disney. It is an entirely practical tool for you to make your own. Nor are elaborate measures necessary. The skull and cross-bones is a symbol, a visual metaphor of sorts, which spells danger to all. An insurance company's use of the Rock of Gibraltar as its emblem draws an analogy with stability. The petrol advertisements that told you to 'Put a tiger in your tank' were setting up a parallel with power.

How do you get these parallels, these comparisons?

1   You decide on the point you want to make.
2   You make a list (old faithful!) of things that symbolise or hold some analogous relationship to that point.
3   You pick the item or items that suit you best.

Put in this stepwise way, the process seems very simple and yet, when the cards are down, it really works.

To show soldiers the value of camouflage, for example, it might help to show such analogies/parallels (which is to say, *related examples*) as deer, snakes and chameleons and how they blend into background. This could be followed by showing how a properly trained and accoutred infantryman can do the same.

Similarly, to glamorise a holiday resort you might introduce slides of Acapulco, Cannes and the Bahamas, thus drawing parallels to your spa and emphasising how much cheaper and more convenient yours is. If that seems too mundane, you could draw an analogy to heaven with various stage sets.

Personification, particularly, is also useful since through it you can so easily create a prototype to fit your needs. Thus, on one occasion, I was desperate for some way to span the history of all humankind so I created a semi-comic character to jump from century to century, in the process bringing in any incident I wished.

In brief, visual and verbal metaphor offer a device that both solves problems and helps to hold the interest of the audience. While the writer certainly should not strain for it, he dare not ignore it or its potential.

The pros and cons of logic

Rudolf Flesch once reduced all logic to two fundamentals: 'Specify,' and 'So what?'

Thus, a generalised diatribe about the brutality of Guatemalan security police does not carry nearly the force of the specific instance of the death of 39 dissidents in the Spanish Embassy fire. The question 'So what?'—that is, 'What difference does it make?' or 'Of what consequence is it?'—leads inevitably to the conclusion that if this is what happens to *campesinos* who disagree with the authorities, political freedom in Guatemala may very well be said to be under severe attack.

This is an approach which, to me, makes sense. But as audiovisual scriptwriters, we all need to move it a step further, via the recognition of the fact that the things you *show* carry greater impact than almost anything else. Thus, any number of words, any intensity of language, is unlikely to outweigh the right visual. What can you say, for example, that will hit harder than a photograph of a napalmed baby?

Similarly, a shot of the great stone warriors guarding Tula is more emphatic evidence of Toltec power than any words. The heaped dead of Auschwitz and Dachau bear horrid witness to Nazism's tenets. The 'wooden shoe' sabotage sticker the IWW slapped on fenceposts and barns across American farm and timber lands just before World War 1 blazed an image of terrorism so sharp that it panicked whole states and helped break the organisation. To countless thousands, the fall of Paris was a balding Frenchman in a business suit with tears streaming down his face.

There may be a lesson here: your best approach sometimes can be to establish mood and let your audience draw its own conclusion. Upon occasion what is not said is far stronger than what is.

Even when the aim is not shock but puzzlement, a picture that magnifies its subject—a fly's eye, a sugar lump—beyond recognition will catch attention. And so will presentations of, for example, unique juxtapositions and unusual compositions of light and shadow and many other things.

This is in no way intended to denigrate logic, indeed assorted aspects of ordered reasoning are considered in the next chapter, but symbolic visuals do constitute an often neglected element that is worth bearing in mind.

Hanging it together 7

I remember seeing a sales film, probably the most visually beautiful I have ever seen. The imagery, the flow of line and the flash of colour caught you, held you tight. Truly, the photographer was an artist. The only trouble was that when the lights went on you could not remember who the sponsors were or what they manufactured.

What had happened was that the photographer's artistry had seduced him. He could not bring himself to subordinate it to his assignment. An eye-catching composition took precedence over any sales point. Spectacular special effects rated higher than product identification.

Unfortunately, this man's failing is not limited to photographers. There is also the client who tries to crowd in unrelated detail; the writer who cannot resist a clever anecdote or turn of phrase; the graphic artist who goes in for psychedelic bursts or 'busy' backgrounds; the sound recordist who lets mood music drown narration. One and all, they suffer from the same ailment: an inability to nail down the job they are paid to do and then build the project itself around it.

To paraphrase Cap Palmer of Parthenon Pictures, certainly one of the finest scriptwriters I have ever known, the goal is never an audience reaction of 'What a brilliant film!' The note you seek is 'Boy, are those great widgits!' or, 'What a wonderful museum! I really must go there next weekend!' or, 'So that's how resistor colour coding works! For the first time, I really understand it.'

How do you achieve this laudable end?

How elements relate

One of the things that occasionally baffles would-be scriptwriters in the AV field is that the field is so diverse. Consequently, no single approach fits all situations. No one solution solves all problems.

On the other hand, the categories into which presentations fall are not all that different. The bonds that join them are every bit as marked as the walls that separate them. The thing that matters is knowing with what issues you are dealing.

Presentations tend to take one of three major approaches, ie they emphasise *instruction, mood* or *experience.* These are not mutually exclusive, though; almost always, a degree of overlap is to be found between them.

Instruction is the most common of the three approaches. Encompassing a high proportion of such forms as slide shows, filmstrips, teaching films, programmed instruction, and the like, it tends to an orderly, linear, logical approach.

Mood, in turn, centres on the creation of a particular state of feeling, ie happy, romantic, mysterious, excited, melancholic, or what have you.

In the experiential approach the emphasis is on letting viewers 'live through' a particular sensory involvement.

All three approaches still centre on what we originally said about audiovisual presentations some chapters back: they change attitudes. It is only the means by which they do it that differs.

Thus, a filmstrip titled 'Great Moments in Music' might offer pictures of famous orchestras, conductors and composers, its narrational comment interwoven with a background of taped symphonic fragments. Its approach could very well be direct, didactic.

The Disney *Fantasia*, in contrast, presents much the same content but in terms of mood. On the surface it is entertainment, pure and simple but it too instructs. It says implicitly, 'Great music can be fun' and, as a correlate, 'Great music does not have to be studied seriously.'

An experiential approach might be one in which the viewer enters a room equipped with one large and several small screens, a bank of push-buttons and volume controls. Each button is labelled with the name of an instrument. When the viewer presses a button, the large screen reveals a symphony orchestra in performance. Simultaneously, the instrument named on the button appears on one of the flanking screens, a performer playing this instrument on another and the orchestra section into which it falls (woodwinds, brass, strings, percussion, etc.) on a third. After a minute or so of solo performance, followed by a minute featuring the section, the orchestra as a whole comes on for a set period. This is again instructional but instruction of a different type and on a different level.

How do you build such presentations, regardless of the category into which they fall? You group their elements in terms of *similarity, contrast* or *contiguity*. That is, as I pointed out when we discussed research in Chapter 3, the first step in organising anything lies in putting like with like. Similarly, things that are *not* 'like' go in a separate class: that of contrast. A third division assembles contiguous bits: those next to each other.

Thus, if your presentation is to be straight instruction, you gather the facts you want to put across, the vital information, pretty much discarding everything else. Remember, though, that the categories are not mutually exclusive. Quite possibly it will seem desirable to add a soupçon of mood material or some sort of experiential audience participation.

To convey mood, you may virtually eliminate facts, save as they contribute to feeling. At the same time, you try to pinpoint precisely the mood that suits your purpose, the idea you seek to sell. Then you figure out how best to evoke it. Other moods, no matter how appealing, go by the boards.

(It also should be noted that distracting, ie contradictory, moods may creep inadvertently into any kind of presentation unless you are careful. When the German Tiger tank first was introduced, for example, it was often described to Allied troops in such fearful terms as almost to paralyse them. An anti-VD film fell flat because the girl on the screen was so attractive the men in the theatre howled for her telephone number. The facial mannerisms with which Bela Lugosi terrified *Dracula* audiences at the time the picture was released now convulse viewers with laughter.)

Often, an experiential programme will centre on whatever cleverness you can devise to involve your public. The trick, as always, is first to make up your mind as to the purpose of the programme in terms of the desired change of attitude. Is the issue a simulation of pilot problems, a demonstration of computer superiority to the human brain in certain areas, or testing mechanically for colour blindness? Again, you go back to grouping your elements as to similarity, contrast and contiguity; add imagination, and work through to a presentation that does the job.

It also helps, especially in straight instructional programmes, if you understand order.

Order and its principles

The project is an in-house television programme; the topic, minor industrial accidents; and the key point, 'When your mind drifts, accidents happen,' or maybe 'Injuries come in when your mind goes out.' The immediate objective is to make employees aware that most accidents are not accidental. The ultimate objective is to improve efficiency and cut down time lost from work due to the many minor industrial accidents which employees too often regard as inevitable and the result of blind fate.

The question to ask yourself is 'What's the mood or tone to be?'

Since relatively minor mishaps are to be featured and since line workers tend to resent or be cynical about pontifical approaches, the handling should perhaps be light, tongue in cheek.

How should the accidents themselves be dealt with? We could include everything from shattered skulls to sliced shoulders but that might make staging complicated, as well as bring in too many serious injuries. It is better to centre on something more common and less critical—maybe a particular part of the anatomy, like fingers.

Fingers give us, out of the blue and with apologies to *Laugh-In*, a tentative title: *The Fickle Finger.*

A good way to open might be with a montage of hands and fingers: fingers typing, fingers sorting, fingers pushing, pulling, poking, pounding.

Then, following the line laid down by our key point ('Injuries come in when your mind goes out'), we could show a series of incidents, black-out bits, in which these fingers get in trouble. The stenographer sees her boyfriend talking to another girl, so she hits a wrong key and spoils a page of typing. A girl bends over, exposing a mouth-watering length of leg; the man who glimpses her closes a door on his finger. A box falls on the hand of a worker frowning over a racing form. A woman, upset because her mother-in-law is coming to visit, receives a bad cut. A man, worried over a sick wife, has a finger broken. A woman, irked by her supervisor, wears a ring while working; a hook catches it and tears her finger. A man with a hangover suffers a finger sprain. Another, his mind on his forthcoming vacation, ends up with lacerations or abrasions.

Meanwhile, the voice-over narrator points out (with an appropriately wry touch) that fingers are faithful friends but they can betray us. This is because they are fickle, inconstant and do not pay attention to business unless our minds do.

Finally, for a climax and to drive home the underlying seriousness of our message, a punch-press operator turns to call to a friend, whereupon the press slams down. We hit a close-up of the man's face contorted in a scream. The next shot is a dissolve to a matching close-up of his unhappy face at a later date and is followed by a shot of a hand sans finger levering the press.

A recap of the earlier, less serious accident shots and maybe a repetition of the opening sequence of busy fingers brings our presentation to a close.

How do you organise such a project?

1   You nail down a key point and objective for your topic.
2   You choose a mood or tone to fit the situation.
3   You pick an approach, a line of logic.
4   You prove each point visually.

We have already dealt with the first two points. The second two warrant a bit more attention.

Thus, for point 3, there are a variety of ways in which you may attack any subject: chronologically, problem to solution, simple to complex, specific to general, general to specific, spatial, and a variety of others. The approach you pick, in turn, is one which provides you with proof that your key point is true, in such a manner as to move your viewers in the direction of the change or changes the sponsor seeks in the present state of affairs.

In our minor-accident example, we worked from *specific instance* (individual mishap) to *general rule* (injuries come in when your mind goes out). Within instances, we worked from *cause* (distraction) to *effect* (accident).

In each case, also, in line with point 4, we prove each point visually, ie we devise incidents which can be photographed. Why? Because, as some sage once observed 'The ear hears, but the eye remembers.' What you see, you believe. When you back that seeing with narrational interpretation and reinforcement, the impact is almost beyond resistance.

This is not necessarily the best way to present the subject; every script is unique and individual circumstances alter each case. We might, for instance, very well have taken a *problem to solution* line, beginning with a series of accidents and then analysing why they occurred. We could also have approached the issue *spatially*, zeroing in on those departments which had the greatest number of accidents.

Whatever our approach, it is vital to always bear in mind that we are trying to prove a key point, ie make a case for a particular core assertion. This demands that some sort of logic and visual evidence support our line of development. Always put your emphasis on *show* far more than *tell*. Narrational statements alone never are enough.

You can learn about *order* of presentation from commercial TV. Virtually every programme starts with a 'teaser' which is an intriguing action designed to catch the viewer's attention. Next, it builds through hills and valleys of varying pressure to a climax, a moment of peak tension in which the mounting excitement rivets every eye to the screen. Finally, the programme ends with some sort of dénouement that cuts loose the strain and ties up the loose ends.

Our accident programme follows the pattern of this sort of television programme. We started with action: busy, fast-moving fingers in a variety of situations. Each injury incident built from a low-tension 'valley' of new characters to a small 'hill' of excitement as preoccupation brought misfortune. Together, the incidents shaped a profile of rising action that climaxed with the tremendous impact of the frightening punch-press episode. Finally, the tension was released and the lesson hammered home by a recap and repetition of the opening.

This approach is not only applicable to in-house TV. It works equally well with film (see my *Film Scriptwriting*, Chapter 3, 'The Film Treatment'), filmstrip, slide show or what have you. Space/time is your only limitation. Indeed, our example could have been developed with equal effectiveness for a five-minute presentation or fifteen.

Of hooks and hinges

The Fickle Finger, you have no doubt noted, was made up almost entirely of illustrative anecdotes—incidents that make a point. The importance of such to the scriptwriter, and the value of the knack of being able to produce them on demand, can hardly be overestimated. They provide hooks to lure viewers into subjects they ordinarily think of as dull; they act as hinges in changing from one segment of a presentation to another; and, they form the backbone of many a programme.

How do you discover or develop these handy items?

A good part of the trick lies in the habit of keeping an eye out for them, both in research and in your thinking. Any time you read a biography or probe the evolution of a process or product or idea, you need to be watching for those bits of action that can be cast into graphic form to help you lead on or manipulate your audience's thinking.

Where creating such out of whole cloth is concerned, your task grows a trifle more difficult—history no longer is providing you with ready-made twists and punchlines—but it can still be managed. The list system, described earlier, is your best tool. Ten minutes with a scratch pad gave me the main details for *The Fickle Finger*.

This needs to be coupled with a process I call 'thinking through,' which you might also term projection, extrapolation, even, perhaps, reduction to absurdity. All it really involves is asking yourself 'What *might* a given person do under such-and-such circumstances that would produce the effect I need?' Extended as far as your imagination will carry it via the list system, you will find you almost always get results. For example, some years ago I needed to create a sloppy girl who could instantly be recognised as such.

Sloppiness is a difficult concept to present on film. The mere fact of dishevelment or slovenliness or soiling may indicate nothing more than being caught in the rain or having to spend a night on a park bench or in a ditch. True sloppiness is much harder to capture in pictures.

I am still proud of my solution which came after some hours of sweating and cerebration. My girl is sitting at a table. A second girl, approaching with a plate of scrambled eggs, trips. The eggs slide off the plate into the girl's lap. Momentarily, though only momentarily, she is taken aback. Then, not at all discomfited, she picks up her fork and starts eating the mess out of her skirt.

It bothers me not at all if this leaves you totally cold. What matters is the mental process involved in creating the tableau and that, I guarantee, you will remember.

Testing your product

Certain qualities characterise every effective script. While their presence will not necessarily guarantee success, the absence of one or all of them definitely will indicate a point or points of weakness.

These qualities are:

1 Unity.
2 Progression.
3 Proportion.
4 Continuity.

Unity means simply that a good script should be all of a piece, addressing itself to a single central idea or theme.

Disunity most often is a result of too many cooks stirring the soup. For example, a sponsor decides he needs an in-house TV programme on pest control. The writer scripts it for him, brilliantly: a bright day appears to be dawning. Only then does the engineer step in. As the show is going to be produced, he thinks that it would be a good idea to include a few shots of the company product's quality features. They could be incorporated easily in the course of showing pest control activities in the various departments.

The sales manager agrees. After all, every employee is, in his way, a potential salesman. A little footage emphasising how the product fits into every decor and colour scheme and its superiority to the competition . . .

Yes, yes! cries the purchasing department. Here at last is a chance to show the company's far-flung network of suppliers and its influence on the international market.

You can see what happens: what started out to be a first-class little show, unpretentious but effective, now ends up hash.

Nor do I mean to put all the blame on others. We writers are ourselves quite capable of being seduced by the extraneous, as when we note that the fluorescent-eyed monster from an old presentation still lurks in an alcove along the route visitors will take as they move through the new mine disaster show. The mood of the disaster programme is sombre but might not the monster popping out add a chill, a laugh—comedy relief to lighten tension?

Please, forego such! Nail down your key point, your objective, your audience before you start. Then stick with them. Comedy relief is something you plan, something in keeping with the rest of your presentation—not cartoon gags stuck in just because they happen to be handy.

Progression is what might be termed the element of forward movement—the fact that you do not just reiterate the same point over and over in Johnny One-Note fashion. In its way a good script is like a wall, built a brick at a time till the whole is complete. A better analogy might be a mosaic: your goal is a particular picture but it takes shape only as you fit in the various pieces.

Indeed, there is an important point to remember here, especially in teaching scripts. Any time you leave out a bit of essential information, it is like failing to put in all the treads and risers when you build a stairway. The student will bog down, just as the climber would fall on the stairs.

To see the element of progression well handled, visit Amsterdam's Anne Frank house. Moving through it, room by room, viewing relics and still photos, you end up with a deep gut feeling for the Frank family's plight.

Proportion is, I think, reasonably obvious. It means that your script emphasises the things you want it to. The place scripts most often fall down in this regard is in the beginning, middle and end; and no, I am not joking.

Thus, the writer gets a great idea for an opening but, by the time he is through, it has become so big and so powerful that it outweighs everything else.

In another situation the writer may come to the end and then does not know quite how to wind the script up. The result is that he tacks on three or four conclusions, one after another and the viewers find themselves irked and frustrated with a sense of anticlimax.

In the body of his presentation, the writer may realise that he does not have enough time or space or frames or whatever to develop the script properly, so he sidesteps and shortcuts, leaving out vital data as he hops, skips, and jumps from high point to high point.

The solution to problems of proportion is to plan thoroughly in advance and allow time for rewrites as necessary. Any script can be given proper form if you work it through.

Continuity is merely a term to indicate that your script—and hence your presentation—hangs together. To a considerable degree, the thing that *makes* it hang together quite possibly may be narration. Words spoken or set forth on title cards or wall posters can perform miracles when it comes to bridging gaps, changing subjects or pointing viewers in new directions. Which is not to say that your visuals, too, should not string together insofar as is practical.

The thing to look out for is jerks or jumps—the sense of momentary bewilderment that assails the audience as it enters a new sequence. Step-by-step development, illustrative anecdotes, parallel constructions, narration, music bridges and stings of sound to mark a change will help. Your main tool, however, remains your own clear eye and straight thinking—your awareness that continuity is an element you need to strive for.

Check your script out consciously, point by point, for unity, progression, proportion and continuity. You will still miss sometimes but not as often as you would without that checking.

By now, though, I suspect you are tired of talk of preparation, planning. In the next chapter, we switch to the actual script preparation—how to go about writing it down.

A young woman I know decided she wanted to be an AV writer. Personal contacts got her an assignment.

The job took her into a shop where a thirty-year veteran also laboured. Day after day, he blithely came up with fresh ideas, new concepts, clever presentations and copy that shone and sparkled. All the while, Suzy continued to sweat on her door-crashing first assignment. If she made progress at all, it was minimal.

Finally she could not stand it any longer. She addressed herself to the old hand.

'Why is it,' she demanded, 'that when you do these things, they look so easy? But when I tackle them, they're so hard?'

The veteran was a kindly man. 'Suzy,' he said, 'they're not easy for me either. But I've got thirty years on you, plus patience.'

He was right, of course. Experience does count, and so does what an old cowboy phrase calls 'staying with the cattle'—sticking with a task, no matter how hopeless it seems or how frustrating it becomes.

I do not know whether you succeed as an AV writer because you have this quality of patience, persistence and perseverance or because, as a writer, you develop it. I do know, however, that you have to have it.

Beyond this quality, however, a system does help, especially when it comes to getting words onto paper. Your best approach is to have some sort of set procedure to follow although this does not necessarily mean that you do a lot of writing. Many projects involve more talk than typing and your sponsor or producer quite possibly will be willing to forego any formal, step-by-step outlining of the unit. Nevertheless, for your own sake, to ensure the clarity and precision of your thinking, you should work out your key point, concept, handling etc on paper, even if only in note form.

I also should perhaps explain my relatively limited use of examples in this chapter. The reason lies in my inclusion of sample pages from a variety of actual working scripts in Part II ('Putting Principles to Work') of this book. I would rather have you study them, regardless of their flaws, than academically perfect examples unsullied by day-to-day work pressures.

On the other hand, I know it is handy to have an on-the-spot guide to go by, so I am including an 'unsolicited' proposal and portions of treatment and production script. You can get an idea of the general approach such take from them but do not assume that they are ideal models.

Ideas, incorporated

Subject: project proposals.

My early days as a scriptwriter saw me develop an almost paranoid orientation where project proposals were concerned. The reason was that I encountered such vagueness among other writers when I tried to find out how to put such on paper properly. One told me one thing, one another. 'You just do it' tended to be the most common and, for me, most frustrating response.

Time passed. Slowly, by trial and error, I discovered that my associates were right. A project proposal was indeed something you 'just do.' Why? Because each project is to a degree different from all others, with its scripting pretty much a law unto itself. No standard approach or handling or format exists. Each writer tends to fall into and develops his own technique. It is hardly the kind of scheme he can recommend or pass on to someone else.

As everyone needs some place to start let us begin with a definition. A project proposal, within the frame of reference of this book, is a written recommendation that a specific AV presentation be produced. Designed to convince a potential sponsoring authority of the project's value and feasibility, it combines a summary of presentation content with such other data as the writer/producer feels may help to catch the sponsor's interest and persuade him that the project is important, desirable and practical.

The heart of a proposal, to my way of thinking, is *interpretation of content*. That is, you build the project around a statement of a concept and its associated key point, core assertion and elaborate all in succinctly persuasive form.

(A concept, remember, is a mode of presentation that might or should exist but does not: a topic plus an idea. A key point is a declaration of your attitude or point of view where this subject is concerned: a clear, concise avowal of the essential thought you propose to sell your audience.)

Proposals fall into two categories: solicited and unsolicited.

Solicited proposals are those submitted in response to an invitation to bid on a project. A government agency, for example, may decide that it needs a particular AV presentation and so sends out notices to writers or producers, asking that those interested give ideas and prices. If you are a

John J. Jones
1234 Medford Plaza
Crossroads, Texas

Prepared for:

CHAMBER OF COMMERCE
Crossroads, Texas

Project Proposal

FOLK ART, CROSSROADS STYLE

(Working Title)

The Crossroads Folk Art Museum's annual festival draws huge crowds and rouses tremendous community enthusiasm... breathes new life and vigor into our regional culture. Its only real weakness is that it lasts so short a time. A week, and it's over.

Couple this with the fact that so many tourists traveling through Crossroads, and so many residents in outlying areas, have no chance to enjoy the festival's color, excitement, and educational benefits. It adds up to a very real loss, both to community and visitors.

This needn't be. Simply, quickly, easily, economically, the festival can be turned into an exciting audiovisual program that will publicize our community, promote our museum, and enable citizens and tourists alike to enjoy our Folk Art Festival all year long.

Here's a created-especially-for-your-benefit project proposal *for a slide show. Note that at this point John J. Jones, our imaginary AV writer, is working almost entirely in terms of persuasion: a presentation designed to sell an idea, a concept, a core assertion.*

(Incidentally, both Crossroads and its Folk Art Festival are, like Jones, totally imaginary.)

Specifically, what I have in mind is a hundred-frame color slide show, backed by tape-recorded narration and appropriate music. Included will be shots of paintings and sculptures...artists and visitors...entertainment features... and the general setting/atmosphere characteristic of the affair.

The key point it all makes will be: "You'll have a great time--a different great time--at the Crossroads Folk Art Festival."

The advantages of this approach are obvious. Since we're talking about a slide show, it can be kept up to date at minimal cost simply by adding new shots of art, artists, and features... eliminating those which are outdated. And narration can be changed for the price of a new tape.

Uses for such a program are numerous. For example, it can be used to promote the annual show in other communities throughout our area. Schools will find it invaluable in helping to build student participation in the Festival's junior division. A mailing about it to art groups outside the state will bring national attention. Tourists visiting our museum during the 51 non-Festival weeks of the year will get a taste of the affair and so be stimulated to come back and see the Festival live. Such a list could go on and on.

From the Chamber of Commerce standpoint, this constitutes an ideal public service project. All Crossroads will benefit-- and the Chamber will get the credit.

Tentative budget? I estimate $3,500 should take care

Project proposal for 'Folk Art, Crossroads Style' continued.

of script, talent, production--the works. And since the
museum already has its own cartridge projector and sound
programmer, purchase of this equipment will not be necessary.

This is an opportunity Crossroads really shouldn't miss.
The profits the show will bring to the business sector alone in
a month will far outweigh the small investment. And Crossroads
as a whole will receive cultural benefits beyond price.

Approved:

For Chamber of Commerce _____ Date _____

For Producer _____ Date _____

Project proposal for 'Folk Art, Crossroads Style' continued.

corporate employee like a writer for in-house TV, perhaps the management may ask you to work up a possible approach for a desired show.

Since the writer or producer involved is attempting to create a market in most cases, the unsolicited proposal may offer a much stronger sales pitch than does the average solicited bid. Which is to say, it tends to radiate what the writer hopes will constitute a contagious enthusiasm for the project.

Solicited or unsolicited, the two things that count most in a proposal are clarity and assurance: the proposal is a form in which understandability and self-confidence run neck and neck. It will also help if, as an aspect of clarity, the proposal is typographically attractive. White space, subheads, indentation and underlining all make a proposal easier to read, comprehend and, quite possibly, approve.

Beyond this, there is little that can be said definitely about proposals. Some are short, some long, with most probably falling between two and ten pages. Some are written sparsely, some go into elaborate detail, though it should be noted that handling that is too fancy may tend to confuse rather than impress. Some tend to the flatly technical, some put emphasis on mood or emotionality or drama. Some consider the treatment form which we will consider now.

Treatment: stepping scriptwards

A treatment is a concise summary of how the content of your project will be developed. Written in the third person, present tense and expository/narrative form, it spells out in greater detail the concept you set forth in your proposal.

It is, in other words, a highly specialised outline and a selling outline, at that, for it emphasises the dramatisation of the material and communicates enthusiasm to the sponsor. Having read it, the sponsor should not only know more or less what the project will show but he should also feel at least a bit of the excitement and fascination with which you hope the ultimate audience will pulse.

How do you write a treatment? Here, as a starting point, is a possible procedure:

1   Record the informational elements you propose to incorporate in your project, setting them down in chronological order of presentation. Informational elements are the factual content, ie the essential data to be included, whether it be historical events, biological processes, machine operations or whatever.
2   Record the interest elements to be developed, again in chronological order. Interest elements are any matters of mood, feeling or drama you want to become apparent.

John J. Jones
1234 Medford Plaza
Crossroads, Texas

Prepared for:

CHAMBER OF COMMERCE
Crossroads, Texas

Project Treatment

FOLK ART, CROSSROADS STYLE

(Working Title)

Our opening slide features a closeup of Gus Faber's
famed "Crossroads Cowboy" folk sculpture. Musical background:
"Keep Comin' Back to Crossroads" (Ken Casey's Crossroads Combo).
Successive slides present titles (OVERLAYS):

The Crossroads

FOLK ART MUSEUM

and

Crossroads

CHAMBER OF COMMERCE

present

Two pages of project treatment, *elaborating on the proposal; spelling out in more detail the idea the proposal set forth. By introducing specifics, telling what happens step by step, Jones paints a picture of the show-to-be with words. Tone is set with 'colour' words, descriptive touches.*

In other words, Jones is still selling, *as well as* telling.

FOLK ART,

CROSSROADS STYLE

(Other titles as desired)

Changing angle, camera hits a MEDIUM SHOT that includes
both the "Crossroads Cowboy" sculpture (on workbench) and Gus
Faber, worn shirt and Levis, shaping up a new piece with hammer
and chisel. Music goes down to background and narrator (GUS
FABER) comes in: "Yep, folks, that's me, all right. Gus Faber,
workin' on a new piece to top my old 'Crossroads Cowboy', right
here at this year's Crossroads Folk Art Festival."

Cued to "Crossroads Folk Art Festival," we flip to a series
of slides that reveal the festival in progress...first in terms
of street scenes (especially Sutter Street, with its huge trees
and beautiful old homes) approaching the museum...the museum
exterior and the lawn show...the interior and Festival proper.
Gus comments on each new slide in his inimitable, wryly humorous,
down-to-earth fashion.

Featured slides will include shots of Ed Rogers and such of
his paintings as "Raspberry Roan," "Doan's Store," and "Bob-Wire
Gal"... Sam Hamilton's branding-iron candlesticks...Laura and
Effie Willis with their quilts...Sam Roper tooling leather...
Miguel Gutierrez blowing wine glasses...Roma Clarke and her
needlework...Wanda Elder with her wheeling hawk paintings...and
so on.

Visitors will be prominent in many of these slides, talking
to artists and artisans, inspecting paintings and craft

The project treatment for 'Folk Art, Crossroads Style' continued.

3   To the best of your ability, interweave these two aspects of your proposed programme in such a way as to give the sponsor, who is reading, the same experience he would receive were he a member of the ultimate audience.

This will hardly be easy. Any old hand will tell you that developing an effective treatment is as difficult a job as any writer can attempt. It is, however, a skill the writer must learn. Without it, he will never pass beyond apprentice level.

Script and its formats

Let us here reiterate a point made earlier. It is quite possible that in scripting an AV presentation, you will never 'write' a script at all in the normal sense of the word. The field is so fluid, the range so wide, the media so mixed, that 'standard' handling frequently turns out to be either inadequate or too restrictive.

For example, take the case of an experiential programme. A simple narrative description of what happens to the audience, event by event and step by step, may be all that is required. An exhibit emphasising mood may focus on sound, lights or the contents of a display. I doubt that the evening park show in the Michigan town where I grew up ever was scripted much beyond the level of 'Fountains leap high into the air. Water cascades over the artificial falls. Varicoloured lights, synchronised to background music, ebb and flow through the entire spectrum.'

Still, a script does help to keep things straight. Which makes this the time and place to learn how to put one together.

You will encounter three basic script formats: the two-column, the one-column and the master scene.

In each case, any success you achieve will in large measure rest on two key factors: your ability to visualise, to see pictures in your head; and your skill at describing the said pictures so clearly that production personnel can capture them on film or whatever.

Visualisation involves a talent all its own. The trick is learning to see, in your imagination, the individual pictures that will ultimately make up your AV programme. Sometimes, as in a slide show or filmstrip, these will be single photographs. In other cases—film, in-house TV, some aspects of multimedia—motion pictures are involved. Again, the issue may be a walk-through exhibit, a display series or a mood or experiential presentation.

Whatever the medium, your job is to imagine what your audience will see or otherwise experience. In effect, you close your eyes, visualise your setting, view what happens there as your show progresses, and then start hitting the keys of your typewriter and describing the scene/experience.

71	MLS, in food booth area.	Hey, now! Art or no art, folks do get hungry, don't they? Well, Crossroads is
72	MCU, happy-looking visitor couple. Man's pointing off slide.	ready for 'em. Come one, come all! It's chow time!
73	MLS, couple from 72. They're headed towards food.	MUSIC: Mariachi group with strongly Mexican number IN, UP, and DOWN to BG.
74	MCU, tamale booth.	The tamale table's great, if you're a border type...
75	MS/MCU, fat, happy Mexican in chef's outfit dipping into tamale pot.	Even if you're not.
76	CU, plate of steaming tamales. They look great.	
77	MCU/CU, 72 couple. Woman's taking bite of tamale. Man holds a partially consumed tamale ...looks delighted.	MUSIC: Combo (strong on bones and banjo) with Dixie IN, UP, and DOWN to BG.

Two pages from the production script *of* Folk Art, Crossroads Style. *Ideas are broken down into individual shots (slides) now, complete with narration and music.*

Note that Jones isn't content with flat, factual description, however. Visuals and narration alike come through in terms of tone, the effects our writer wants to create.

Festival script--12

78	MS, barbecue booth... different couple. Black woman (Delia Walker?) is serving.	Barbecue ribs, Crossroads style. Old South eatin'. You-all don't know how good ribs can be till you taste these.
79	CU, different couple at booth. Angle favors man as he bites rib, sauce dribbling down chin for laughs.	MUSIC: Combo with <u>Deep in</u> <u>the Heart of Texas</u> IN, UP, and DOWN to BG.
80	Frame-filling CU, steaming bowl of chili.	Tex-Mex chili. The flavor folks dream about clear 'round the world.
81	MCU, Adolph Fredericks in chef's cap at chili booth ...giving bowl to visitor.	
82	CU, visitor's enraptured face.	
83	Facial CU, Adolph. He looks ferocious	That chili...Men have fought an' died to protect their private recipes.
84	MCU, Adolph. He grips a six-gun stuck in belt.	

The production script of 'Folk Art, Crossroads Style' continued. Jones will probably have to rework many details after shooting's completed, in order to make everything fit together smoothly. It's all part of an AV writer's job.

```
                                        Festival--11


             INT. - EXHIB. HALL - DAY

      71     MLS, to take in food booth

             area.


             GUS: Hey, now!  Art or

             no art, folks do get

             hungry, don't they?  Well,

             Crossroads is ready for

             'em.  Come one, come all:

             It's chow time!


      72     MCU, happy-looking visitor

             couple.  Man's pointing

             off slide.


      73     MLS, couple from 72.

             They're headed towards

             nearest food booth.


             MUSIC: Mariachi group

             with strongly Mexican

             number IN, UP, and DOWN

             to BG.


             GUS: The tamale table's

             great, if you're a border

             type.  Even if you're not.
```

Here our Folk Art Festival production script is cast into one-column format. Personally, I prefer two-column, since it allows you to line up narration, music, and sound effects against the slides more precisely. But some directors like one-column because of the extra space it gives them for production notes. Your copy column may go on either left or right, or even down the middle. Suit your producer's preference.

Festival--11

INT. ; EXHIB. HALL - DAY

71   MLS, to take in food booth area.

                    GUS
            Hey, now! Art or no art, folks
            do get hungry, don't they?
            Well, Crossroads is ready for
            'em. Come one, come all! It's
            chow time!

72   MCU, happy-looking visitor couple. Man's pointing off
      slide.

73   MLS, couple from 72. They're headed towards nearest food
      booth.

      MUSIC: Mariachi group with strongly Mexican number IN, UP
      and DOWN to BG.

74   MCU, tamale booth.

                    GUS
            The tamale table's great, if
            you're a border type...Even
            if you're not.

75   MS/MCU, fat, happy-looking Mexican in chef's outfit--
      Diego de Vegas, maybe. Have him dipping into tamale pot.

76   CU, plate of steaming tamales. They look great.

77   MCU/CU, couple from 72. One's taking a bite of tamale.
      The other holds a partially consumed tamale. He/she looks
      delighted.

      MUSIC: Combo (strong on bones and banjo) with Dixie IN, UP,
      and DOWN to BG.

78   MS, barbecue booth...different couple. Black woman (Delia
      Walker?) is serving.

                    GUS
            Barbecue ribs, Crossroads
            style. Old South eatin'.
            You-all don't know how good
            ribs can be till you taste
            these.

79   CU, different couple at booth. Angle favors man as he
      bites rib, sauce dribbling down chin for laughs.

      MUSIC: Combo with Deep in the Heart of Texas IN, UP, and
      DOWN to BG.

Another one-column format—this one page width.

9   INT. - EXHIB. HALL - DAY
                              GUS
             Hey, now! Art or no art,
             folks do get hungry, don't
             they? Well, Crossroads is
             ready for 'em. Come one,
             come all! It's chow time!

    Our slide takes in the entire food booth area. Picking
    up a happy-looking visitor couple, we point them towards
    the provender...zero in on the tamale booth. MUSIC builds
    mood with a strongly Mexican number.

                              GUS
             The tamale table's great, if
             you're a border type...Even if
             you're not.

    Our couple's at the tamale booth. It features a fat,
    happy-looking Mexican in a chef's outfit--Diego de Vegas,
    maybe. He serves the couple. They eat, looking
    appropriately delighted.

    The barbecue booth. MUSIC (strong on bones and banjo) hits
    Dixie.

                              GUS
             Barbecue ribs, Crossroads
             style. Old South eatin'.
             You-all don't know how good
             ribs can be till you taste
             these.

    A different couple eating...black woman (Delia Walker?)
    serving. Man's played for comedy--head thrust forward,
    sauce dribbling down his chin as he bites a rib.

    The chile booth. MUSIC comes on strong with Deep in the
    Heart of Texas.

                              GUS
             Tex-Mex chili. The flavor
             folks dream about clear
             'round the world.

    An enraptured visitor eating chili. It's serviced by Adolph
    Fredericks. He looks ferocious--glaring, mustache quivering,
    etc.

                              GUS
             That chili...Men have fought
             an' died to protect their
             private recipes.

The master scene format, as applied to our Folk Art Festival slide show. While it's fine for entertainment film, I really don't care for it in other AV situations. Use it only when you're flying blind and are in no position to spell out your shots.

Why? Because this format gives the director total control. Whether he'll bring back the slides you need remains ever open to question.

Note that you number by sequences only in the master scene format.

We will take up how to put those pictures onto paper, shortly.

It is not enough to look just for single images, however. You also need to watch for relationships between them so that your finished package will be tied together neatly rather than jumping about in all directions.

Such relationships can be established in two ways: a visual link may be set up between single shots, as in the cutting of continuity sequences in motion pictures; or, the link may be created through narration, as in compilation sequences. (These subjects are discussed fully in my *Film Scriptwriting*.)

Unless you propose to make a speciality of film, however, your best procedure is simply to spend as much time as possible watching effective presentations of the type you propose to script. Do not run each just once; a dozen times will serve you better. Note how a shot may seem to flow from the one preceding. Sometimes this is because it is of the same subject, but larger, or smaller, or from a different camera position, or following continuing action.

On other occasions, markedly different pictures will be tied together by what the narrator says. Alternatively, both means of relating material—visual and narrational—will be used together.

The script samples in Part II of this book will help sharpen your awareness of these procedures.

The two-column format is the one that is most commonly used. On the left side of the page, ie the left-hand column, it describes the material that the viewer is to see. Anything heard—narration, dialogue, sound effects, music—appears on the right-hand side, roughly parallel with the visual content it will accompany. The visual content is broken down into individual shots, ie still pictures or a series of pictures taken in the same run by a motion picture camera.

The one-column format contains the same material as the two-column but presents it with both visual and sound (often termed *video* and *audio*) in a single column. This column may be set on the left, like the video side in the two-column script, or it may extend clear across the page.

The master scene script extends across the full page width. It differs from the other two formats in that it simply tells what the audience sees and hears, making no effort to break its content down into shots. Although extremely popular in the entertainment film industry, the master scene script is seldom used for AV presentations.

What about narration?

An important aspect of nearly every script is narration: words spoken (generally voice over) to point up, complement or supplement the visual portion of a programme.

In audiovisual media, video (what is seen) by and large dominates audio (what is heard). As much as possible, the visual elements should tell the story. Words, narration, are based on and cued to the graphic aspect.

On occasion, however, you will find that you have no choice but to resort to what is termed the 'illustrated lecture' approach. In this, narration keeps the ball rolling, with pictures thrown in to point up, complement or supplement the audio—an exact reversal of what I said previously.

There are, indeed, programmes that involve no narration whatsoever. *Small World* comes instantly to mind and so do the Chaplin films, *The Red Balloon*, assorted dance and art presentations, and a host of silent filmstrips.

The value of such materials runs high in the right circumstances. Perhaps the most obvious case in point is that of the AV unit which is to be used with audiences that do not speak the language in which the programme was produced. There, the narrated module may prove next to useless, whereas the one without words makes its teaching point or creates its mood or provides its designated experience nicely.

In other words, narration can go in a variety of directions; it can be handled in a host of ways or sometimes eliminated. As in so many aspects of AV, there are times when you have to use your own judgement but, going back the full circle to the starting point, *in general* video should dominate and tell the story.

This is just as true whether you are scripting lines to be recorded on cassettes to guide visitors touring an art gallery or museum or when you are working up a slide show; the same goes for button-activated commentaries at displays, exhibits, or dioramas.

(Lip-synchronised dialogue, by and large, finds little place in AV work, save perhaps for in-house video. To a large degree, you learn the skills involved by doing. For a detailed appraisal, see my *Film Scriptwriting*.)

Your starting point for writing effective narration, it seems to me, lies in your project treatment, the organisation of your material. As you develop your production script from the material, you arrange your visuals in an appropriately logical order and, simultaneously, set down whatever interpretive commentary, ie narration, seems desirable.

The next step is to check back to make sure you have included all factual information which is not conveyed by the visuals and which *must* be presented.

It is essential, in narration, to hold down length. Do your best to avoid being lulled by the allure of your own words into a lecture approach. Do not be afraid of silence or letting music or sound effects fill a void or create a mood. Your viewers may need time to absorb particular visuals.

Somewhere along the line, you will also need to decide on the tone you want to strike in your narration. Is it to be light, pontifical, folksy, formal, colloquial, voice-of-doom, or what have you? Here, experimentation is your best tool. Try key lines first one way, then another, until you find an approach that sounds right. Do not be too quick to compromise on the 'almost.' Tone can be vital!

Beyond this, as you work up and smooth and polish, strive for our old friends clarity and simplicity. You will find the second person (the 'you' approach), active voice ('he saw the snake' not 'the snake was seen') and the simple declarative sentence ('they moved to the next mound') help sharpen your lines immeasurably.

Strive, too, for 'talking writing,' ie the effect of speech rather than a literary style. Avoid figures and statistics as much as possible. Do not describe precisely what is seen; interpretive comments will make your point better. Certainly, do not talk about things that are *not* seen, except if you are interpreting things that are.

Anything you can do to rouse interest with narration also will be appreciated. Dramatisation, humour, the use of more than one voice— each, in its place, can be effective. Do not be afraid to experiment.

As you write, read your narration aloud or persuade a friend to do so while you listen. You will be shocked at the awkward twists and stiffnesses that will be revealed.

In addition, such reading will help you with cueing, ie timing out the precise moment or point within a visual at which narration should begin and determining how long any given segment of narration should run. While all sorts of formulas have been devised for setting narration length, your own ear is still the best judge as to how long a speech can run before boredom sets in.

Keeping it simple

Using the two-column script, descriptions of visuals on your typewriter will ordinarily run from spaces 15 to 40 and sound descriptions from 45 to 70 (pica type and the left edge of the paper at zero). The page number will come two spaces below top of page, the first line of text, four lines below page number. All copy should be double spaced and there should be four spaces between shots.

As you will see from the samples in Part II, it is pretty much up to you how you describe the visuals. The big issues are clarity and simplicity. For my money, that means emphasis on pictorial nouns, action verbs and simple declarative sentences.

I also have prejudices about this phase of format. If a presentation is to include both art and photographs, I like to have each labelled as such.

Further, I believe crews work faster and better if there is no confusion as to the setting of the work: whether a picture is INT (interior) or EXT (exterior); where it is located (PARK, GROCERY STORE, COTTAGE,

SURGERY); and the time (DAY or NIGHT). This information should be typed ALL CAPS at the start of the visual.

Below the setting, you should describe how large the subject is to appear in the picture relative to the background and what the said subject is doing. Film terminology on this works from three basic positions: LONG SHOT (LS), which describes the subject in relation to background; MEDIUM SHOT (MS), a shot that takes in the subject but not much else; and CLOSE-UP (CU), an emphasis shot, calling attention to some limited portion or specific detail of the subject.

Other common designations include ELS (extreme long shot), MLS (medium long shot), MCU (medium close-up), ECU (extreme close-up). There is an assortment of others but, in all of them, the important thing to remember is that each is relative. Consequently, the image size designations are meaningless unless you name the subject, for example ELS, brown cow; CU, dagger handle; or MCU, Genevieve.

On the audio side of the page, you set down anything that should be heard: MUSIC, SOUND EFFECTS (FX, SFX), NARRATOR (NAR.), or dialogue (ED, CORNELIA, GOD). If the music you want is 'Ride of the Valkyries,' obviously you must say so. Same holds for thunderbolts, Porsche motors revving or the chirping of crickets where sound effects are concerned. The narrator (actors, too) will appreciate knowing how you want him to speak, for example wearily, angrily or hoarse with fright.

One-column scripts take the same road, as per the examples on pp. 70–71.

The master scene script describes action from spaces 15 to 75 on the typewriter, gives dialogue lines or narration from spaces 30 to 60, sets up parenthetical business (the manner in which speeches are delivered) from spaces 40 to 55, and names speakers from space 45. Speeches/narration and action are single spaced; everything else is double spaced.

As you will see from the samples in Part II, however, this is a business full of individualists and not all follow the same line. Some will single space where I say double, some will use capitals where I recommend lower case letters, while others will describe shots and settings in a manner to make my hair stand on end. The variety does not matter; you have a guide of sorts to go by and adapt to whatever circumstances you find yourself confronting.

Making it complex

One of the first things you learn in any kind of writing is never to let anyone see rough or unfinished copy, and this is doubly important for AV shooting scripts.

The reason for this is that the best script you can write is still rough and unfinished as far as your sponsor is concerned. He is thinking in terms of the completed programme or presentation. The fact that it goes through a 'paper' stage en route or that this stage might conceivably be beyond his comprehension is an item which eludes him.

This is in no way calculated to question the sponsor's intelligence or good intentions. He may be a saint already canonised and a genius at electronics or finance or mass production. Yet in all too many cases, the script *is* beyond him—so far beyond that he will probably never grasp it. The reason is that he and millions like him, lack the power to visualise. He simply will not be able to make the jump from words to pictures—to hear sound and see pictures from the pages you present him.

Naturally, this is not true of *all* sponsors. Occasionally, you will be fortunate and find yourself working with one who sees your concepts every bit as vividly as you do, and maybe more so.

More often than not, however, you will not be so lucky. In addition, your sponsor almost certainly will insist on seeing your shooting script. Then, having seen it, he will panic. I can offer no sure-fire solution to this dilemma. My only suggestion is, in essence, cautionary: do not join him in panic.

To this end, put yourself in the sponsor's place. Imagine that he is a microbiologist. Called into his laboratory, you are told to look into his microscope. Will you see the same things he does? Interpret them in an identical manner? The answer, of course, is no. The microbiologist, as a specialist, sees and interprets with a specialist's knowledge.

You, as a specialist in scripting for the audiovisual media, are in a similar position. Looking at a script, you see things in it and interpret them differently than does—indeed, than *can*—a non-specialist.

How should you cope with this? For one thing, do not just hand the sponsor the script. That is no more fair than it would be for the microbiologist to command you to use his microscope. It is better to make it a point to let him know in advance that script interpretation calls for its own brand of expertise. It will do no harm, indeed, if you parade a few polysyllabic technicalities—refer to Marshall McLuhan, Eisenstein, Vorkapich, Korzybski—and throw in overtones of the esoteric.

Then, *act out* your presentation, shot by shot and step by step. Do not hesitate to dramatise, gesticulate and even leap about, if that seems to be called for. Radiate enthusiasm. Pulse reassurance. Make it clear to the sponsor that all is clear sailing, that there are no problems. A bit of flattery in regard to the sponsor's acumen and insight might not be amiss.

The sponsor, in his turn, will have ideas. Listen to them, separating them into two categories as you do so. Part will be generalities, ie overall reactions to your product; others, probably the majority, will focus on specifics and pinpoint details.

Check the generalities carefully. It just may be that the sponsor has caught some weakness that you have overlooked or a strength that rates larger attention.

Pay attention to the second group too, for again the sponsor may have noted flaws or errors. By and large, however, what he has to offer will be nit-picking based on ignorance of the field. Typically, he will complain about your choice of words in describing visuals, not realising that these words are intended to make things clear to the crew and so have only indirect bearing on what reaches the screen. He may think that a close-up means that the camera is physically close to the subject, or that the punctuation does not follow the rules he learned in school, or that all sorts of miscellaneous background information needs to be incorporated into shot descriptions.

Whatever the sponsor says, however, work through the script with him step by step and shot by shot. Within the framework of so doing, bow to his every whim. Let him change commas and abort adverbs to his heart's content. You can accept all this with good grace and cheerful mien because, if you have handled things skilfully, all that is sacrificed is a little time; you know that he will not spoil your brain child after all.

The storyboard approach

A storyboard is a script translated into still pictures. It consists of a series of photographs or sketches, each showing a successive slide/frame/action segment of the proposed AV presentation. Ordinarily, the storyboard reveals only what the audience will see on the screen, though occasionally a writer will include diagrams, floor plans or the like, for either his own or the director's benefit.

A special pad may be used for storyboarding. It has space for sketches down the left-hand side, while the right is reserved for narration/sound/comment. Alternatively, the pictures may be centred and the narration typed or written in beneath each.

Another way of handling the job is to present each picture on a card or sheet of paper which has a ratio of approximately three units of height to four of width ($3 \times 4''$; $4 \times 6''$, or $5 \times 8''$ pads often are used). These pages then are pinned to a corkboard or other display surface where they can be rearranged at will if concepts change or additions or deletions are made.

The function of the storyboard is to help the writer, the sponsor or their associates to see the script's visual relationships and development more clearly. The reason for this is that an amazing number of people simply cannot visualise from words. Also, quite often, the writer himself has trouble finding language to convey to others the image he seeks. When that happens, a storyboard is a handy tool to have in reserve.

On the other hand, do not let the difficulties scare you off if a storyboard

FILM: PEST CONTROL #5   FRAME NUMBER: 1

FILMSTRIP FRAME DIMENSION

35mm SLIDE DIMENSION

FINAL MEDIA - PHOTOGRAPH: X   ART: OTHER:

EDUCATIONAL OBJECTIVE: TO DEMONSTRATE PRECAUTIONS NECESSARY IN PUBLIC AREAS OUTDOORS.

VIDEO:

SHRUBBERY BEING SPRAYED BY WORKER. THE AREA IS ROPED OFF.

AUDIO:

APPROVED BY:

[PLEASE MAKE ADDITIONAL COMMENTS ON BACK OF FORM]

Storyboard excerpt used by permission of Postal Service Training and Development Institute.

FILM: _PEST CONTROL #5_   FRAME NUMBER: ___ 2

FILMSTRIP FRAME DIMENSION
35mm SLIDE DIMENSION

FINAL MEDIA - PHOTOGRAPH: ___X___   ART: ___   OTHER: ___

EDUCATIONAL OBJECTIVE: TO DEMONSTRATE THAT PUBLIC AREAS ARE TREATED AFTER HOURS IF POSSIBLE.

VIDEO: AUDIO:

WORKER SPRAYING BASEBOARDS IN
WINDOW AREA. THE AREA IS CLOSED.
ALL WINDOWS OBVIOUSLY CLOSED.
LIGHTS ARE OFF.

APPROVED BY: ___

[PLEASE MAKE ADDITIONAL
COMMENTS ON BACK OF FORM]

Storyboard excerpt used by permission of Postal Service Training and Development Institute.

FILM: PEST CONTROL #5   FRAME NUMBER: 3

FILMSTRIP FRAME DIMENSION
35mm SLIDE DIMENSION

FINAL MEDIA - PHOTOGRAPH: ___X___   ART: _____   OTHER: Burn/In

EDUCATIONAL OBJECTIVE: DEMONSTRATE IMPROPER PRECAUTIONS IN OPEN PUBLIC AREA.

VIDEO:

BAIT STATION IN THE MIDDLE
OF THE FLOOR IN A POST
OFFICE BOX AREA. B/I
LARGE "X".

AUDIO:

APPROVED BY: _____

[PLEASE MAKE ADDITIONAL
COMMENTS ON BACK OF FORM]

Storyboard excerpt used by permission of Postal Service Training and Development Institute.

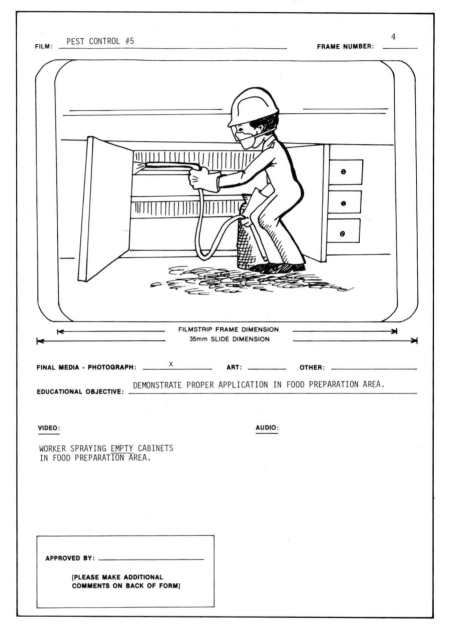

Storyboard excerpt used by permission of Postal Service Training and Development Institute.

is needed. Plan out your presentation shot by shot; then sketch the key shots, however roughly, as you see them in your mind's eye. Practice is the key, and it is a great way to pass the time during television commercials.

Forget presentation or shooting boards. They should be the decision and responsibility of producer or director, not writer.

In the art storyboard examples shown on pp. 80–83—they represent a 'shooting' board—every detail is spelled out. Even 'educational objective' is nailed down, shot by shot. Note, too, how costly this sort of procedure is. In a large organisation, however, it can be justified in terms of reduced shooting time later.

The photo board, in turn, establishes its value by virtually eliminating the possibility of error in the finished filmstrip by the precision with which it shows details that could never be put across in words.

Words *are* the writer's tools, however; and nowhere are they more important than when he gets down to

Again: continuing elaboration

A script is built, not born: each time around, you flesh it out in greater detail.

From topic you go to idea.
From idea to concept.
From concept to key point.
From key point to proposal.
From proposal to treatment.
From treatment to production script.

It does not end there, though, if the finished product is to reach its full potential.

First glances and first guesses can be good sometimes but not always. When they are not, you need second looks and second guesses and maybe even third.

It is vital, therefore, that you do not try to go too fast or freeze your thinking before it is complete. Rather, bide awhile and brood awhile. Make further notes. Question your shots, your approaches, your ideas.

If your pages have become too cluttered, you may need to retype and, possibly, rework as you go. Talk things over with the producer; you might even go so far as to listen to what he has to say, that is *really* listen. Some of the sponsor's notions may not be as crack-brained as you first thought; do not shut them out just because he is the one who voiced them.

Above all, try to visualise your finished project: the programme you hope ultimately to see or feel or experience. Analyse it, step by step, shot by shot and display by display. Try to spell out your goals more clearly.

You will never reach a state of total satisfaction, of course. Nirvana is something to dream of, not attain, and deadlines put an end to every project. Hopefully you will know at least that you have given the job your best shot. That is worth something.

Your job is not done just because the script is finished. You still have to cope with the production stage.

Production and its problems

9

A client knocked at my door one day with an assignment. The organisation he represented had a personnel-training textbook which needed to be made more palatable to its employees/students. To this end, the said organisation wanted me to script a series of tape cassettes that would dramatise the principles the book presented.

This is hardly a unique situation. Every audiovisual writer who has been around awhile frequently finds himself signed on to adapt material from one medium for use in another. The writing seldom offers any major problems. Such headaches as do arise ordinarily spring from issues over and beyond copy, for example, balancing the budget, dealing with assorted tempests in teapots, coping with what appear to be crushing catastrophes, or estimating elements that range up to—and sometimes beyond—the fourth dimension.

Most of these difficulties involve what might loosely be termed production problems. More often than not, when the cards are down, the writer will be called upon to help solve them. He will be asked to 'write around' them.

Balancing the budget

The tape cassette assignment, I eventually learned, involved salvaging a large textbook investment. Rather than throw out or do the whole programme again, those in charge had decided to add the supplemental tapes. This was an intelligent and perfectly legitimate approach, of course, and one from which I gained a considerable profit. It does illustrate, however, the way in which an AV writer may be drawn in to help solve non-AV problems.

Another situation, which did not end so happily for me, grew out of a state agency's assignment of an employee to script an urgently needed film. Production had to meet a rigid deadline.

Less than knowledgeable in the film field, the employee slopped through the job and then quit. The agency was stuck with a disastrous combination of tight schedule and unshootable script. To make matters worse, they had previously contracted a producer to make the film. All the available money was tied up in the said contract.

At this point, the agency asked me how much I would take to redo the script. I spent several days and a fair amount of travel money investigating, then quoted them a figure. They came back with an offer of a third of what I had asked, on grounds that the producer would finance only a treatment fee from his contract money. I refused. Whereupon, the agency flew into a rage and refused even to return my phone calls to discuss the matter further.

There are other cases when you have scripted a job and the circumstances change in the course of production. I remember one such instance when bad weather killed a week's shooting time. That meant an extra week's pay for the entire crew. The producer promptly turned to me, the writer, and blithely demanded that I change the script to eliminate a week's time elsewhere.

Again, the council of an Indian tribe abruptly decided that an exorbitant fee must be paid into its coffers if shots of various artifacts were included in a filmstrip. Who do you suppose was asked to devise a way to dodge the issue and eliminate the problem?

Closely related to, and often overlapping, these budget-balancing crises are a second type of trouble, one which I call 'tempests in teapots.'

Tempests in teapots

Subject: A colourful Indian sheep drive.

Problem: The current low price of mutton leads the tribal elders to decide that this year the drive is not worth the bother. So no visuals are available for the programme you have scripted.

Subject: A leading science fiction writer.

Problem: It suddenly dawns on this writer that the opulence of his habitat may arouse the greed of larcenous types. He therefore refuses to have any of the background vital to the presentation included.

Subject: A scientist's review of his investigations.

Problem: The narration that the scientist wants included is far too long and there are no visuals that fit it.

I put the above tempests in the teapot class because they are relatively easy to resolve. Thus, the sheep drive project can be saved by a bit of fakery that combines landscapes with close-ups. The science fiction writer can be shot against a cheap star map, with only economy class mementoes displayed on the table before him. A programme can be made up of visuals that capture the essence of the scientist's work; he is then limited to comments on them and opening, closing and bridging narration that summarises his philosophy over shots of him at work in his laboratory.

Other problems include: the brilliant lines that you have written that will just not read; the new industrial equipment that has to be incorporated at the last moment; the room with a ceiling too low for the display that you have planned; the exhibit that has to be moved to quarters with too few cases or bad acoustics or wiring inadequate to handle the lights; the colours that looked good on paper but prove hideous in production.

In each case, you the writer will probably be called on to remedy the situation. Do not resent it. It is better for you to help work it out than to have the producer or crewman simply chop the project to pieces.

The worst problems are yet to come. What do you do about the headaches that aspirin will not cure?

Coping with catastrophe

It is one of the largest wooden churches extant. Your slide show will examine the fascinating details of its architecture.

Only now, one night half-way through the shooting, the church burns down.

An in-house TV tribute to a company official is scheduled for showing next week.

Today, it is revealed that the official has had his hand in the till all these years.

A sports short on your school's top high-jumper.

He breaks his leg at the penultimate meet, the one just before the one at which he was rated to win the championship.

These are disasters and it is entirely possible that you will not be able to do a thing about them. On the other hand, do not let a mood of gloom envelop you too quickly; victory *has* been snatched out of the jaws of defeat more times than you might imagine.

Your three best tools for coping with disasters, in my experience, are ingenuity, attitude and symbolism. They are tied together so closely that it is hard to separate one from the other.

Ingenuity just might provide a way out of the problem of the church that burns. You could, for example, substitute simple sketches, art work, for some of the photographs you had planned to use, especially if you, the writer, had the foresight to take your 35mm camera along when you researched the project, shooting everything but the kitchen sink, as the saying goes. Your contact prints from that film may very well give an artist just the detail he needs in order to reproduce the church's minutiae as line drawings. Intercut with your crew's photography, you may end up with a first-class slide show after all.

If you also rewrite your narration a bit, to add a nostalgic tone and emphasise the sense of loss, you may, indeed, find yourself with a better and more intriguing presentation than you had counted on in the beginning.

What about Company Official? The odds are that, most of the time and in most companies, your show is as good as junked already. Executives are sensitive about corporate image. They want to play ostrich, hide their heads under the board table and pretend that the official never existed and defalcation never took place. There is, however, the remote chance that, given the right *attitude*, you may be able to salvage something.

Let me show you what I mean. Years ago I knew a man who, in his youth, had spent several terms as mayor of an Arizona mining town. His original election is a shining example of how attitude can turn the tide in impossible situations.

The day before the polling, a mass meeting had been arranged at which the populace could hear each candidate express his views. At this meeting, our man's most bitter opponent had revealed that the candidate's mistress was the town's most notorious lady of pleasure.

It was the kind of disclosure that should have dealt the candidate's chances a mortal blow. He refused to accept it as such, however. Instead, he called the shady lady up out of the crowd and onto the platform.

'This is Susie,' he announced. 'If there's any man here who don't wish he was sleeping with her like I am, I want him to vote against me.'

He won the election by a landslide.

In case you think this is too far-out an example, I cite you the case of the town of Wetumka, Oklahoma. Thirty years ago, Wetumka was visited by a confidence swindler who successfully mulcted the local business community of everything except their drawers.

The town, however, had a sense of humour. After the first shock had worn off, one and all collapsed in a gale of laughter at the way they had been gulled. They then established a special holiday—Sucker Day—that is still celebrated with the area's most feastive annual event. They just wish the original con man would join them for it but so far he has stayed clear despite the community's promise to grant him immunity from prosecution.

Bearing these two instances in mind, a tongue-in-cheek account of the embezzling company official's deeds and misdeeds might prove wildly successful. You could perhaps use two narrators, one reciting the official's achievements in glowing terms as they would have appeared in the originally scheduled programme, the other describing his transgressions over cut-in footage of cash being lifted, hands juggling books, safes being opened, and the like.

I would like to do the script myself, in fact, but I will not pretend that I think most companies would go for the idea—not when I still cannot persuade the Oklahoma Tourism people to let me include Wetumka's Sucker Day in their promotion programmes.

The high-jumper with a broken leg offers special difficulties. First, of course, comes the fact of the fracture. For the year, at any rate, he is out of the running (no pun intended). If he is a senior pupil, it is the end of his chances for championship status in the school competition. Even if he is a junior, it still means putting your project on ice for a year while you pray that next season will see him back in the winner's circle.

The issue of attitude intervenes again here. Who says sports shorts can concern only winners, champions? Why do the hard-luck guys never get any limelight?

I am living in Costa Rica as I write this and the country's first entrant in Olympic skiing competitions has just finished next-to-last. He fell down before he completed his runs on the slalom! And yet, here in the tiny Central American republic of Costa Rica, this man is a hero. Only three years a skier, his way to Lake Placid paid for by donations, he arrived with no coach, no crew, no doctor and no team-mates, but he still entered and he still finished. Next to last or not, he finished. To his countrymen, therefore, he is a hero.

Ingenuity and attitude can help you, as a scriptwriter, salvage programmes but how does *symbolism* help?

A symbol is something that represents another something: the lion stands for Britain, the donkey for the Democratic party, the cross for Christianity, the arrow-pierced heart for love, and the black armband for mourning. This makes symbolism a handy tool for the scriptwriter. Under the right circumstances he can substitute a symbol for an unavailable or expensive visual.

The cliché file offers us a plethora of examples of symbols. Remember the calendar's flipping leaves that indicate the passage of time; the moving clock hands; the snow-laden tree branch that dissolves into bloom, greens out, goes bare and stark as autumn leaves fall; the walking feet, the spinning wheels, the whirling propellers?

Symbols need not necessarily be clichés, nor do we have to cast them out forever in the name of sophistication. You can still use a map or road sign to pin-point a place, thermometers or seasonal scenes to indicate time of year, tools or hands at work to establish setting. Book jackets, newspapers, programmes, tickets, passports, menus, placards and money all add up to a convenient shorthand limited only by the imagination of those who use it.

Sound too may be a symbol. Voices chattering in Cantonese mean one thing, German gutterals another. A Viennese waltz sets a different mood than does the tinkle of marimbas. The clicking of a telegraph key represents a period separate from that of the teletype's clatter.

One word of caution is necessary: do not be too subtle with your symbols. The Russian postage stamp or Euclidean equation that has great significance for you may totally elude a less discerning viewer. Also, be sure that the symbols mean what you intend. The yellow chrysanthemums you find so bright and cheerful are the flower of death in Mexico; purple is the colour of mourning; and, the 'mujer alegre' from your phrase book is not just the happy woman you think she is in Spain.

These are points to ponder at your leisure.

The art of estimating

Soon after you enter the AV field, you will become acquainted with what is called 'budget writing.' Which is just another way of saying, 'Keep it cheap, Jack! We haven't the mint behind us.'

Since estimating and budgeting actually are the writer's problem only indirectly, there is no need to go into their technicalities here but the producer *will* appreciate it if you have at least some minimal awareness of the factors involved.

The key issue, straight down the line, is time: the more time a job takes, the higher the cost. This being the case, you will be dealing with a fair range of variables once you get out of the shoot-it-in-an-afternoon-at-the-lab-bench class. These include:

1 Construction.
2 Lighting set-ups.
3 Sound.
4 Cast.
5 Travel.
6 Shooting.
7 Opticals/special effects.
8 Art/animation.

AV writers sometimes assume that *construction* refers only to building mammoth sets in the *Intolerance* mould. They could not be more in error. Huge stagings are seldom an issue in AV.

Miniatures, on the other hand, are a considerable factor. When you write the Baths of Caracalla, the Hanging Gardens of Babylon or pre-Fire London into your script, you are calling for endless hours of research and labour by skilled specialists. The same can be said for relief maps of the Mindanao Deep, a reproduction of the Acoma Pueblo or a termitary. This does not mean that such are *verboten* but you do need to ask around among the people who will be doing or paying for the work just how practical your ideas are. Their answers quite possibly may lead you to modify your thinking.

Lighting set-ups are another major cost factor. Why? Because it takes time to put up, adjust, take down and move the lights necessary for good photographic work. The more space that has to be lighted, in all probability the more lighting set-ups are needed. Changes in locale (and that means even from room to room) are also cost factors as is the setting itself. For example, a grimy engine room is going to eat light the way a whale engulfs plankton; shiny sterile hospital facilities offer their own problems.

Again, the answer is to talk to your workers—your camera people, in this instance. Find out *before* your script is frozen whether what you have called for is going to prove a disaster area.

Sound can make or break you. Original music or out-of-this-world sound effects have a price. Can your project afford it?

You will find lip-synchronised dialogue far more expensive than voice-over narration. The reason is not just that recordists and mixers must be hired; more important, often, is the fact that with lip-sync you give more people more chances to make mistakes. Consequently, your crew may have to spend extra hours getting satisfactory takes. This also runs up the costs for your cast.

The people who will be performing in your epic are the *cast*. It should go without saying that the smaller your cast, the better. If you are using professional talent, they will cost money. If you are using amateurs, scheduling, coordinating and working with them will take time which, as we pointed out earlier, is an expensive item.

Most AV packages do not really call for much talent on the part of their actors. As the writer, you should do your best to keep it that way. Virtuoso performers are hard to come by and proper planning and scripting will eliminate the need for them.

This brings up another practical matter: the use of animal actors. Please, avoid it! Coaxing animals into the behaviour your script calls for—while at the same time not committing indiscretions on the set—can be a maddening task. It is better by far to write them out. If you *must* have animals, limit your demands on them to the prop level.

Travel can be a snare and a pitfall. In the first place, the cost of transporting and maintaining even the smallest crew can be incredible. In the second, staging in an unfamiliar locale involves small—and sometimes large—nightmares, ranging from inadequate power sources to delighted natives who come to observe (read: 'gawk') and otherwise disrupt your crew's work. In the third, you may in the end discover that you really could have done the job better back home where conditions can be controlled.

Hollywood did not build everything from Les Halles market to atomic submarines on its sound stages for no reason.

The actual business of *shooting* would seem to be a simple, easily figured matter but here again there may be problems. Have you written in such items as time-lapse photography, in which more time than usual passes between successive frames of film, so that an apple tree's bloom changes to ripened fruit before you eyes? Have your included microphotography, where the intimacies of aphid life loom three feet tall, or high-speed work that sees speeding bullets stopped in mid-flight or travelling leisurely across the screen?

All these and many other matters take time and trouble and so cost money.

Lastly, there is a package I tend to group together: *art/animation/opticals/special effects*. Each of these is a subject unto itself on which whole books have been written. Each is vital in certain situations. Each costs— sometimes astronomically—because it requires the work of specialists. Rather than discuss it here, inadequately, I refer you to such works as the John Halas/Roger Manvell volume, *The Technique of Film Animation*, and Raymond Fielding's *The Technique of Special Effects Cinematography*. Every AV writer should be familiar with them.

Reactions and revisions

10

Back during World War 2, aircraft recognition was a vital matter for servicemen. Often, improvised audiovisual aids were used to help teach it. These, generally, involved association of a cartoon drawing of some particularly toothsome, scantily-clad female with each aircraft. Plane and drawing were flashed on the screen simultaneously. The servicemen/students then shouted out a descriptive appellation—frequently unprintable—designed to identify both girl and plane.

The technique worked beautifully. Kept alert by their yen to catch yet another eyeful of the luscious lovelies, the woman-starved troopers soon had little difficulty in telling a Messerschmitt from a Spitfire, a Wellington or Lancaster from a Dornier.

Impressed by all this, some of us attempted to carry the principle back into civilian audiovisual practice. There complications arose. Specifically, we soon learned that service situations frequently were a good deal more free and easy than those on the outside. So when I introduced the girl gimmick into a filmstrip designed to teach safety practices to oil field personnel, I found myself confronted by an ageing, choleric executive whose purple wattles shook with rage and righteous indignation as he informed me that the strip would never see screen in the state of Texas so long as it carried frames portraying 'that huzzy!'

Needless to say, the girl came out and I learned a lesson significant to every writer: it is not enough to write a script; you also must live—and cope with—the frequently unpredictable reactions that follow.

The maiden's blush

An elderly gentleman with whom I was for a time associated had a pet phrase that came up at least half-a-dozen times during the preparation of any script. 'Remember,' he would warn, 'these lines will fall on virgin ears!'

We writers used to laugh about it; it came across that corny. As the years roll by, however, I find myself thinking that whether or not the old gentleman was right about the ears, at least he was definitely on target as to how a good many people react to blue lines or off-colour remarks in AV programmes.

Thus, I recall a technical course in which students had to remember an involved list of colours in exact order. To help them with it, the instructors had worked out a mnemonic phrase, a nonsense sentence that served as a memory aid. Dull rather than obscene or even naughty, it still served its purpose very well.

Then someone came up with the bright idea of incorporating core course data in a filmstrip. One of the items included was the naughty nonsense sentence.

Put into service, however, the filmstrip got an instantaneous and well-nigh violent reaction. Students whom no one had ever thought of as even remotely moralistic proclaimed their indignation and filed protests with the administration. In a matter of days, the offending programme was withdrawn until the writer—not me, praise be!—could wearily work up a new, unsullied sentence, pure as the driven snow.

On another occasion a rather elaborate multimedia resort promotion presentation was the target of censorial attention. Thinking in terms of what he knew of his potential audience, the writer incorporated a fragment at the end of a sequence on indoor sports activities in which the camera focused on a bedroom. Illumination was a small nightstand light, the room itself visible only in vaguest outlines. A man's hand reaches over and turns off the light.

A moment's silence. Then, out of the black, a woman's hoarse, passionate whisper, 'Oh, darling ... '

Do I need to tell you it was killed?

In other words, you will save energy if you forego any hint of such, unless you know in advance that the sponsor will go along.

The fatal flaw

Some years ago Broadway had as one of its more colourful attractions a musical review called *Star and Garter*, starring the renowned ecdysiast (read: strip-tease artist) Gypsy Rose Lee. One of the show's better numbers featured a gentleman yclept Professor Lamberti performing a xylophone solo.

Audience enthusiasm for the act apparently knew no bounds. The professor was, of course, delighted.

What he remained apparently oblivious to was that, while he hammered out his numbers, a luscious young lady (I do not remember whether or not it was Gypsy) was parading seductively about the stage behind him, divesting herself of garment after garment. The xylophone's tinkling music had nothing whatever to do with the applause.

Well, it was a good act and I, for one, certainly enjoyed it. I recall it now, however, not for its entertainment value but for the parallel it draws with what I term the *fatal flaw*: the elements or aspects of a situation of which an audiovisual writer is not aware but which can prove disastrous for him and his project.

Here are three cases in point.

Your programme deals with an ultra-conservative religious sect that clings to its traditional ways. Completed, it contains stock shots that show tractors at work, allegedly in sect's fields.

Only then do you learn that one of the group's tenets disallows the use of power equipment.

You script a presentation on computer function. It centres on a formula which you have picked up from a textbook for calculating a key mathematical aspect of the work.

When the programme is proudly unveiled to an audience that includes a top computer expert, the sponsor—and you—learn with horror that the expert considers the programme amusing. Your prized formula was discarded as inadequate 25 years ago.

Your script specifies a 'saddled horse.' The saddle with which the horse is equipped in the finished presentation is a high-pommelled Western type when the situation calls for an English one. Comments run a kindly gamut from 'absurd' to 'ridiculous.'

All these are, regrettably, true incidents. They illustrate the reason why every writer, on every project, should insist upon having a technical advisor.

He also should research his script in painstaking detail—and not just in books.

Then, he should be sure that his statement of the case is so clear that not even a production crew can misunderstand or misinterpret it.

Failure to take these precautions will certainly force rewrites—rewrites at the writer's own expense if he is the one at fault. It also will lead to embarrassment, producer irritation, and to the producer's eyeing the writer's claims to reliability and competence with a certain cynicism in the future.

This is not to say that you can always avoid such traps, no matter how careful you may be. Thus, the writer in the computer fiasco described *had* a technical advisor. The trouble was that the advisor had been working in the field at the base level rather than keeping up with new developments.

Similarly, an outdoor-type producer would have known from context the type of saddle needed in the horse bit. Unfortunately, the man involved had no taste at all for animal husbandry. To him, a saddle was a saddle, and that was that. In fact, if the situation had turned out to be funny rather than calamitous, the producer would have belonged down in our next category.

The gags you didn't plan for

Ernie was a good man but rigidly teetotal. Lips that touched wine were not even going to get into the same room with his if he could help it. So it was a mistake to put him to work on a show that had included a scene in which a character took a drink.

Ernie's interpretation was to fill a water-glass to the brim with stage whisky for the actor to gulp down. The actor must have been equally inexperienced because he did precisely what he was told to. It gave the producer and writer a good laugh when they looked at the rough cut but it also necessitated reshooting.

The lesson to be learnt is: be sure that your script says what it means and that the cast and crew understand that meaning.

Another mirthful occasion involved a mental health film on coping with anger. The key point was: anger is contagious. Often you take out the rage brought on by one event on something unrelated and entirely unoffending.

In the script, a man has a bad day at work. He vents his spleen on his wife. She turns her wrath on their little boy. The boy kicks the family dog.

When the crew shot the scene, all went according to plan up to where the boy kicked the dog. At that point, the dog took the initiative and lunged at a passing cat. The cat, in turn, took off at full speed with the dog in hot pursuit, in an S-curve that would have delighted D. W. Griffith.

The scene proved far and away the most effective in the picture. Audiences by the thousand have doubled over with laughter at it and I still meet people who insist on telling me about it. Yet it was an incident totally unplanned for.

The lesson to be learnt is: you can have good luck as well as bad but it is not something to count on.

This incident is one of those that taught me how dangerous it is to put yourself at the mercy of animal actors. While they may, and sometimes do, give you wonderful effects, your lack of control over them can prove disastrous.

Similarly unplanned, but necessitating a good bit of rewriting and reshooting, was an incident involving a director/photographer friend of mine. He was working on a presentation featuring a young woman who wore her hair in the long, straight, flat-ironed style of the '60s and '70s. In the course of the job, she became enamoured of the director.

Unaware of this fact, he made a crucial mistake. He vocally admired the hairdo of another young lady who wore her tresses in a short, tight-waved, upswept mode.

Fate enters. The director is called out of town unexpectedly for a week. Another photographer unfamiliar with what has been done, takes over.

On returning, the director discovers that his star has decided that she would be more attractive to him if her hair were more like that of the girl he had regarded so approvingly. So, not even thinking of how this might affect the work she was engaged in, she had her locks shorn and coiffed to resemble those of her imagined rival.

How do you cope with a situation in which half the shots of your show feature a young woman with long hair and the remaining half, the same young woman, waved and upswept, particularly when the two halves are not in sequence?

You call in the writer. He goes quietly crazy trying to figure out ways to space out the long-haired shots so that they will intercut with close-ups without making it too obvious that what was going to be a neat little presentation has now become a salvage job.

Blooper time

Every shop has what is variously called a 'goody reel' or 'blooper box' or whatever, in which are gathered the hilarious relics of disaster. Here stands the medical show star who, forgetting that hospital gowns hang open in the rear, inadvertently turns his back to the camera. Here, too, is the actor who, picking up the telephone, speaks into the receiver. The man who stalks dramatically to the set door, prepared to jerk it open as per the script—only the knob comes off in his hand. The girl who, staring soulfully into her lover's eyes, flips cigarette ash into his dinner.

If these bits happen to have been recorded in lip-sync sound, you will also hear some of the most colourful language you are likely to encounter anywhere.

The tradition of 'Blooper Time', the moment when someone abruptly decides to thread up the reel or load the slides, is, I think, a highly desirable one. This is a business in which people tend to get up tight. Painstaking care can, under stress, deteriorate into fussiness. The time comes when you know you will scream or smash if someone reminds you just one more time that the elected term this year is 'lodge' and not 'resort.' The fact that sooner or later you will find a way to make minerals come alive for grade-school pupils or the display on the Talmud compete with soccer still does not keep you from wanting to drown your own blank-brained inadequacy in a bottle.

When such moods take over, it is good to know that this also can be a silly business, populated by lunatics fully capable of de-pantsing a radio announcer while he is on the air and cannot fight back. When some clown plays games with possible homonyms in your script, substituting a bag of flour for a bunch of flowers, it lightens and brightens.

Reworking an old show is never the happiest of tasks but it need not be so bad.

Updating the easy way

Mini skirts, billboards, Trans Ams and beehive hairdos all offer hazards for the AV writer. In each case, they are identifiable with a period and, consequently, they date a presentation. Yet often, dating is the last thing a sponsor wants. He is eager to have his programme appear sharp, current. Indeed, any time it loses that pristine edge his impulse is to, in the phrase, 'update' it.

Can you see the problem that develops? In order to eliminate dated styles and scenes, the entire project may have to be re-done and that can be expensive. Besides, people age. The cute blonde may have added 40 pounds in the past ten years. The handsome young scientist or salesman now may peer myopically from beneath a bald spot.

How can you deal with such and update without anguish?

It is not easy and sometimes it is totally impossible, especially when theories or attitudes are revised. Psychiatry offers some beautiful examples. Pre-frontal lobotomy held the spotlight as the answer to all sorts of emotional problems. Then styles changed and lobotomy was hastily swept beneath the psychiatric rug or even paraded as a 'chamber of horrors' exhibit. Now, under the name of psychosurgery, it may be making a comeback.

Most stumbling blocks are not that extreme, however. They centre on externals, surface details, and not core content. Also, there are a few tricks of the audiovisual trade that can blunt the horns of your dilemma. The trouble is, though, that most of these tricks are steps you need to take not when time for revision is at hand but back at the beginning, when you script the original package.

Specifically, what you need to do with any programme that may stay in use for a protracted period is to plan it so that *colour* is separated from *content* insofar as practical. (Colour may be called atmosphere, background realism or interest elements; content, in contrast, may be described as information which your programme must convey to viewers if it is to fulfil its function.)

What I am suggesting, then, is that you avoid interweaving the colour and content components inextricably, where possible.

Thus, on interiors, avoid extremes of style as much as you can, even to the point of specifying that the crew frame their shots so as *not* to feature the brand new IBM electric typewriter in an identifiable manner. Walk wide of Carnaby Street gear; costume your cast in simple, clean-lined garb—maybe not the traditional 'basic black' but on that order. Treat hair, footgear and decor in the same way.

If the sponsor *wants* the latest thing, modern stylings, this is fair enough. Plan for such but limit it to 'colour' shots and sequences. Try to keep the content segments as timeless as possible.

Apply this principle even more rigidly to exterior shots. Car styles change like other fashions. Close-ups of crowds reveal the year in which they were shot. Billboards vending products long off the market are always good for inexpedient laughs. Buildings erected or torn down can kill you.

As the writer, set it forth in your script that crowds appear in extreme long shots only, that billboards are shot around where possible, that appearances of cars are restricted and skylines limited.

What should you do about the bald spot and the now-plump pigeon in content shots? To a degree, you can manage by cutting in close-ups of hands, equipment and background details, especially if you had the forethought to have the crew shoot lots of facial close-ups and broadly pertinent action when the original programme was prepared.

How well all this will work out remains to be seen. In general, I am dubious about updates. Film deteriorates, and matching cuts and colour even in slide shows can prove tricky if not impossible. However, if the sponsor insists, you will have to make the best of it. Always remember that the most successful efforts are those planned out in careful detail back when the presentation was first scripted.

11   Setting it in context

Her name was Elise and she very much wanted to become an AV writer. The trouble was that she lacked experience and no one was willing to trust her with an assignment.

The obvious answer was for Elise to do a few scripts for free, for public service groups or clubs or churches or whatever. Such frequently are poor enough to be grateful for any volunteer service. Elise would thus have gained experience and ended up with a finished product which she could have shown to potential paying sponsors.

Elise elected not to play it that way, however. As a secretary with a firm that frequently produced slide films and the like, she discovered that, first, her immediate boss often was involved in these productions and, second, he absolutely detested doing the informational brochures or teacher aids ('poop sheets' as they are often called) which went with the films.

That was enough for Elise. She took it upon herself to prepare this material for her boss, dropping it onto his desk in rough-draft form.

The boss at first was startled, but Elise made it a point to act as if she considered her rough drafts to be merely a part of routine secretarial service. The boss would have been less than human had he not accepted such relief from what he considered an odious chore. After all, it is easier to edit and correct less-than-perfect copy than it is to produce a guide from scratch.

For her part, Elise learned from the corrections. Soon her work was going through virtually untouched; the boss's approval was hardly more than a matter of form.

The next step was the scripts themselves and then Elise was on her way.

Over and beyond any ideas Elise's procedure may stimulate in you, it remains a fact that most audiovisual presentations are backed by printed matter. You as a writer probably will be required to prepare it. How do you go about it?

Among your souvenirs

You have designed a spectacular three-room, 16-case display on missile development, from the thrown stone to the thermonuclear warhead. Included are all sorts of working miniatures, viewer-participation devices and action-plus-sound units.

This kind of set-up can take a lot of explaining. Also, and no matter how meritorious the presentation, there is a limit to how long it will remain on display.

It is at this point that supplemental print materials come in. A flyer, a brochure or a souvenir programme all serve to preserve your masterpiece both as memorabilia and for future research reference. You will be surprised how often items ranging from old playbills through advertising pamphlets to leaflets calling for strike meetings end up as invaluable sources of data on all sorts of subjects.

Frequently, too, the management loves such addenda. A souvenir booklet on your mine tour simulation or dramatisation of the rise and fall of the hollow earth theory or the Bermuda Triangle, sold to viewers at a modest sum, may help make the presentation yield a tidy profit.

Preparing this kind of thing is much on the same order as writing a newspaper feature story. Your goal is to interest and entertain your reader, as well as to inform him.

To this end, try to begin by yelling 'Hey, you!' at him with something that catches his attention. Good ways to start include a brief, easily read *summary* of the contents, an intriguing *question*, a thought-provoking *quotation*, a striking *statement*, a colourful *description* or an interest-catching *anecdote* or story.

As your piece develops, make it a point to throw in more interesting facts, contrast bits and unusual twists, specific details, examples and quotations. Use short words, short sentences and short paragraphs with plenty of sensory and 'colour' content along with the facts about your topic.

Speaking of those facts, you will find your task simplified if you attack your topic systematically, looking into its past, its future and the people, places, things and processes involved. That does not mean that all will be included in your brochure, of course (and certainly not in the order I have given here), but you will stand less chance of missing vital aspects if you check it out as described.

In organising your material, in general follow the AV programme that is its *raison d'être*. Beyond this, try to relate your bits and pieces logically, tying each sentence to the one ahead where practical. At the end, tie up your package with a line or two that summarises the facts and feelings you have incorporated—a sort of 'So this is the way it stands' touch.

Writing is by no means the whole thing where this kind of package is concerned, however. If at all possible, make it a point to work things through with the art director (if any) and printer. Introduce pictures that add interest and/or clarify copy. Lay out pages to provide white space. Use subheads, indentations and captions—all the small, vital typographic tricks that help create attractive, uncluttered pages.

Bear all these things in mind also when you move over to preparing supplemental material for AV teaching programmes.

Is there a textbook in the house?

An amazing number of audiovisual presentations are designed to augment or supplement published textbooks. Thus, not long ago, my wife and I were handed a thick manual on industrial electricity and asked to script a variable-speed filmstrip, with sound, on electrical symbols to go with it. The instructors had found that their students just did not memorise symbols from the printed text. Presented as audiovisual instruction, however, with frequent tests and reviews within the programme the students had no choice but to master the subject.

Working in this way with textbooks is not particularly difficult but you do have to bear a few basic principles in mind. Ordinarily, for example, programmes must be coordinated with chapters and must follow the same organisational pattern. Whether AV units should use the same examples as the text is a matter of opinion and policy. Many authorities believe it is desirable. Others, however, feel you should introduce new examples illustrating the same concept. Alternatively, you can simply review text content.

There are other situations in which a text may strike a teacher as one-sided on a particular subject. He/she may wish to use audiovisuals to present another viewpoint: the Civil War from the South's angle, disease from the witch doctor's point of view, or apartheid as the Afrikaaner sees it.

In other cases it may be deemed desirable to offer pupils enrichment materials, ie data related to but not covered by the text. An English instructor may want background/biographical information on authors; a chemistry teacher, an outline of efforts other than Lavoisier's to identify and isolate oxygen; or a history department, sociological insights from Mayhew's *London Labour and the London Poor.*

All such can be developed nicely in audiovisual form. The only issues for the writer are careful advance appraisal of audience and purpose, and proper research to assure factually accurate content.

It should go without saying that a competent subject specialist is a tremendous asset in such work. Do not be so short-sighted as to begin without one. This will prove even more true when you undertake the projects covered in our next section.

Your guide to guidebooks

Most textbooks do not stand alone. For, though pupils seldom realise it, the teacher ordinarily has an extra edge in the form of a guidebook or teaching guide: a pamphlet or special edition of the text which provides related information or anecdotal material designed to make teaching simpler for the teacher.

Such teaching guides are not limited to textbooks. More and more, they are also provided for audiovisual materials so that the said materials may be presented with maximum effectiveness.

The preparation of such guides most often falls to the AV programme's writer. Indeed, a clause obligating him to provide his services in this regard very well may be included in his contract.

To make best use of an AV programme, it is generally agreed that the teacher should introduce it with comments designed both to impress the students with its importance and to rouse their interest in it. After the programme has been shown, in turn, there should be a discussion to help clear up possible confusions, sharpen insights and reinforce learning. There may also be quizzes on the programme content.

This approach also sets the pattern for teacher aids and supplementary teaching material. You, as the writer, probably should begin your guidebook text with a brief essay designed to orient the teacher to the audiovisual presentation. A list of points to watch for in the programme is also helpful. Frequently, the teacher must rely heavily on this because circumstances make it impossible for him/her to see the programme before showing it to a class.

Quite possibly, too, for a slide show or filmstrip, you will be asked to include a frame-by-frame commentary—perhaps with reproduction of each frame and of narration—in order to help the teacher not to get lost. This commentary should incorporate information not included in the narration so that the teacher will have material to use in his/her introduction and/or the discussion following the programme. Remember that he/she may know next to nothing about the topic. To appear knowledgeable to their students, teachers want all help possible.

Specific dates and facts should be brought in, as well as correct spelling of names and places. Definitions or identifications and important vocabulary will all be appreciated.

Another item that will win you the teacher's gratitude will be a questionnaire, with answers, to help stimulate class discussion after the presentation. Sample quizzes are valuable, too, as outlined in our next section.

Testing, testing ...

It would be nice if we could forego tests in AV scripting. Unfortunately, the field does not work that way. A high proportion of presentations are designed first and foremost to instruct. Only through quizzes and examinations do they attain their full potential. Presentations that in effect constitute programmed instruction attack this issue one way; other types of AV aid, another.

In programmed instruction, you can handle testing by inserting questions on the material covered every few frames. The student answers by filling in blanks, checking squares, circling statements, pushing buttons or the like.

This should give you a hint as to the kind of questions favoured. True/false or multiple choice types of answer obviously rank high for three reasons: they are simple to prepare, easy to grade, and require recognition rather than the ability to dredge up information from the mind's inner reaches. How much or how thoroughly they teach is something else again; many pedagogues dislike them heartily. For the moment, though, they are pretty much standard.

To prepare a true/false question, you simply make a simple statement either agreeing with or contrary to the information provided in the frame or segment over which testing is to take place. If the student then pushes the button that says it is right, when it is wrong (or vice versa), he is put in a position of having to repeat the frame/segment. If he is correct in his appraisal, he moves ahead to the next bit of data.

Multiple choice simply increases the student's potential opportunity for error since it gives him three or four possible answers to choose from instead of two. When you give him a blank to fill in, with no hints as to the proper statement, you introduce a whole new ball game in which his chances to go wrong are virtually unlimited. (Opportunities for confusion and ambiguity also are virtually limitless in this last instance, which is one reason why it is not too popular.)

Once you leave the programmed instruction area, testing becomes more complicated. You may be asked to prepare quizzes on various levels of pupil competence, for example. Alternatively, you may be required to give the teacher two or more tests so that he/she can use the programme in more than one class or for more than one year without repetition.

You will also need to bear in mind that dates are difficult to remember from an AV presentation unless some device for dramatic emphasis is invoked. Similarly, the students may not have seen many words from your programme's vocabulary written down and therefore do not know how to spell them; try to ask questions that do not require spelling beyond the students' normal range.

Whatever your topic and whatever your level, your subject specialist still will be your greatest aid. Your handling, too, remains much the same. True/false and multiple choice tests are easy to grade, so teachers love them.

You should not, however, let this restrain you from including at least a few essay questions, with lists of points students should include on the basis of facts given, plus notes to help the teachers in grading, evaluating and commenting.

Closely related to such are the ideas and information to be covered in review sections.

Looking backwards

Remember how your school textbooks ended chapters? Almost always there was a section titled 'Questions for Review' or equivalent.

It was a pedagogically sound approach. Newly acquired information needs reinforcement. One of the most effective ways to do this reinforcing is to refresh the students' memory of the subject matter through review.

As always, teachers welcome your help. In preparing aids for them, you should provide both review material and suggestions for how best to approach review situations.

Questions for review need not necessarily call for specific answers. Quite possibly they may be open-ended and designed to provoke thought, speculation or discussion of course content. Do not be content to evoke only the parrot syndrome.

At the same time, do not leave the teacher stranded. You may be dealing with subjects outside his/her field. Recognising this, you need to provide answers and ideas as well as questions.

An approach teachers may forget—and one of which you certainly need to remind them—is the effectiveness of AV itself for review purposes. In language training, for example, vocabulary originally presented on laboratory tapes may now come forth in filmstrip dialogue, supplemented perhaps by workbook exercises.

Similarly, field trips and the like take on fresh interest when slides or film of the expedition are used as review material. Recollection and excitement alike are stimulated. Each pupil brings a personal recall factor to the fore. Anecdotes, incidents and colour all come into focus to sharpen the memory of the experience and thus reinforce the learning pattern.

In brief, the thing to bear in mind is the importance of using the various media to reinforce each other. Print backed with slides or tapes or puppets or graphs or paintings (or vice versa) will, when skilfully and knowledgeably handled, increase learning. This does not mean just playing back materials viewed before. Often, the introduction of new presentations will whet attention and so do a better job than the familiar.

Finally, while we are on this topic of review, remember that as an AV writer you have an obligation to construct your own programmes and presentations on sound educational principles. Each should include some sort of recapitulation or, perhaps, self-test at the end—a summary to remind the viewer of what he has learned, its importance and the interpretation you want him to give it. This applies even when, on the face of it, your unit allegedly exists only to show the beauties of Pago-Pago, the excitement of a wrestling match or the colour of the Horse Guards.

This all need not be a tremendous lot of work, even if it does sound like it, especially if your take the easy way out.

The easy out

Years ago I developed a habit of never throwing away a scrap of paper connected with a project until the project was over and done. Colleagues laughed at me about this. Sometimes I laughed too. It seemed so ridiculous, heaping up all those unused notes and filling file drawers with print, calligraphy and blue-pencilled typing.

Then along came my first teacher guide chore (maybe the second or the third) when it finally dawned on me why, unknowingly, I had been saving all that scrap paper. Those notes and jottings and false starts and good-tries-gone-wrong were the well from which good AV-related 'poop' sheets spring. Instead of racking my brain and pacing the floor, I found I had only to go back through my files of clutter and out would pop facts and ideas that were ideal for my purpose. Even though they had not been used in the presentation itself because of space or other limitation, they offered just the kind of cues and colour that I now needed.

Although, perhaps, I am exaggerating a little, it still remains a fact that you can reduce time spent in working up supplementary materials by 50 per cent or more if you, too, hang onto those seemingly useless notes you made back when you were trying to find an idea or a concept or a key point. Many of them will fit into your present chore.

The same thing holds true of your notes on sources. Knowing where you previously found useful material will give you a happy hunting ground for data you can use today.

You can carry the collection of data to extremes. What role will I ever find for the dusty, long-obsolete books on the Dutch East Indies that I accumulated for an assignment just after World War 2? Yet they still sit on my shelf and probably will continue to occupy space there. After all, who knows when the phone will ring?

Deals and how to make them　　**12**

Once upon a time, a novice writer was approached by representatives of a civic club who wanted a slide show on the evils of alcoholism in their community. The writer liked the idea, especially since the price was right. Soon he was up to his eyeballs in books and pamphlets and interviews with psychologists and social workers. His preliminary treatment was received with enthusiasm, acclaim and loud accolades.

The writer settled down to working up the script ... proudly carried the finished product to his mentors. The reception was again enthusiastic.

The writer glowed. Then, although he hated to introduce such mundane matters, he asked about when he would receive the agreed payment.

His mentors referred him to the sponsoring group where he learned an interesting fact. Although the project indeed had been discussed, final approval never had been given. The treasurer, a power within the organisation, stood firm and steadfast in his opposition to the project.

To make a long and painful story shorter, the writer never did receive his money. The fact that I can still remember it so clearly after more than forty years tells you how much it galled me.

I hope that you, as writers, never will be faced with a similar disaster. To that end, let us consider a few of the steps you can take to prevent it.

The range of contracts

Contracts—or perhaps I should say agreements—come in a variety of forms. Most writers have done jobs under terms ranging from a producer/sponsor's suggestion of 'Why don't you work that up?' to documents so multi-claused and replete with legal jargon as to make one's hair stand on end.

Each of us has his chosen way of dealing with this issue. My own tends to involve avoiding either extreme in favour of a simple letter of agreement in which I outline what I propose to do, for how much and under what terms. When my client signs and returns a copy of this to me, acknowledging his acceptance, the deal is made. Since each project is different, so is each letter, though the difference is more in details than in outline.

There are two reasons for my preference to such a letter rather than the simple handshake type of agreement. First, your man may die or quit or be transferred. His successor may either be unaware of or choose to deny your project's existence. Your letter protects you from this.

The second reason is that misunderstandings arise in even the most cordial relationships. When that happens, it is nice to have some point of reference to fall back on—not hair-splitting legalese but just general terms to remind each of you as to details which might otherwise be forgotten.

What is wrong with the other end of the stick, the total legal instrument? Firstly, I am not a lawyer, so I really would not know how to write or read such a document. Paying a legal eagle to draw one up would take too large a proportion of the profit out of most script jobs.

Even more to the point, however, is my conviction that no legalistic contract really means much. That is to say, I enter any agreement with the intention of fulfilling my part of the bargain. I do my client the courtesy of assuming that such is his intention likewise. Indeed, if I do not trust him, I prefer not to do business with him at all. Life is too short to waste trying to second-guess thieves.

Why bother with detailed contracts? The letter of agreement serves as well. But it would not be true to say that I never deviate from this approach. Often, when old and trusted friends have called, we have never got round to putting anything in writing. Again, when I am dealing with some major government agency or corporation, I recognise that their red tape is sacred to them and so solemnly affix my signature to some ponderous compilation of verbiage which, in the end, means no more than my one-page or two-page statement.

Within your contract, however you draw it, you should cover at least four things: how much you get; how you get it; cutoff points; and, approvals. Of course, you should also have a statement as to what you are supposed to do as your part of the bargain.

How much you get paid is a somewhat involved subject that we will take up in the next section. How you get your money is a simpler matter because I can give you some definite advice. Specifically: *accept no assignment that does not pay you as you go along, step by step.*

The woods are full of AV projects that never have been completed and never will be. In each case, the writer who agreed to script the job 'on speculation'—that is, on the gamble that it would be produced and make money, and that he thereupon would be paid a set fee or share of the profits or both—ended up with empty pockets and a lot of time lost.

I'm not proclaiming this from any superior height. I too have listened to honey-tongued promoters and been persuaded to 'work up' ideas that just could not miss. The only trouble was, they *did* miss—and there went a week or a month or more of work unrewarded, as surely as if that much cash had sifted through a hole in my pocket. Now when tempted to gamble, I try to limit myself to proposals for books which I can peddle from publisher to publisher until they hit. Where AV ideas are concerned, I will talk up an idea to a producer for an hour any day but that is as far as I go. Beyond, I want to see money on the line.

But back to our point: *accept no assignment that does not pay you as you go along.* How do you set this up?

A good system for arranging fees, it seems to me, is to write your letter of agreement to call for three equal payments: one for research and development at the start, when the agreement's signed; one for working up the proposal and/or treatment, payable when you deliver the treatment; and, one for preparing the production script, again payable on delivery.

You may split payment into quarters instead of thirds, with final payment on completion of the project, but this can be hazardous, since you have no way of knowing when or if production will be finished.

Payment on delivery of treatment/script does not mean that the client is stuck if your work is unsatisfactory. I take it for granted that, within reason, you will try to straighten out any kinks that develop. If you fail— well, we will consider that when we talk about cutoff points.

In many cases, as a beginner you will not be able to get these terms. You certainly should strive for them, however, and you certainly should not work on pure speculation unless you are at that total novice stage where experience is its own reward for you.

In any event, do not hesitate to point out to your client that research, for example, is work, tedious and time-consuming. The proposal and treatment centre on creativity, conceptualising and talent. Precise description of visuals in the production script, logical development and smooth handling of narration cut production costs sharply.

Consequently, the payment for your work should not be tied to someone's whim. A script is the bedrock of any project. If the client is serious, he should be willing to invest your fee to get it.

A cutoff point is, in effect, a contract cancellation clause. It permits a client to end a writer's connection with a project if his work proves unsatisfactory.

This is entirely legitimate. The client has a picture in his mind of the script he wants or, at least, he can recognise the ones that he does not want. If it becomes obvious that the client and the writer just are not on the same wavelength, therefore, the client can pay for the work done up to that point and cancel the agreement.

If the client is going to cancel, ordinarily he does so on completion of the treatment. Cancellation does not necessarily reflect in any way on the writer's competence; it may result from anything from personality conflict to loss of anticipated financing.

Cutoff points should be specified in your letter of agreement, just to avoid possible misunderstandings. All it takes is a simple statement like, 'This agreement may be cancelled by either party upon written notice following delivery of and payment for treatment.' The cutoff point could equally well be at the proposal stage or first-draft screenplay (if you are writing for film) or whatever.

Suppose you and the client get along famously and make it through all cutoff points without event. Your agreement should still include a paragraph calling for approvals—'sign-offs' as they are sometimes termed—on completion of each stage. In other words, when you finish the proposal and the client cries 'Gee, that's great!' he also should give you some sort of written statement that says 'Proposal is satisfactorily completed and approved.' A similar statement should also be written for treatment and shooting script, and maybe even final narration.

It is quite possible that this sort of formality is not important if you are dealing with a small producer on a one-on-one basis. But it may be. Producers and sponsors alike have been known, in the later phases of a project, suddenly to become wildly enthusiastic about a new idea. Forgetting the fact that the writer already has devoted a considerable number of hours to preparing a first version, they demand that he proceed with the new concept as if the original never existed.

This just is not cricket. So the writer needs to be able to produce a signed approval for each step of the job already completed, backed by an agreement clause that says any major or non-routine changes required after approval are to be paid for as if a new project were being launched. This can make the world much brighter for the writer.

The right price

I write this with a simple time sheet beside me. Of loose-leaf lined paper with a place for a project title at the top, it is divided into five columns headed: Date, Aspect, From, To, and Time. The column for Aspect is rather wider than the rest and details the particular phase of the job I am working on: planning, proposal development, treatment development, production script, etc. Sitting down to work, I fill in the date, aspect and starting time. When I finish, I scribble the quitting time under To and hours worked under Time.

Hardly an elaborate system, it still enables me to know pretty much the number of hours I have devoted to a given endeavour. This is important because, when I divide it into the price I got for the job, it tells me how much per hour I have earned.

This figure is, obviously, not very accurate. You cannot cover the minutes you spent trying to devise an incident or an angle as you drove from here to there, or that sudden wide-awakeness in the middle of the night when you scrawled a solution to a problem on a scratch pad. The figure is, however, better than picking a price out of thin air which is the way to disaster. (I wrote a script some years ago, only to find that in the end I had netted—so help me!—a grand total of 43 cents an hour on it.)

I have two other reasons for favouring this sort of time-analysis approach. One is the fact that having at least a rough idea of the hours involved in carrying through a particular type of assignment—be it slide shows or suspense novels—enables you to allocate your time more accurately and bid more intelligently next time that sort of chore comes your way.

The other reason is that too low a bid for a job merely convinces your client that you do not think you are worth much and that does neither of you any good.

In calculating your bid, how much you should charge per hour is, obviously, a matter for personal decision. An approach that makes sense, however, suggests that you base your figure on the amount you could earn at a regular job. Thus, if you have reason to believe an employment agency might place you at five or ten dollars an hour, then surely your work as a writer should rate at least a similar amount.

When free-lancing full time, another factor needs to be considered: there will be times when you have no assignments and yet you will still have to eat and pay rent.

Your script fees, therefore, must cover this dead time as well as days you actually work. Hours spent soliciting assignments must also be entered, plus office and equipment overheads and the like. All should be adjusted to take account of the going rate, if any, in your area.

None of the above is designed to lay out iron-clad rules for you. My only goal is to nudge you in the direction of treating AV writing as a business. Believe me, you need to do so if you are to survive!

Two final items should be mentioned in regard to this matter of price and pricing: travel and cutoffs.

Travel, particularly, is an item to consider in every bid. It not only ups your costs when you have to work away from home, it may also knock you out of the running in competitive situations. Often, I have been able to snag a job just because I could bid $500 less for not having to add in air fare, car rental and hotel bills.

Even more important, writing away from your home base cuts you loose from contacts and research materials while, on the other side of the coin, attempting to carry out an assignment by remote control invariably involves you in situations in which you have to make extra trips to confer with specialists or technical advisors, resolve questions of authority or time out tricky sequences.

This is not to say you should not travel but you do need to include it in your budget.

The cutoff snare. The cutoff is, as mentioned earlier, a perfectly legitimate contract provision. Occasionally, however, you will encounter a sponsor or producer who will use it in a less than forthright fashion. To this end, he signs you to prepare a presentation for him. When you submit your treatment, however, he rejects it on whatever grounds. Later you discover that he is not only perfectly happy with it but that he proposes to shoot the programme from it.

Whether he pays you for the treatment or not, you are entitled to be irked at this procedure on two counts: artistic and financial.

Artistically, the issue is that the client probably will not do much of a job when it comes to expanding the treatment into shots. The fact that he will go to such extremes to dodge your fee is hardly indicative of orientation to a quality product. If you are like me, you like anything you do to stand a fighting chance of looking good.

Financially, you are being treated very shabbily indeed. The preparation of the proposal and treatment constitute the most creative—and nail-gnawing—aspects of scripting any programme. Conceiving an approach and thinking through its development are the really difficult parts of audiovisual writing.

Further, by the time you have written the treatment, a high proportion of the shots for the final script already are blocked out in your mind. The fact that they are not yet down on paper is primarily a matter of typing. To be knocked out of this portion of your fee on meretricious grounds falls just short of highway robbery.

How should you deal with situations like this? As outlined above in my comments on contracts, *insist* on an arrangement that gives you one-third payment on signing, for research and development of the project; a second third on delivery (*not* approval) of treatment; and the final third on submission of the shooting script. By handling the deal in that way, you are assured of at least two-thirds of your full fee, even should you be cut off after the payment for the treatment.

Incidentally, all this is not to imply that most sponsors/producers will resort to such attempts to bilk you. On the contrary, the overwhelming majority are totally honest. As in any business, however, there always are a few who cut corners and these are the ones you need to know about when you are beginning.

Entirely apart from chicanery, doing business as a writer has other hazards you should be aware of.

Danger! Specifications ahead!

They stick the doggonedest clauses into AV script contracts sometimes. As a writer, you need to be acutely aware of all of them. Nowhere is the old line about 'read it before you sign it' more vital because you will have to live with those terms, those clauses. Failure to understand or pay attention to them can commit you to totally impossible conditions—and that is a conservative statement! Overlooking an apparently routine detail like 'The script will include frame counts which must coincide with the timing of the narrative' may prove disastrous.

In general, specifications fall into two categories: *technical* and *image*.

Technical specifications are pretty much the kind of thing you would expect: lip-sync dialogue, voice-over narration, or mixed; age level for narration vocabulary; music included or excluded; and, visuals of particular equipment or action.

(Visuals of equipment can be a headache. You need to find out exactly where the said equipment may be observed in operation. Down the street is one thing but if it can be seen only in London, Montreal, Manila or 'Lower Slobbovia', some travel money needs to be written in. Similarly, are you to centre on representative plants or parks or state prisons, or must all types be pictured? If all, how much attention must be devoted to each? Will single slides be adequate, or is glowing descriptive narrative for individual operations required?)

It is in image specs that contracts can really go crazy. My wife worked on a show which specified that all the physicians were to be American Indians. (It turned out there were only 42 in the entire United States.) Where nurses and other health professionals were shown, Indians were to be in the majority. Caucasians were permitted only in incidental roles.

You will also encounter clauses that require women in certain parts (Women's Lib marches on!); that specify that all women wear skirts and men wear ties; that restrict dialogue forms of address to Mr, Mrs and Miss; or that exclude drinking, smoking, profanity, long-haired men. You name it, it has appeared in a writer's contract somewhere.

Be aware of these restrictions and their possibilities for handicapping you.

The same principle applies to time schedules. Study them carefully and be sure you can meet them.

How can you be sure? Partly, you judge by the material. Are you sufficiently familiar with the programme's subject that you can run it through in a hurry or is it something that will involve you in endless reading, field work and conferences with experts?

Equally or more important are the time sheets I described under 'The Right Price,' earlier in this chapter. Nothing can help you more in appraising a time schedule than your knowledge—based on past performance—that you can come up with a generally acceptable proposal of the type required in three days, expand it into a treatment in five more and then produce the final script at the rate of ten pages per day.

Producers like it when you can talk in such terms. They see it as the mark of the professional. The writer who is unsure of these matters, on the other hand, they see as the eternal amateur—a genus they tend to walk wide around as unreliable. (Incidentally, this kind of thinking applied to a marked degree in The Old Hollywood. A studio assigning a picture to a writer often expected him to be able to deliver an average of three pages of script a day.)

It goes without saying, of course, that no estimate you make should pretend to be absolute. As a rule of thumb passed on to me years ago says, 'Always write bad luck into your contract.'

My prize example of this centres on an incident that occurred while I was living in Mexico. A firm with which I had had happy relations for years sent me an assignment for a series of AV programmes to be prepared from tape recordings. Since it was a time when cash was in short supply for me, I was delighted. I cleaned up my typewriter and prepared to settle down to work.

There was a catch, however. The tapes did not come—and the job had a rigid deadline.

Finally I got on the telephone to find out what had happened. No one could give me any answers. Even worse, no transcript of the tapes was available.

Days passed, then weeks, then the deadline and still no tapes arrived. Months later, they did arrive. They had, it turned out, been held by Mexican Customs as dutiable items. I had to pay a ridiculous fee to get them out of the post office.

By then, of course, it was too late. To make matters worse, I lost not just the assignment but my edge with the company. As they explained, if I chose to live in a place where mail did not even reach me on schedule, they could see no way to utilise my services further.

Snowstorms, sickness (your own and others'), equipment breakdowns (I now have four typewriters) and unavailability of people or information all go to emphasise that you should 'Always write bad luck into your contract.'

If you are like most writers, such doom-saying holds little charm for you. What you are interested in is getting down to business and seeing how professionals in the field perform. I feel the same way about it. Indeed, that is the subject of the second part of this book.

Part II
Putting principles to work

13 Some basic forms: ground rules

In the last analysis you learn by doing. Along the way most of us also pick up valuable hints from observation—checking out other people's projects to see just how they attack the problems.

This is particularly true in a field like audiovisual, where demands, approaches and formats differ so widely. This being the case, I offer you herewith bits and pieces from all sorts of presentations—a pot-pourri of mechanics, handlings and concepts. The range is as wide as I know how to make it: tape cassettes to multimedia, in-house video to programmed instruction, as well as trips down a number of off-beat bypaths.

This is not to say that any of these samples constitute pure perfection. They do, however, represent professional products, work bought and paid for, and they do show more clearly than any set of arbitrary rules just how many variations may spring from basic principles and formats.

I have also included material from various operations' guidesheets, plus specifications laid down by sponsoring/producing groups. While obviously only indicative, they at least give you some notion of the kind of requirements you may encounter where your own efforts are concerned.

Case study

What happens when you take on a job for a major organisation?

My wife and I have done a good many scripts for the US Postal Service's Training and Development Institute. Since the Institute knows precisely what it wants and operates within the framework of quite rigid specifications, the procedure followed in preparing work for it is in many ways applicable to other large bodies.

The process starts with the writer's receipt of a 'Request for Quotations' and 'Statement of Work.' These generally arrive accompanied by a thick textbook or other research materials on the subject, designed to indicate to the writer what kind of a task confronts him.

If the writer wishes to be considered for the assignment, he decides what kind of a price he wants, completes the request form and returns it.

Note that in this case we described the job as 'two film strips.' Actually, this terminology is to a degree a misnomer, since (as the Statement of Work indicates) the Beseler Cue See unit is a specialised, variable speed AV projection system. Probably what we should have said was 'two filmstrip scripts' or 'two Beseler System scripts.'

Although sometimes modified in practice, the 'Statement of Work' means precisely what it says. Woe be unto the writer who fails to read it carefully! Observe, for example, how the 'Script Format' section specifies emphasis on 'single frame concept' and 'live photography,' limits 'graphics and animation,' and warns against 'lip sync motion.'

Note, too (under 'Subject Matter'), that the writer is required to prepare 'supporting workbook materials' and the like, plus quizzes.

The 'Delivery Schedule and Production Elements' offers its own perils. The schedule set forth in general, individual scripts are specific. Thus, a particular piece of work may require a good deal longer than the time allotted. It takes careful study and a thorough knowledge of how rapidly you can turn out copy in order to estimate a job accurately.

The statement of module objectives which comes as part of the 'Statement of Work' tells you what you should try to accomplish in your scripts. Again, careful study is called for.

In this particular case, two scripts (not reproduced here) for previous films covering the same body of information were included as part of the work statement.

The bid we submitted in response to the 'Request for Quotations' was accepted, with notification given us via an 'Order-Invoice-Voucher.'

Note that, at our request, 'The delivery schedule listed on page 3 of the statement of work is the time required for each module.' In other words, we were granted *double* the time originally allotted. In view of the complexity the assignment developed, we were glad!

Our first move where the actual assignment was concerned was preparation of treatment outlines. Partly, this was because the Institute staff wanted assurance that our approach was in keeping with their thinking. Equally, however, we had no desire to jump in blind when we wrote the full-scale production script.

The treatment outline shown on page 124 is that for Unit 2 of the project, that is the Module 12 mentioned in the statement of objective.

The signed approval at the end of the treatment is an important item; it shows proof of delivery and is a protection against forgetfulness and/or changes in policy or personnel.

	U.S. POSTAL SERVICE **REQUEST FOR QUOTATIONS** *(THIS IS NOT AN ORDER)*		PAGE 1	OF 1

1. REQUEST NO. 104234-79-C-0056	2. DATE ISSUED 01-11-79	3. REQUISITION/PURCHASE REQUEST NO. 79-7615-130

4. ISSUED BY U.S. Postal Service Officer of Contracts, Norman Branch P.O. Box 1400 JOHN R. DEPE Norman, OK 73069 405-325-1916 FOR INFORMATION CALL *(Name and tel. no.) (No collect calls)*	5. DELIVER BY *(Date)* See below
	6. DELIVERY [X] FOB DESTINATION [ ] OTHER *(See Schedule)*

7. TO NAME AND ADDRESS   TO BE COMPLETED BY BIDDER
 	
(Street, City,
State and
ZIP Code)
     J.R. Swain & Associates
     1304 McKinley Avenue
     Norman, OK 73069
	8. DESTINATION *(Consignee and address including ZIP code)*
	
	U.S. Postal Service
	Training & Development Institute
	(PST&DI) Media Branch
	P.O. Box 1400
	Norman, OK 73070

9. PLEASE FURNISH QUOTATIONS TO THE ISSUING OFFICE ON OR BEFORE CLOSE OF BUSINESS __01-26-79__ SUPPLIES ARE OF
                                                              (Date)

DOMESTIC ORIGIN UNLESS OTHERWISE INDICATED BY QUOTER. THIS IS A REQUEST FOR INFORMATION, AND QUOTATIONS FURNISHED ARE NOT OFFERS. IF YOU ARE UNABLE TO QUOTE, PLEASE SO INDICATE ON THIS FORM AND RETURN IT. THIS REQUEST DOES NOT COMMIT THE POSTAL SERVICE TO PAY ANY COSTS INCURRED IN THE PREPARATION OR THE SUBMISSION OF THIS QUOTATION, OR TO PROCURE OR CONTRACT FOR SUPPLIES OR SERVICES.

SCHEDULE

10. ITEM NO.	11. SUPPLIES/SERVICES	12. QUANTITY	13. UNIT	14. UNIT PRICE	15. AMOUNT
1	Furnish the necessary personnel and services to produce a script for use with the Beseler Cue See oriented audio visual training course titled "Bulk Conveyor System", PEDC Course No. 55501-00 Modules 1 and 12. The furnishing of the scrips shall be in accordance with the Statement of Work for preparation of scripts and workbooks for Super 8 Variable Motion Training Films dated 1-10-79 on 4 pages.	2 film scripts FOR THE JOB		$1600 ea. Total	$3200
a.	PLEASE COMPLETE THE FOLLOWING The offerer certifies that he (x) is, ( ) is not, a Small Business Concern and that he ( ) is, (x) is not, a Minority (Small) Business Concern				

16. PRICES QUOTED INCLUDE APPLICABLE FEDERAL, STATE, AND LOCAL TAXES.

DISCOUNT FOR PROMPT PAYMENT:_____% 20 CALENDAR DAYS;_____% 30 CALENDAR DAYS; _____%_____ CALENDAR DAYS.

17. NAME AND ADDRESS OF QUOTER *(Street, city, county, State, including ZIP Code)* J.R. Swain & Associates 1304 McKinley Avenue Norman, OK 73069	18. SIGNATURE OF PERSON AUTHOR-IZED TO SIGN QUOTATION 20. SIGNER'S NAME AND TITLE *(Type or print)* J.R. Swain	19. DATE OF QUOTATION Jan 24, 1979 21. TELEPHONE NO. *(Include area code)* (405) 321-4982

PS Form
Oct. 1972 **7318**   ☆ GPO 1971 750-625/57
                                                              829-625

Request for a quotation from the US Postal Service Training and Development Institute.

STATEMENT OF WORK

FOR PREPARATION OF
SCRIPTS AND WORKBOOKS FOR SUPER 8 VARIABLE MOTION TRAINING FILMS
10-26-78

GENERAL

The writer will produce training scripts for the Super 8mm film format using the Beseler Cue See variable speed projection system. Demonstration materials which show the characteristics of super-8 variable motion are located in the Media Branch, Norman, OK, or Bethesda, MD. The Cue See format consists of a continuous loop super-8 film cartridge and an audio cassette tape. There are 3,600 frames of visual information available for the writer. The system uses variable motion from still frame through any film speed up to 24 frames per second. The advance of the film is controlled by inaudible pulses on the audio cassette. The projector is primarily designed for individual instruction, but will also project an image on a 4' x 5' screen for use in group instruction. The program development contracted for here will be primarily in the individual format. Work will be performed under a delivery schedule (attached) and will be monitored by a PST&DI Project Support Manager.

SCRIPT FORMAT

The writer will prepare a script describing the visuals and audio segments of the program. Visuals will be specified in detail in support of narration in an adjacent column. The script and visuals will be in vertical column format. The super-8 system is basically an advanced version of filmstrip or slide projector with the added feature of variable motion. The writer will seek to emphasize in the script the single frame concept enhanced by filmography and live motion where these clearly contribute to the effectiveness of the training program.

As a general rule, live photography will be used where possible production cost savings are indicated. Graphics and animation will be limited by the writer to program elements requiring such treatment.

The writer will plan the script to use any number of visual frames not to exceed 3,600 frames in the aggregate (the capacity of the film cartridge). The script will include frame counts which must coincide with the timing of the narrative. Where motion is to be used the writer should consult the Project Support Manager to determine the appropriate frames per second for the motion. Lip sync motion will, as a rule, be avoided. The individual program will be between 12-20 minutes in duration for the AV segment. Time required for the workbook exercises will be in addition to that required for the AV.

-1-

Statement of work from the US Postal Service Training and Development Institute.

SUBJECT MATTER

Course design principles associated with program instruction will govern the writing of the material. The writer will be furnished with those student performance objectives around which the instructional material will be developed. The writer will be provided with information regarding the skills and knowledge already possessed by the target population. Content direction will be provided by the Postal Service. The training program should be characterized by interaction between the learner and the content. To achieve this, short question and answer exercises will be written into the program to test for understanding as the student progresses through the program. A student exercise at the completion of the formal AV segment to test understanding and summarize key points in the program is to be considered by the writer.

The writer will be responsible for the writing of supporting workbook materials and administrator guides to be used in conjunction with the program, should these be required.

The writer, using the performance objectives, will prepare a twenty-question criterion examination to evaluate student achievement of each criterion objective around which the course is designed. These questions will be used to validate the training module. The writer will be responsible, as necessary, for incorporating script changes resulting from the validation phase.

RIGHTS IN DATA—SPECIAL WORKS (July 1971)

(a) The term "Data" as used herein includes writings, sound recordings, pictorial reproductions, drawings or other graphic representations, and works of any similar nature (whether or not copyrighted) which are specified to be delivered under this contract. The term does not include financial reports, cost analyses, and other information incidental to contract administration.

(b) All Data first produced in the performance of this contract shall be the sole property of the Postal Service. The Contractor agrees not to assert any rights at common law or in equity or establish any claim to statutory copyright in such Data. The Contractor shall not publish or reproduce such Data in whole or in part or in any manner or form, or authorize others so to do, without the written consent of the postal Service until such time as the Postal Service may have released such Data to the public.

(c) The Contractor hereby grants to the Postal Service a royalty-free, non-exclusive, and irrevocable license throughout the world (i) to publish, translate, reproduce, deliver, perform, use, and dispose of, in any manner, any and all Data which is not first produced or composed in the performance of this contract but which is incorporated in the work furnished under this contract, and (ii) to authorize others so to do.

(d) The Contractor shall indemnify and save and hold harmless the postal Service, its officers, agents and employees acting within the scope of their official duties against any liability, including costs and expenses, (i) for violation of proprietary rights, copyrights, or rights of privacy, arising out of the publication, translation, reproduction, delivery, performance, use, or disposition of any Data furnished under this contract, or (ii) based upon any libeleous or other unlawful matter contained in such Data.

(e) Nothing contained in this clause shall imply a license to the Postal Service under any patent, or be construed as affecting the scope of any license or other right otherwise granted to the postal Service under any patent.

(f) Paragraphs (c) and (d) above are not applicable to material furnished to the Contractor by the Postal Service and incorporated in the work furnished under the contract; *provided*, such incorporated material is identified by the contractor at the time of delivery of such work.

Statement of work (continued) from the US Postal Service Training and Development Institute.

DELIVERY SCHEDULE AND PRODUCTION ELEMENTS

The following is the script production delivery schedule requirements and their schedule for completion. Note that one week each is required for management review as part of activities 3, 4 and 5. The time for these reviews is included in the schedule. Individual schedules may vary based on complexity of material. In the space provided insert your proposed delivery schedule, if it varies from the schedule listed.

ACTIVITY	POSTAL SERVICE SCHEDULE	CONTRACTOR PROPOSED SCHEDULE
1. Briefing on project	7 days after award	_____ days after award
2. Research completed	21 days after award	_____ days after award
3. Treatment	28 days after award	_____ days after award
4. First Draft	42 days after award	_____ days after award
5. Final Draft	56 days after award	_____ days after award
6. Possible rewrite after validation	3 days after validation completed	_____ days after validation completed

NOTE: The writer should include one day for consultation with graphics and photographics staff as development of the approved script progresses.

-3-

Statement of work (continued) from the US Postal Service Training and Development Institute.

OBJECTIVE

Bulk Conveyor Systems
Course /55501-00

The objective of this course is to provide the student with an
understanding of the operating principles and design limitations of
belt conveyor systems, the function of the various component parts,
preventive and repair maintenance requirements, and fault isolation
procedures.

MODULE 1

The objective of this module is to provide a set of reference pictures
and audio descriptions for use previous to and during the period the
student is completing modules 2 through 11 of the text. The audiovisual material should provide an overview of subjects and lessons
contained in modules 2 through 11.

MODULE 12

The objective of this module is to provide a set of reference pictures
and audio descriptions for use previous to and during the period the
student is completing modules 13 through 26 of the text. The audiovisual material should provide an overview of subjects and lessons
contained in modules 13 through 26.

Note: This contract is for the development of two (2) Beseler Cue-See
variable speed motion scripts. Each script in motion format will run
approximately 20 minutes. The two (2) variable speed motion programs
will serve as an orientation to the student who will complete the
existing text book course which contains a total of 26 modules.

While the attached filmstrip scripts will provide a good guide as to
content, the writer is expected to enlarge upon the student's orientation
to Bulk Conveyor Systems and their applications in the Postal Service.

ATTACHMENT A

*Treatment outline used by persmission of Postal Service Training and
Development Institute.*

| MARK ALL PACKAGES AND PAPERS WITH ORDER NO. AND (IF ANY) CONTRACT NO. | & Seq. No. | U.S. POSTAL SERVICE ORDER-INVOICE-VOUCHER | | | DATE OF ORDER 01-31-79 | | PAGE 1 | OF 2 |

CONTRACT NO. (If any)	C/C (1)	ORDER NO. (2-14)	DELIVER BY (29-34)			GROSS AMT. (60-67)	SEQ. NO. (72-77)	S/M	ITEM CODE
	1	104234-79-P-0071	MONTH 0 4	DAY 1 1	YEAR 7 9	$3,200.00	D 78783	A	FAAS

ISSUED BY	REQUISITION NO.	GOVERNMENT BILL OF LADING NUMBER(S)
U. S. Postal Service Office of Contracts, Norman Branch 1524 Asp Ave., P.O. Box 1400 Norman, OK 73070 405-325-1916	79-7615-130	

DISCOUNT TERMS: NET

DELIVER FOB: ORIGIN ___ (City and State)   [X] DESTINATION ▼

CONTRACTOR/VENDOR (Name and address, including ZIP Code)	SHIP TO (Consignee and address, including ZIP Code)
TO: J. R. Swain & Associates 1304 McKinley Ave. Norman, OK 73069	U. S. Postal Service Training & Development Institute (PST&DI) Media Branch 79-P-0071 P.O. Box 1400 Norman, OK 73070

TYPE OF ORDER: PURCHASE [X]   DELIVERY [ ]

REFERENCE YOUR **written quote of 1-24-79**. PLEASE FURNISH THE FOLLOWING ON THE TERMS SPECIFIED ON BOTH SIDES OF THIS ORDER AND ON THE ATTACHED SHEETS, IF ANY, INCLUDING DELIVERY AS INDICATED. NEGOTIATED PURSUANT TO POSTAL CONTRACTING MANUAL 3–203.

EXCEPT FOR THE BILLING INSTRUCTIONS ON THE REVERSE, THIS DELIVERY ORDER IS SUBJECT TO INSTRUCTIONS CONTAINED ON THIS SIDE ONLY OF THIS FORM AND IS ISSUED SUBJECT TO THE TERMS AND CONDITIONS OF THE ABOVE-NUMBERED CONTRACT.

ACCOUNTING AND FISCAL DATA: [X] SEE BELOW   [ ] SEE ATTACHED

C/C (1)	VENDOR (2-7)	BUD. FIN. NO. (8-14)	FAC (15)	W/C (16-17)	SUB. LOC. (18-20)	PROP. ACCTBL. FIN. NO. (21-27)	W/C (28-29)	SUB. LOC. (30-32)	PCN (33-38)
2		107610							

NO. OF ITEMS (39-42)	DISC. (43-47)	TRADE-IN (48-52)	ACCT. (48-52)	SUB. ACCT. (53-55)	F/ACT. (56-59)	GROSS AMT. (60-67)	SEQ. NO. (72-79)		A/C (80)
			52172					0	1

SCHEDULE

ITEM NO.	SUPPLIES OR SERVICE	QUANTITY ORDERED	UNIT	UNIT PRICE	DOLLAR AMOUNT	QUANTITY ACCEPTED
1.	Furnish the necessary personnel and services to produce a script for use with the Beseler Cue See oriented audio visual training course titled "Bulk Conveyor System", PEDC Course No. 55501-00 Modules 1 and 12. The furnishing of the script shall be in accordance with the Statement of Work for preparation of scripts and workbooks for Super 8 Variable Motion Training Films dated 1-10-79 on 4 pages.					
A.	Module 1	FOR THE	JOB	1,600.00	1,600.00	
B.	Module 12	FOR THE	JOB	1,600.00	1,600.00	
	NOTE: The delivery schedule listed on page 3 of the statement of work is the time required for each module.					

SEE BILLING INSTRUCTIONS ON REVERSE

SHIPPING POINT	GROSS SHIPPING WEIGHT	INVOICE NO.

CONTRACTOR, IF DESIRED, THIS ORIGINAL ORDER-INVOICE MAY BE USED IN LIEU OF A SEPARATE COMMERCIAL INVOICE, PROVIDED THE FOLLOWING STATEMENT IS SIGNED AND DATED. PAYMENT IS REQUESTED IN THE AMOUNT OF $_____. NO OTHER INVOICE HAS BEEN OR WILL BE SUBMITTED.

_____ (Signature)   _____ (Date)

TOTALS:
FROM OTHER PAGES   0
GRAND TOTAL ▶ $3,200.00
NET (if discounts)
(See reverse for rejections)

UNITED STATES POSTAL SERVICE

John R. Depe (Signature of Contracting Officer)

JOHN R. DEPE — NAME OF CONTRACTING OFFICER (Type or print)

MAIL INVOICE TO: XXXXXXXXXXXXXXXXXXXX Issuing office (see above) XXXXXXXXXXXXXXX NY

PS Form 7334 Aug. 1975

1. Vendor's Copy - Original

Notification of acceptance of bid on an 'Order-Invoice-Voucher' from the US Postal Service Training and Development Institute.

```
J.R. SWAIN & ASSOCIATES
1304 McKinley Avenue
Norman, OK 73069
Tel. (405) 321-4982



                          Proposed

                    Film Treatment Outline


                   BULK CONVEYOR SYSTEM

                        -Unit 2-

                     (Working Title)
```

Opening titles will be (1) sponsoring organization's name, and (2) main titles.

These titles will appear over the same fast-cut series of shots of postal conveyor belts that was used with titles in Unit 1.

Titles off. A frame-filling shot of a stopped conveyor belt, loaded with mail.

Narrator observes that in Unit 1 we saw how the bulk belt conveyor helps the Postal Service meet the volume crisis. Now, in Unit 2, we turn the spotlight on servicing...with a continuing overview of more of the mechanical and electrical components which must be serviced to keep the bulk belt conveyor system operating.

The treatment outline for Unit 2 (Module 12 in the statement of work).

Unit 2--2

We focus on the maintenance and repair of parts neccessary
to make the belt actually move: gear reducer, couplings,
accessory-drive equipment, roller chain, and the motor itself.

Next we shift to the electrical problems involved in
keeping conveyor belts functioning. Basically, this is a brief
introduction to various aspects of electrical circuits, wiring
practices, measuring instruments, and motors and generators.

Once again, the responsibility of maintenance personnel
for the safety of users will be stressed, with a reminder that
after any maintenance and/or servicing of equipment all guards
must be replaced and all safety rules carefully observed.

Concluding narration reiterates the importance of proper
servicing. Faced with today's mail volume, the Postal Service
could not operate without the bulk conveyor. The worker who
helps to keep it functioning efficiently and safely is performing
one of the Service's most vital jobs.

End titles come on over a repitition of the opening shots.

The End

Prepared for:

U.S. Postal Service
Training & Development
Institute

Approved: _____ Date: 3-28-79

The treatment outline for 'Bulk Conveyor System' continued.

Conveyor 2--1

FADE IN:

INT. - POST OFFICE - DAY

1 REPEAT: Opening MONTAGE from   MUSIC: In and up.
   Unit 1...fast-cut shots from
   varied angles of postal
   conveyor belts of all types:
   long, short, wide, narrow,
   fast-moving, slow-moving, on
   the level, up and down
   inclines, carrying mail bags,
   boxes, letters, etc.

TITLES OVER:
     As desired.

Conveyor script excerpt used by permission of the US Postal Service Training and Development Institute.

Conveyor--2-2

2 Frame-filling shot of stopped   MUSIC: Down and out.
   bulk conveyor, loaded with
   mail. Two concerned   NARRATOR: Unit 1 of these films
   employees consider it...one   showed how the bulk conveyor
   standing, perhaps; one   helps the Postal Service to
   hunkered.   meet the volume crisis. Now,
                                     in Unit 2, let's turn the
                                     spotlight on service...take a
                                     look at more of the things you
                                     need to know in order to keep
                                     these same conveyors running.

   STOCK SHOTS
3 MONTAGE: Assorted power   First and foremost, what we're
   symbols...rushing rivers,   dealing with here is power...
   dams, hydroelectric plants,   because power's what drives
   turbines, etc...including   conveyors...whether it comes
   batteries and generators.   from batteries...generators...
                                     or AC sources.

   EXT. - POST OFFICE - DAY
4 MS/MLS, post office building,
   name prominent.

Conveyor script excerpt continued—used by permission of the US Postal Service Training and Development Institute.

Conveyor 2--3

INT. - POST OFFICE - DAY

5 MONTAGE: Employees working on all sorts of downed conveyors.

Any time you're concerned with maintenance, the issue's likely to be the same: keep power flowing.

6 MCU, employee plugging male plug into wall socket. Room features conveyor motor.

Most often, you start from an AC power source. Energy moves from it through wires...that is, conductors...into the drive motor.

7 CU, wire to plug.

8 MS/MCU, drive motor...to favor lead-in wire.

ART

9 Diagram, motor. Dotted lines indicate magnetic field. Arrow labeled MAGNETIC FIELD points to dotted lines.

There this energy...the ability to do work...activates a magnetic field.

10 POP OFF dotted lines, arrow, words.

Conveyor script excerpt continued—used by permission of the US Postal Service Training and Development Institute.

There are several points worth noting in the three pages from the shooting script itself. The use of stock shots, for example, helps reduce cost. (This also holds true of use of shots from Unit 1 in the opening montage.)

Use of art in shot 9 shows an element that could not be photographed live. Probably the dotted lines and labelled arrow should have been set up as an overlay, however.

Note that much of this material was planned so that it could be shot either as motion-picture footage or as single-frame still photographs. This is true of shot 2, for example, or shots 5 and 6. The reason for this is the Beseler unit's variable-speed capacity. If the film 'ran tight,' length could be reduced by going to single-frame coverage; if it was loose, or if detailed study of some element became important, filmed action could be used. This gives director and producer valuable leeway.

When first submitted, no numbers were included on the shots/-sequences, so that shots or sequences could be dropped, changed or added without disrupting everything before and after. It developed that the Institute people were happy enough with the initial version, however, and they suggested penning in the numbers rather than retyping the whole business. What changes were necessary were limited to a few pages.

A month or so later the cheque came through, and that was the end of the job. Or was it?

No, of course not. To begin with, there were a fair number of hours spent studying the background information provided. Next came conferences (which is to say, lengthy discussions) with Will Gibson, the project supervisor, and with Richard Thorp, Institute media supervisor for the Norman unit, plus a couple of trips to Postal Centres to see bulk belt conveyor systems operating in their natural habitat.

Where the writing of the treatment and script themselves were concerned, false starts were made, mistakes incorporated and dead ends reached. Screams and suggestions from our technical advisors/supervisors got us back on the track each time. Eventually the job was, indeed, completed.

It was hard and sometimes dreary work. It was also a stimulating project for much of the time and in the process we acquired a great deal of interesting information we had not had before. In the end, we found it highly satisfying—and not at all badly paid.

Of dialogue devices

No matter what anyone tells you, radio is not dead. Its techniques survive alive and well in AV, as witness the series of tape cassettes I mentioned in Chapter 9.

Do not flip the page just because you do not see anything to be interested about in radio or tapes. As Don Gillis aptly observes in *The Art of Media Instruction*, 'In this age of super-systems and advanced television technology, the lowly audio area is often sorely neglected. It has, however, an infinite capacity to deliver information and is a much more cost-effective teaching-learning tool.'

With this in mind, let us scan an excerpt from a cassette script.

At least six things are worth noting about this fragment:

1 Its low cost.

'A radio documentary may be produced with virtually no budget and little equipment save two or three tape recorders and some tapes,' remarks Robert L. Hilliard in *Writing for Television and Radio*. He is right, though I would add the additional element of a writer's imagination.

2 Its utilisation of medium.

Radio/tapes involve sound. Everything else is a matter of script and production technique.

Sound, for our purposes, may be conveniently divided into three sub-categories: voice, music and effects. The effects refer to any sound from any source other than voice or music.

In this cassette, all three aspects of sound come into play. We hear 'football-type band music', 'football crowd noise and cheers', the voices of the narrator and three characters, Petarski, Vitti and Client 1. Their interplay creates a small, temporary world of sound for the listener.

3 Its concentration of emphasis.

'If your instruction requires showing real people in interpersonal action situations, to be convincing you will need lip-sync dialogue. But realistic sync conversation is "spready" and when it carries an entire situation, the scene can run too long and even diffuse the instructional point.

'On the other hand, voice-over narration, though fast and direct, loses the convincingness of *real* inter-character talk.

'The "Duo-Dialogue" system combines the two. The action is played with voice-over narration up to nearly the high point, at which time the real lip-sync dialogue "pops up" through the recording (the speaking character usually in CU or MCU) to make the significant point of the scene, with the narrator's voice then returning to nail down the finish.

'The instruction becomes more effective because the emphasis *automatically* goes to the significant instructional point, hence is better remembered. And money is saved, because less expert actors can be used, and they require less rehearsal and fewer takes.'

The speaker is Charles A. 'Cap' Palmer, veteran writer and producer. Although he is talking about film, what he says can be applied equally well to tape.

Goal--1

CASSETTE SCRIPT: GOAL TO GO!

MUSIC: FOOTBALL-TYPE BAND MUSIC IN...UP...DOWN
                      TO BG.

SOUND: FOOTBALL CROWD NOISE AND CHEERS IN...UP...
                      DOWN TO BG.

NAR.:   Tony Petarski was as hot a halfback as ever
                      played for Jarvis High. "Goal-to-Go
                      Petarski," they used to call him...Well,
                      it's twenty years later now, and Tony's
                      carrying the ball as a CSR. Question is,
                      how's he handling goals these days? Here
                      he is, over at Vitti & Sons...

SOUND & MUSIC: DOWN...OUT.

PETARSKI: That picture, Mr. Vitti. Is that your
                      father?

Vitti: How'd you guess?
     (PLEASED)

PETARSKI: You favor him...He's a fine-looking man,
                      Mr Vitti. Is he the one founded this
                      business?

CSR cassette excerpt used by permission of the US Postal Service Training and Development Institute.

Goal--2

NAR.:   Aimless chitchat? Hardly! Before you sell
                            anything, you have to open up channels of
                            communication...establish rapport. Tony
                            knows that. So, rapport's his first goal
                            whenever he contacts a new customer. Other
                            angles come later...

PETARSKI: Good deal, Mr. Calhoun...Before we go on,
                            though, maybe you'd better clue me in about
                            just how your setup works. What channels
                            do we go through? Who makes the final
                            decision?

NAR.:   Nailing down authority can be a big, vital
                            goal. Ask any CSR who's discovered too
                            late he's wasted his best efforts on the
                            wrong man. Though even when you zero in
                            on the right one, you can still be a long
                            way from scoring...

CLIENT 1:   All right, mister, sell me! Just what is
                            it you want us to do?

PETARSKI: Operation as complex as yours, I'll need
     (GOOD-NATURED)   information before I go sounding off. Like
                            specifically...

CSR cassette excerpt continued—used by permission of the US Postal
Service Training and Development Institute.

4 Its sharp focus on audience.
Not only does this tape zero in on situations characteristic of those encountered by its audience—CSRs, consumer sales representatives—it also recognises that a high proportion of its listeners will be sports fans, that most will not have gone beyond a high school education and that they are goal-motivated, used to thinking in terms of striving, achieving.

5 Its dramatic approach.
In other words, it tells its story, presents its message, in terms of people doing things—a highly desirable handling in view of the audience attitude noted in the final point of 4, above. Nothing captures people's interest more.

6 Its high emotional impact.
As observed previously, effective AV shoots for the heart as well as the head. To that end, here, desire is coupled with danger, the potentiality of failure. This grips the imagination, creates empathy and drives home instruction. Facts that alone fall flat and dry come to life when you wrap them in the warm glow of human feeling.

Purely from a writing standpoint, the lessons noted here transfer nicely to more complex or elaborate projects. You may be surprised how often your ability to come up with low-cost, imaginative shortcuts can win you jobs that otherwise might go to the competition.

14   Assessing the slide show

Basically, a slide show is a presentation made up of a number of 35mm slides set up for viewing in a predetermined order and accompanied by some sort of voice-over commentary. The simplest may have the person in charge inserting slides into a projector one by one and talking about the pictures as they flash on the screen. More sophisticated versions use magazine-fed automatic projectors with commentary read aloud or played on tape or disc.

The slide show is one of the commonest audiovisual forms. It can be one of the simplest to produce. Both audio and visual aspects are easily changed, simply by making a new tape and/or substituting/inserting/deleting slides.

Now, let us look at five pages (the first three and last two) of the working script of a reasonably advanced, strongly fact-oriented, industrial product promotion show.

Our comments, analysis and interpretation this time come from my old friend Bill Pryor, the show's writer/producer and a man well worthy of your attention. For years a writer, writer/director and writer/producer at such firms as Perceptoscope and The Calvin Company, he now has his own operation, Wm. E. Pryor Creative Services, in Kansas City, Mo. His observations almost constitute a short course on the slide show form.

Enclosed is a script I just finished. Not a complete script; changes were made, as usual, in the narration, etc. And, it is not really good on the visual side because I write that side for myself because I present the scripts in person and then I shoot the whole thing myself, so it doesn't have to be very thorough.

Slide shows are a big deal this year . . . If the script is to be produced by someone other than the writer, it should be *at least* as thorough as a motion picture script. Slide shows have to 'cut' properly just like a film. In the case of the enclosed script, if there is a sequence of a truck loading asphalt, the writer should specify that the green truck that was in the long shot must be the same green truck as in the MS and CU. This is because a lot of still photographers shoot slide shows. Angles should be

Third Draft--Load Management System slide show　　　12/1/79

1 - Title slide with　　　MUSIC FADES IN, THEN DOWN UNDER SOUND
logo.　　　　　　　　　　SOUND EFFECTS THROUGH OPENING MONTAGE.

2 - Opening montage -

--Driver talking into
intercom.

--Truck drives onto
scale

--Operator dials in
information

--Truck stops under bin.

--Operator presses load
button.

--Truck loads.

--Truck pulls up to
get ticket.

--Driver gets ticket.

--Truck leaves.　　　　　MUSIC AND SFX FACE UNDER NARRATOR.

3 - Overall shot of　　　NARRATOR:
LMS and printer
　　　　　　　　　　　　What you have just seen is a typical

　　　　　　　　　　　　truck loadout sequence at a hotmix

　　　　　　　　　　　　plant equipped with the new Intecon

　　　　　　　　　　　　Load Management System--the most

　　　　　　　　　　　　advanced truck loadout and business

　　　　　　　　　　　　management system available to the Hot mix

　　　　　　　　　　　　industry today.

*Load Management System script excerpt used by permission of William E.
Pryor.*

2

④ *overall SRO*

4 - ECU - Lapsed
time digital display
(1:04).

Use 2 shots—
truck loads/
truck leaves

At this hotmix plant, the average
time during an early morning rush
period for a driver to pull onto the
scale, load, receive his ticket and
begin to leave the yard was *is* just over
one minute.

5 - Another truck

add shot of truck

It is a normal, everyday occurrance
for this plant to load and ticket 200
tons of hotmix in ten minutes. In fact,
five hundred tons in half an hour--
that's five hundred tons in thirty
minutes--is not unusual.

6 - Operator's point
of view to show LMS
and truck loading

What makes this production rate
possible on a day-to-day basis is the
plant's Load Management System,
used in conjunction with its surge storage
equipment.

7 - High angle -
Truck leaves bin.

But the transfer of hotmix from bin
to truck is only part of the story
of what has happened *here* in sixty seconds
here...

*Load Management System script continued—used by permission of William
E. Pryor.*

3

8 - Same as above,   ...because by the time the driver
truck is further
from bin   pulls from under the bin to the
                           TICKET
                          pneumatic tube ~~outlet~~...

9 - Printer area   (SFX: PNEUMATIC SCHLUURRRP)
(SRO) as girl
sends ticket.

10 - Driver gets   ...his ticket is waiting for him.

11 - Tickets on SRO And that tickets contains <u>complete</u>
counter.
                          information, with customer name,

                          address, project and truck number,

12 - ECU - Ticket,   the time, date and <u>of course</u> gross,
close enough for   of which was
readibility   tare and net weights. All printed of which

                          out automatically in seconds. by the load
                          Management System.

13 - Overall shot   In addition, all data on the
of LMS.
                          transaction is recorded automatically

                          and retained in the system's central

                          memory.

Load Management System script continued—used by permission of William E. Pryor.

13

68 - SH corporate logo   *(Bobbling)*   At Standard Havens, ~~your business~~ *hot mix* is

(S. shot / Japanese shot / Bobbling / Down CRT / Michigan CRT)

our business. We produce a full line

of equipment for the hotmix production

industry--including Surg-Stor systems,

plants, air pollution control

equipment, ~~and~~ *repair* parts, and *plant* accessories,

and ~~service~~ *electronic controls.*

69 - Building shot   More than a decade ago our

equipment

Surg-Stor ~~system~~ began leading the *way in*

70. *Pix of SH Surge Bin System – possibly CRO*   *(the)* revolution that changed hotmix

2 S-S shots

plants from start-stop operations

into continuous, steady production

systems.

70 - Several shots   A Surg-Stor system frees your plant
of Surg-Stor systems
from dependance on truck availability.

/You produce more hotmix in a day

because you are filling bins from

the plant instead of one truck at a

time./ If you have surge-storage on

your plant, you know how it has

helped you increase your efficiency

and make more money...

Load Management System script continued—used by permission of William E. Pryor.

14

70 - Cont'd

...But, if you don't have a Load
Management System, then you are
~~wasting~~ missing a big part of ~~your~~ the potential profits

71 - LMS shot;
truck loading
in background

investment ~~in~~ surge-storage. By
automating the loading, ~~and~~ ticketing,
~~and~~ record keeping and invoicing
procedures, ~~internize~~ the Intecon

72 - Another
LMS system

Load Management System frees your
plant personnel from manual and
tedious paperwork, increases accuracy
and improves the business end of your
business.

73 - Owner type
with LMS, printer,
operator handing
him reports from
printer x; maybe
use two different
angles.

The bottom line is this; with a
Load, *pause* Management System you not
only load out more hotmix in less
time--you minimize errors and ~~you~~
improve ~~your~~ *invoicing* turnaround on receivables. *and cash flows*
It all adds up to greater operating
efficiency plus a better profit
picture.

74 - Overall shot
of SRO with flag,
bins, full truck

(MUSIC UP)

End on product
shot

add something on
business informat

Load Management System script continued—used by permission of William E. Pryor.

specifically spelled out. (Once again, *I* don't write like that because I shoot and produce it myself.)

Sound effects and music are more important in a slide show than a movie. You can do more with them. You can have stereo if you want. Sound quality is much better, because normally it will be a magnetic cassette with good speakers being used during the presentation, rather than the less-than-sparkling quality of a 16mm optical or Super 8 mag print.

Things to beware of: The client always wants to overdo the verbiage in a slide show. Note the enclosed script. It was a committee abortion. I won about 50 per cent of the battles and gave in on about 25 per cent and threw up my hands on the rest just in order to get the job done on time.

Note that this slide show is all live photography. No artwork except title and logo. Much better than charts, drawings, graphs, etc. Lots of people think in terms of artwork on a slide show. It costs a lot, and it's dull. The audience wants to see the equipment working.

The writer must be aware of the way the show is going to be presented. He should know all about the equipment. He should direct the narration and edit the show himself. He should program the tape himself. If he doesn't somebody will mess it up. Even at most AV companies that I am aware of, the writer does most of the production—he may not direct it or photograph it, but he usually edits and programs the show. The writer must let the photographer know what kind of equipment the show is going to be projected on. All of the playback units vary. They crop differently. Is the show going to be presented with dissolver units, ie multiple projector setups? Great! You can make it almost like a movie. Example: Long shot of a person, then dissolve to an ECU of him, then dissolve to MS at another angle, or something. You can get in three shots to cover a paragraph rather than just one. Looks good.

Clients want to talk in terms of *number* of slides in a show—how much per slide, etc. That is none of their business. Every slide show conference begins with someone saying, 'We want this to be about 45 slides or so; I've heard that a slide should be on the screen for about 20 seconds.' Etc. The enclosed script runs for less than *eleven minutes*; there were *102 slides* in the finished presentation. Make it move fast. Tell the photographer to get LS, MS, CU, ECU and different angles of every shot. That gives you programming options. Slide shows are hideously dull if you have only one slide for every paragraph of narration.

The writer should charge as much for a slide show script as for film. It usually takes longer to write. An hourly or daily rate is best. If you say $2,000 for a filmscript, that's OK; but if you say the same for a slide script somebody will have a fit. But if you establish your rate immediately and let them know how much time you're spending and on what, then the same amount of money is OK.

A slide show is not necessarily cheaper than a film—though of course it may be. It takes just as many lights, just about as long to set up a shot. You have to pay more attention to certain things in production. In a movie if somebody blinks, no big deal. On a slide, the person will be on screen for awhile. You have to establish shots better. You can't zoom in, so your establishing shots must be better thought out. You still have to do narration, music, etc. You can do all that, including mixing, on quarter-inch tape at recording studios that are cheaper than film labs, so music costs can be cheaper. Film and lab are cheaper, obviously.

Everybody wants a multi-screen slide show. Talk them out of it if possible. Two projectors, a dissolver and a sync playback unit are as complex as they should get. Because all that other stuff isn't portable. I made $8000 converting a multi-screen slide show to 16mm film a couple of years ago because the guy who made the slide show never thought about how to transport eight projectors, etc., on a plane.

There are, however, sometimes good reasons for multi-screen things. One is that the producer always makes more money: therefore the writer should charge more. The other is that if your subject matter leaves a lot to be desired, you can always snow the audience with sight and sound.

Things to avoid in slide shows: The same as in films. Don't have lists of stuff; you see a lot of slide shows where every succeeding slide for about 20 slides builds up another title with a different color—and the narrator reads the stuff to the audience.

And there you have it, friends: the straight goods, alive and breathing. Only the expletives have been deleted.

We are still not through with slide shows, simply because they come in so many shapes and sizes. Bill's script, above, is a good example of one written to fit a situation where control is, to a degree, limited by circumstance. This is all that is needed most of the time and the pattern you encounter where most work is concerned. That is, you write within the framework of actual events taking place. Consequently, there is a fine line beyond which you cannot make reality conform to your artistic/technical needs.

In some slide shows, however, well-nigh absolute control is demanded in order that a particular emotional effect may be achieved. To that end, the show may eliminate reality completely in favour of a 'story' approach—a fictional dramatised *simulation* of events.

As a sample of such, consider *Candles on the Cake*, a retirement annuity sales slide show I scripted for Rocket Pictures in Los Angeles some years ago. It was intended for use by salesmen in table-top rear-screen projectors. The idea was to persuade the prospective client to grant 15 or 20 minutes of uninterrupted time in his own office. There the salesman would set up the automatic slide-plus-sound projector. For the allotted period the client was transported into the world the show created, with no telephone or secretarial interference. When the presentation ended, the salesman moved in for the kill, adapting the annuity idea to the client's personal situation and needs.

For me as writer, the issue was to come up with a script that, transmuted into audiovisual form, would sell retirement annuities. The method was to appeal to the deep-rooted, near-compulsive hunger for security and,

```
                                           Candles--1


   1    FOCUS FRAME              (SILENT)


   2    ART: TITLE              (MUSIC: INTRO)
        "B.S.B. PRESENTS..."


   3    ART: MAIN TITLE         (MUSIC: UP)
        "CANDLES ON THE CAKE"
                                (MUSIC: TO B.G.)


   4    ART: ILLUSTRATION       NAR: This is a story of birthdays
        CU, BIRTHDAY CAKE WITH  --the birthdays of
        CANDLES BURNING BRIGHTLY

   5    PHOTO: INT              John Horton, chief clerk at Acme.
        CU, JOHN IN LIVINGROOM,
        LAUGHING DELIGHTEDLY AT Today he's 65.  So,
        MATCHING CAKE ON TABLE
        BEFORE HIM


   6    PHOTO: (CONT.)          the Hortons are having a little
        MS, HORTON FAMILY
        GROUPED ABOUT TABLE.    family celebration.  For this is
        SHOT FAVORS JOHN.
        ALSO INCLUDED ARE       a turning-point for John; more
        ETHEL, BOB, DOROTHY,
        AND TWO CHILDREN        than just an ordinary birthday.


   7    PHOTO: INT.             Acme gave him his first formal word
        MCU, JOHN AT DESK IN
        OFFICE, READING LETTER. on the subject: official notice
        HIS EXPRESSION IS ONE
        OF PLEASURE--MAYBE EVEN that he's reached mandatory
        REPRESSED TRIUMPH AND
        EXCITEMENT.  A          retirement age.  It's a moment
        DISTINGUISHED-LOOKING
        MAN STANDS BESIDE HIM   John's been looking forward to--
```

'Candles on the Cake' script used by permission of Dick Weston, Rocket Pictures, Inc.

Candles--2

8	PHOTO: (CONT.) CAMERA DRAWS BACK TO MS. MAN PATS JOHN ON BACK. BOTH ARE BEAMING	--a chance to relax and enjoy life. Now, thanks to the company rule, he can do it. He's even relieved of responsibility for making the decision to quit.
9	PHOTO: (CONT.) CU. JOHN'S BEAMING FACE	That's the way it is in business. and he's glad. Business retires you; you don't retire from business.
10	PHOTO: (CONT.) MS, OFFICE, DIFFERENT ANGLE. JOHN IS CENTER OF GROUP OF FOUR OR FIVE MEN, WITH GIRL SECRETARY IN BACKGROUND. THE DISTINGUISHED MAN IS INCLUDED. ONE MAN IS GIVING JOHN AN OPENED CASE WHICH CONTAINS A WATCH. ANOTHER HOLDS A SCROLL-TYPE PAPER, AS IF READING A PROCLAMATION	The watch they gave him at the plant today--as John sees it, it's a symbol of success and of fulfillment...recognition that the company has observed and appreciated all the years of hard work he's put in.
11	PHOTO: INT MCU, SHOT 6 PARTY, JOHN GESTURING AND SPEAKING, CAKE STILL BEFORE HIM. OTHER MEMBERS OF FAMILY (THOUGH PROBABLY NOT ALL) ARE INCLUDED	That makes John feel mighty good. --In terms of the future, even more so. Because it looks like a clear track ahead.

'Candles on the Cake' script continued—used by permission of Dick Weston, Rocket Pictures, Inc.

Candles--3

12   PHOTO: (CONT.)   A man couldn't ask for a better
     CU, ETHEL, LAUGHING
                              wife than Ethel.

13   PHOTO: (CONT.)   Son Bob is a boy any father would
     CU, BOB, LAUGHING
                              be proud of.

14   PHOTO: (CONT.)   Dorothy's a fine daughter-in-law;
     CU THREE-SHOT, DOROTHY
     WITH HER ARMS ABOUT THE and the grandchildren--well!
     TWO CHILDREN.   ALL ARE
     LAUGHING.

15   PHOTO: INT.   Through the years, John's liked
     MCU THREE-SHOT, JOHN
     CONFERRING WITH TWO   his work and the people he's
     OTHER MEN IN SHOT 9
     OFFICE.   ALL LOOK   worked with.
     GOOD-NATURED AND
     FRIENDLY

16   PHOTO: INT.   His terms on the church board--
     MS, CONFERENCE ROOM,
     CLEARLY IDENTIFIABLE AS they prove he's responsible and
     IN CHURCH.   SEVERAL
     MEN ARE SITTING ABOUT   respected.
     TABLE--ONE (NOT JOHN)
     AT HEAD, OTHERS ALONG
     SIDES.

17   PHOTO: EXT   His neighbors are all his good
     MCU TWO-SHOT, JOHN IN
     YARD, LEANING ON RAKE   friends.
     AND TALKING ACROSS
     HEDGE TO NEIGHBOR.

'Candles on the Cake' script continued—used by permission of Dick Weston, Rocket Pictures, Inc.

Candles--4

18 PHOTO: (CONT.)   Sure, he and Ethel have had their
    MS, THAT PORTION OF
    YARD IN WHICH JOHN AND   share of trouble--
    NEIGHBOR STAND. ETHEL
    KNEELS SOMEWHAT TO ONE
    SIDE OF THE TWO MEN,
    PRUNING ROSES OR THE
    LIKE, AND JOHN IS
    GESTURING IN HER
    DIRECTION. THIS SHOT
    ALSO SHOULD INCLUDE
    ENOUGH OF THE HORTON
    HOME TO ESTABLISH IT AS
    A COMFORTABLE, WELL-CARED
    FOR, MIDDLE-BRACKET
    PLACE

19 PHOTO: INT.   --the period when Ethel was in
    MS, BEDROOM. DOCTOR
    SITS BY BED, READING   such poor health...
    THERMOMETER, MEDICAL
    CASE ON STAND BESIDE
    HIM. ETHEL LIES IN THE
    BED, SO PLACED AS TO
    CHEAT ON HER AGE. JOHN
    (HAIR DARK) STANDS TO
    ONE SIDE, BACK TO CAMERA

20 PHOTO: EXT.   ... the long layoff during the
    MS, JOHN STANDING AT
    FACTORY GATE, BACK TO   depression...
    CAMERA. HE'S WEARING
    HAT, COAT COLLAR TURNED
    UP AS IF AGAINST THE
    COLD. HE IS READING
    PROMINENT SIGN: "NO
    WORK TILL FURTHER
    NOTICE"
    (or)
    ART: ILLUSTRATION
    NEWSPAPER WITH HEADLINE:
    "ACME CLOSES; 3000
    JOBLESS" OR THE LIKE

21 PHOTO: EXT.   ...Son Bob's months as a prisoner
    MLS, BOB, SHOT THROUGH
    HIGH BARBED WIRE FENCE. of war...
    AREA IS BLEAK. BOB
    WEARS SHABBY ARMY UNIFORM.
    HE STANDS SLUMPED, HANDS
    IN POCKETS

'Candles on the Cake' script continued—used by permission of Dick Weston, Rocket Pictures, Inc.

Candles--5

22	PHOTO: INT. MCU, FRAGILE ELDERLY WOMAN IN WHEELCHAIR IN BEDROOM	...the years Ethel's mother stayed with them before she died.
23	PHOTO: CLOSE MS, PARTY GROUP AS IN SHOT 6. SHOT FAVORS JOHN. HE STILL LOOKS HAPPY ENOUGH, YET THERE'S A SOBER, THOUGHTFUL NOTE BEHIND HIS PLEASURE	But troubles pass, John knows. So he's worked hard and played his breaks straight...brought home his paycheck each and every week.
24	PHOTO: (CONT.) MS, ROOM. PARTY IS STILL IN PROGRESS, BUT JOHN HAS RISEN AND IS LOOKING AWAY FROM THE PEOPLE, ADMIRING THE ROOM ITSELF WITH HIS HEAD COCKED SLIGHTLY	Now, the house is free and clear; all paid for.
25	PHOTO: (CONT.) MS, LIVINGROOM CORNER. JOHN IS TAKING PIPE FROM RACK ON END TABLE THAT STANDS BESIDE A COMFORTABLE-LOOKING OLD OVERSTUFFED VELOUR CHAIR WITH FOOTSTOOL. A LIGHTED FLOOR LAMP, VINTAGE 1925, FLANKS THE CHAIR. A SMALL SHEAF OF PAPERS AND LETTERS, AND A FEW BOOKS, ARE ON THE END TABLE NEXT TO THE PIPE RACK. BANKBOOK IS ON TOP OF HEAP	The furnishings--well, a man gets used to familiar things. Comfort's more important than a lot of fancy doodads.
26	PHOTO: (CONT.) MCU, JOHN SEATED IN CHAIR FROM SHOT 25. HE'S PUFFING AT HIS PIPE. HE HOLDS BANK- BOOK IN HIS HANDS, STUDYING IT. HE LOOKS COMFORTABLE AND WELL- SATISFIED. SHOT FAVORS BANKBOOK	There's even a little money in bonds and in the bank. So,

'Candles on the Cake' script continued—used by permission of Dick Weston, Rocket Pictures, Inc.

Candles--6

27 PHOTO: (CONT.)   John figures the years ahead are
    CLOSE MS, JOHN AND
    PART OF PARTY GROUP.   going to be good years. Because
    ETHEL(AND PERHAPS
    OTHERS) HAS RISEN AND   all he and Ethel want from
    STANDS FAIRLY CLOSE TO
    JOHN. SHOT STRONGLY   retirement, really,
    FAVORS JOHN AND ETHEL
    AS THEY GAZE FONDLY AT
    EACH OTHER, SMILING

28 PHOTO: (CONT.)   is independence. They plan to
    CU, JOHN GAZING UP
    THROUGH HIS PIPESMOKE   settle down to the pattern they've
    INTO THE WORLD OF HIS
    DREAMS   chosen...enjoying the simple

                             things--

29 PHOTO: INT   --sleeping late...
    MCU TWO-SHOT. JOHN
    LIES ABED, STRETCHING
    SLEEPILY. ETHEL STANDS
    BESIDE HIM, ONE HAND ON
    HIP, LAUGHING AND SHAKING
    A BIG KITCHEN SPOON AT
    HIM AS IF DEMANDING THAT
    HE GET UP

30 PHOTO: EXT.   ...fishing...
    MS, JOHN AND ANOTHER
    MAN OF SIMILAR AGE IN
    ROWBOAT. JOHN IS
    CASTING

31 PHOTO: EXT.   ...gardening...
    MCU, ETHEL CUTTING
    BOUQUET OF ROSES

32 PHOTO: EXT (STOCK SHOT) ...taking an occasional scenic
    MS-MLS, GRAND CANYON,
    NEW YORK CITY SKYLINE,   trip...
    OR THE LIKE

*'Candles on the Cake' script continued—used by permission of Dick
Weston, Rocket Pictures, Inc.*

33   PHOTO: EXT.   ...spoiling their grandkids.
     MS, AMUSEMENT PART RIDE
     TICKET STAND AREA.   --Only then comes a rude
     JOHN"S BUYING TICKETS
     WHILE THE GRANDKIDS   awakening--
     EAT COTTON CANDY.
     ETHEL HOLDS LITTLE
     GIRL'S HAND

34   PHOTO: INT.   --the day when John suddenly
     MCU TWO-SHOT, JOHN AND
     TV REPAIRMAN IN TV   realizes that he's drawn his
     REPAIR SHOP. MAN HOLDS
     PICTURE TUBE AS IF HE   last paycheck.
     WERE EXPLAINING
     SOMETHING. JOHN HOLDS
     CHECKBOOK IN ONE HAND,
     PEN IN OTHER. HE'S
     FROWNING DOWN AT THE
     BOOK'S ENTRIES; PAYING
     NO NEED TO THE
     REPAIRMAN. SHOT FAVORS
     JOHN

35   PHOTO: INT.   Nor does it help then the Hortons
     MCU TWO-SHOT, JOHN AND
     ETHEL BY FRONT DOOR.   learn that social security and
     ETHEL HOLDS A SHEAF
     OF MAIL. JOHN HOLDS   John's pension, both together,
     TWO CHECKS IN ONE HAND,
     THEIR ENVELOPES IN THE   simply won't be adequate for them
     OTHER. BOTH HORTONS
     LOOK A TRIFLE UPSET AS   to live on.
     THEY GAZE AT THE CHECKS

36   JOHN AND ETHEL LOOKING   It dawns on them, then, that
     AT EACH OTHER. THEY
     REGISTER WORRY, FRIGHT   they've made their retirement

                                 plans well enough. But they've

                                 forgotten to plan for a steady,

                                 continuing income--the income

                                 that anyone, retired or not, must

                                 have, in order to meet the bills

                                 that go with living.

*'Candles on the Cake' script continued—used by permission of Dick
Weston, Rocket Pictures, Inc.*

Candles--8

37   PHOTO: INT.
     MCU, JOHN TAKING BONDS
     FROM BOX IN BANK'S
     SAFETY DEPOSIT VAULT

Economizing isn't enough. Before
John knows it, he's dipping into
savings, cashing bonds.

38   PHOTO: INT.
     MS, BIRTHDAY PARTY.
     REDRESS TO DIFFERENTIATE
     FROM SHOT 6

Another year, another birthday
party. More and more often now,
extras seem to come up--

39   PHOTO: INT.
     MCU TWO-SHOT, JOHN AND
     MECHANIC IN GARAGE.
     THEY STAND BESIDE
     WORKBENCH.MECHANIC
     HOLDS TOOL

MECHANIC: Sorry, Mr. Horton. It's
going to have to be a valve job
this time. These older cars--

40   PHOTO: INT.
     MCU TWO-SHOT,
     OPTOMETRIST SEATED AT
     FITTING TABLE IN
     OPTOMETRIST'S OFFICE.
     OPTOMETRIST HOLDS
     GLASSES

OPTOMERIST: Yes, Mrs Horton,
you definitely do need new glasses.
I'm surprised your headaches aren't
worse than they are.

41   PHOTO: INT.
     MCU TWO-SHOT. JOHN AND
     DENTIST STANDING BESIDE
     DENTAL CHAIR. DENTIST
     HOLDS AND TAPS PLATE.

DENTIST: A plate that's cracked
this badly <u>can't</u> be repaired, Mr.
Horton. You'll have to have a
new one.

42   PHOTO: EXT.
     MCU TWO-SHOT, JOHN AND
     ROOFER IN YARD, HORTON
     HOUSE IN BACKGROUND.
     ROOFER HOLDS PAD AND
     AND PENCIL

ROOFER: That's the best price I
can make you, Mr. Horton. Putting
a new roof on a house just plain
costs money.

'Candles on the Cake' script continued—used by permission of Dick Weston, Rocket Pictures, Inc.

43 PHOTO: EXT.   NAR.: John's first thought is to
    MS, JOHN CHECKING
    CLASSIFIED ADS IN   find another job.
    FOLDED NEWSPAPER AT
    OFFICE BUILDING
    ENTRANCE

44 PHOTO: INT.   PERSONNEL MAN: I'm sorry, Mr.
    MCU TWO-SHOT, JOHN AND
    PERSONNEL MAN. MAN SITS Horton. But we need someone a
    BEHIND DESK WHICH BEARS
    SIGN "PERSONNEL MANAGER" bit younger for this position.
    JOHN STANDS BEFORE HIM,
    HAT IN HAND.

45 PHOTO: INT.   NAR.: Worse, John learns that
    MS, JOHN TALKING TO
    CLERK ACROSS COUNTER.   any work that pays more than
    HE LOOKS DEPRESSED.
    SIGN PROMINENT IN $100 a month, $1200 a year, cuts
    BACKGROUND SAYS THIS
    IS "SOCIAL SECURITY   down on his social security
    LOCAL OFFICE" OR THE
    LIKE   benefits.

46 PHOTO: EXT.   The car goes--John has to raise
    MS TWO-SHOT, MAN
    HANDING JOHN CHECK.   cash somewhere.
    THEY STAND BEFORE A
    BIG USED AUTO LOT SIGN
    "CASH FOR YOUR CAR" OR
    THE LIKE

47 PHOTO: EXT.   Church donations? Entertaining?
    MLS, JOHN AND ETHEL
    PASSING TOY STORE   Presents for the grandchildren?
    WINDOW DISPLAY. THEY
    WALK WITH HEADS DOWN,   No more. Pride takes a beating
    SHOULDERS SLUMPED,
    NOT LOOKING AT THE   when financial security fades.
    DISPLAY

'Candles on the Cake' script continued—used by permission of Dick Weston, Rocket Pictures, Inc.

Candles--10

48 PHOTO: INT.   John's next birthday isn't quite
   MCU, BIRTHDAY PARTY
   FAVORING JOHN. HE   so happy. If he and Ethel didn't
   LOOKS DEPRESSED AND
   HARRIED DESPITE HIS   own their home, they might be in
   CANDLE SPARKLING CAKE
                           real trouble.

49 PHOTO: INT.   John's health begins to fail.
   MCU TWO-SHOT, DOCTOR
   TAKING JOHN'S BLOOD   Bills pile up. Even with Bob and
   PRESSURE AGAINST
   MEDICAL OFFICE   Dorothy helping, the Hortons'
   BACKGROUND
                           pension money won't go around.

50 PHOTO: EXT.   The Hortons' house costs more to
   MS, HOUSE. JOHN AND
   ETHEL STAND NEAR THE   keep up than they can afford. But
   ENTRANCE, JOHN IN
   SHIRTSLEEVES AND ETHEL it's hard to let a place go when
   IN HOUSEDRESS. THEY
   LOOK UPSET. A MIDDLE- you've 30 years of memories in it.
   AGED COUPLE IN STREET
   ATTIRE STAND OFF TO
   ONE SIDE, SURVEYING
   THE HOUSE CRITICALLY.
   WITH THEM IS A REALTOR-
   TYPE MAN IN BUSINESS
   SUIT, SPEAKING AND
   GESTURING.

51 PHOTO: INT   Now, though, there's no choice.
   MCU TWO-SHOT, CRASS-
   LOOKING MAN AND WOMAN Worst of all is the auction--
   WITH NEEDLEPOINT CHAIR
   OR THE LIKE TURNED   cherished possessions pawed over,
   UPSIDE DOWN SO THEY
   CAN INSPECT THE JOINTS sold to strangers.

'Candles on the Cake' script continued—used by permission of Dick Weston, Rocket Pictures, Inc.

52 PHOTO: INT.   The watch Acme gave John when he
    MCU TWO-SHOT, JOHN
    AND PAWNBROKER AGAINST   retired goes to the pawnshop.
    PAWKBROKER BACKGROUND.
    JOHN IS PUSHING WATCH   Time's run out for him, and he
    ACROSS COUNTER AS
    PAWNBROKER EXTENDS   knows it.
    CASH

53 PHOTO: INT.   SON: Dad, I'm sorry. But Dorothy
    MCU THREE-SHOT, JOHN
    ETHEL AND BOB.   and I won't have you living this
    BACKGROUND IS LIVING
    ROOM OF EXTREMELY   way. You'll have to move in with
    SLEAZY-LOOKING
    APARTMENT   us.

54 PHOTO: INT.   NAR.: The birthday that follows
    MS, BIRTHDAY PARTY SET
    IN COMPTEMPORARY-STYLE   the move is a sort of private
    LIVINGROOM OF BOB'S
    HOUSE. ETHEL IS   nightmare for John.
    APPROACHING TABLE,
    CARRYING LIGHTED CAKE.
    DOROTHY IS COMING CLOSE
    BEHIND AND TO ONE SIDE
    OF HER, CARRYING TRAY
    WITH DISHES OF ICE
    CREAM.   THE GRANDKIDS
    STAND IN DOORWAY TO ONE
    SIDE.   JOHN AND BOB ARE
    ALREADY SEATED AT THE
    TABLE. SHOT FAVORS JOHN.
    HE LOOKS EXTREMELY
    DEPRESSED AS HE STARES
    AT THE CAKE

55 PHOTO: (CONT.)   All he can think about is how he's
    MCU THREE-SHOT, JOHN,
    ETHEL AND DOROTHY.   failed the one he loves the most,
    JOHN WATCHES ETHEL AS
    SHE TALKS TO DOROTHY.   even though she'll never say a word
    THERE'S AN AIR OF
    RESIGNATION ABOUT HER.   about it.
    SHOT FAVORS ETHEL

'Candles on the Cake' script continued—used by permission of Dick Weston, Rocket Pictures, Inc.

Candles--12

56 PHOTO: (CONT.)   Crowding both grandchildren into
    MCU TWO-SHOT, THE
    GRANDKIDS. THEY'RE   one bedroom--well, John knoss it
    STARING SULLENLY OUT
    OF FRAME   can't help but change the way

                             they feel about him and Ethel.

57 PHOTO: (CONT.)   Dorothy's a wonderful daughter-in-
    MCU TWO-SHOT, ETHEL
    AND DOROTHY. ETHEL   law. But what young woman wants
    IS LEANING FORWARD TO
    SET DOWN THE CAKE.   her husband's mother telling her
    DOROTHY IS LOOKING AT
    ETHEL (WHO CAN'T SEE   how to run her kitchen?
    HER FACE) WITH JUST
    THE SLIGHTEST EXPRESSION
    OR IRRITATION. SHOT
    FAVORS DOROTHY

58 PHOTO: (CONT.)   John sees the friction it creates
    MCU TWO-SHOT, DOROTHY
    AND BOB. THEY'RE   between her and Bob.
    STARING AT EACH OTHER
    WITH CLEARLY
    ANTAGONISTIC EXPRESSIONS

59 PHOTO: INT   In the days that follow, the kids
    MCU THREE-SHOT, DOROTHY
    AND THE GRANDKIDS, IN grow more rebellious.
    KITCHEN. DOROTHY IS
    SCOLDING ONE OF THE
    CHILDREN, AND THE
    CHILD'S SNARLING BACK.
    THE OTHER YOUNGSTER
    STANDS SULLENLY IN THE
    BACKGROUND.

60 PHOTO: INT   Noise, confusion, humiliation--
    MS, LIVINGROOM. THE
    KIDS ARE RACING THROUGH John hates every aching moment of
    OR FIGHTING. JOHN
    STANDS IN ONE CORNER, it! Is this the independence in
    HOLDING HIS EARS. HE
    LOOKS MISERABLE.   retirement that he dreamed of?

'Candles on the Cake' script continued—used by permission of Dick Weston, Rocket Pictures, Inc.

61 PHOTO: INT
    CU, JOHN STARING AT   Another year...another birthday
    WALL CALENDAR. NO
    YEAR SHOWS, BUT THE   coming up. John dreads it. No
    DAY OF THE MONTH IS
    CIRCLED   party for him, this time; no

                                 candles on his birthday cake.

62 PHOTO: INT.   Too late, he's learned a bitter
    MS, BEDROOM. JOHN
    SITS ON THE EDGE OF   truth: It's just as bad for a man
    THE BED, HEAD IN
    HANDS, ELBOWS ON   to live too long as it is for him
    KNEES, A PICTURE OF
    DEFEAT   to die too soon. --But why must

                                 a man live till he's past 65 to

                                 find it out?

                       (END OF PART ONE)

63 PHOTO: INT.   Yes, that's the way it usually
    REPEAT SHOT 28
                                 happens, when a man doesn't plan

                                 for retirement income. But for

                                 John Horton, fortunately, it came

                                 to pass only in his imagination;

64 PHOTO: (CONT.)   a fantasy at his sixty-five
    CLOSE MS, PARTY GROUP.
    ALL ARE LAUGHING AS BOB   birthday party. The reason dates
    AND DOROTHY PULL JOHN
    UP FROM HIS CHAIR   back some years, to John's

                                 memories of old friends--

'Candles on the Cake' script continued—used by permission of Dick Weston, Rocket Pictures, Inc.

Candles--14

65	PHOTO: INT. MS, PRODUCE STORE, ELDERLY SAM REDDICK SWEEPING IN FOREGROUND. HE LOOKS PITIFUL AND INADEQUATE	--like Sam Reddick. Sam couldn't manage on social security, after he retired. So he ended up as sweeper at a produce store.
66	PHOTO: INT. MS, LARGE BLEAK- LOOKING ROOM WITH SEVERAL ELDERLY PEOPLE. ED ROBERTS STANDS LOOKING OUT WINDOW IN FOREGROUND, FRAGILE AND FORLORN	Ed Roberts' girls put <u>him</u> in a rest home, just to get him out from under foot.
67	PHOTO: EXT. MS, LILLIAN'S FRONT DOOR. THREE DO-GOODER TYPE WOMEN STAND JUST OUTSIDE WITH COVERED DISHES. LILLIAN IS IN THE OPEN DOORWAY, GREETING THEM WANLY	Lillian Goss's church circle made her their private project after she lost all her money on those bad investments.
68	PHOTO: INT. MS, JOHN (AGE 45) IN SILHOUETTE AT DUSK AT WINDOW, PONDERING, HIS BACK TO CAMERA	John saw that a man who wants independence needs to plan ahead for it. For earned income stops when he retires.
69	ART: CHART LIFE EXPECTANCY AT 60, 65, 70 AND SO ON	Could he <u>save</u> enough to support him and Ethel for the rest of their lives? The life expectancy tables said no.

'Candles on the Cake' script continued—used by permission of Dick Weston, Rocket Pictures, Inc.

70 ART: ILLUSTRATION
BALANCE-TYPE SCALE
WITH ONE PAN MARKED
"$40,000", THE OTHER
$100

Investments? For an income of only $100 a month, John would have to accumulate thirty or forty thousand dollars!

71 ART: ILLUSTRATION
FRAME-FILLING DISPLAY
OF STOCK CERTIFICATES,
FEATURING OFF-BEAT
ITEMS

To get higher interest, bigger returns, he'd have to gamble on speculative ventures--and maybe lose his shirt

72 PHOTO: INT.
CU, JOHN IN BED, NIGHT
LIGHTING. HE LIES ON
HIS BACK, BACK OF
WRIST ACROSS EYES

He began to wonder if there <u>was</u> any such thing as retirement security, where the average man was concerned.

73 PHOTO: INT.
MS, OFFICE, AGENT AND
JOHN SHAKING HANDS
ACROSS DESK. CAMERA
IS BEHIND AND TO ONE
SIDE OF JOHN, FAVORING
AGENT STRONGLY

Then, one day, his insurance agent came by to talk with him about retirement income annuities.

74 PHOTO: (CONT.)
MCU, AGENT SPEAKING.
BOTH MEN NOW ARE SEATED

AGENT: In effect, Mr. Horton, you'll be buying financial security on the installment plan!

'Candles on the Cake' script continued—used by permission of Dick Weston, Rocket Pictures, Inc.

Candles--16

75 ART: ILLUSTRATION   NAR.: Under the plan John chose,
      BULGING MONEY BAG
      MARKED "$30,000"   when he retired he'd receive either

a lump sum payment of $30,000 on

a predetermined date,

76 ART: ILLUSTRATION   or a regular monthly income for
      FAN OF MONTHLY
      CHECKS   the rest of his life. In either

case, it would be ample to

supplement social security.

77 ART: ILLUSTRATION   The sum could equally well have
      MCU, JOHN'S HEAD AT
      AGE 40 IN SILHOUETTE. been $15,000, $25,000, $50,000,
      SURROUNDING IT, ALL
      ANGLES, ARE QUESTION   or more. The decision was his,
      MARKS OF ASSORTED
      SHAPES AND SIZES, AND based on his own needs and
      SUCH LUMP SUM FIGURES
      AS "$25,000", "$35,000", resources.
      "$50,000"

78 ART: ILLUSTRATION   To retire <u>before</u> sixty-five, all
      MONTAGE OF VIGNETTES OF
      IDEALIZED RETIREMENT   he had to do was state in advance
      ACTIVITIES--MAN PLAYING
      GOLF, LUXURY LINER   the age at which he wanted to
      ENTERING TROPIC HARBOR,
      COUPLE BENEATH COLORFUL receive the money.
      UMBRELLA ON BEACH,
      COUPLE IN EVENING GARB
      ENTERING THEATRE, ETC.

79 REMUNERATION XXXNG ON Because he invested in the annuity
      DESK. HEADING SHOULD
      READ "RETIREMENT   at an early age, the premiums
      ANNUITY PREMIUM TABLE"
      OR THE LIKE   were low.

'Candles on the Cake' script continued—used by permission of Dick Weston, Rocket Pictures, Inc.

Candles--17

80   ART: ILLUSTRATION   Had John died before retirement
      SILHOUETTED FIGURES
      OF ETHEL (AGE 40) AND   age, Ethel and Bob would have
      BOY (AGE 12) STANDING
      IN FRONT OF STYLIZED   received the full amount of his
      SKETCH OF HORTON HOME.
      ETHEL HAS HER ARM   policy--income to replace the
      AROUND THE BOY. A
      CIRCLE OF GOLD LINKS   money he'd have earned.
      COMPLETELY SURROUNDS
      HOUSE, BOY AND ETHEL

81   ART:ILLUSTRATION   Best of all, annuity income was
      CU, PAPER HEADED
      "ANNUITY CHECKLIST" A   free and clear; non-taxable. It
      LIST OF FOUR ITEMS
      FOLLOWS: "SECURITY?",   wouldn't cut down on social security
      "RETURNS?", "NON-
      TAXABLE?", "SOCIAL   benefits.
      SECURITY?" AFTER EACH
      IS A HEAVY, RUBBER-
      STAMPED "OK"

82   ART: ILLUSTRATION   When John retired, he decided to
      CU, ANNUITY CHECK
      MADE OUT TO JOHN HORTON   take his annuity in regular income

                                 form, so that he'd have a check

                                 coming in each and every month,

                                 even if he lived to be 99!

83   PHOTO: INT.   Because he'd planned ahead, John
      REPEAT SHOT
                                 could afford to be happy at his

                                 party. He knew what his financial

                                 future held in store for him!

84   PHOTO: INT.   Today, social security and the
      MCU, JOHN AND ETHEL
      WITH SUPERMARKET CART.   company pension plan take care of
      JOHN'S AT THE HELM,
      ETHEL TAKING SOME ITEM   the Hortons' basic necessities
      FROM SHELF
                                 well enough.

'Candles on the Cake' script continued—used by permission of Dick Weston, Rocket Pictures, Inc.

Candles--18

85	PHOTO: EXT. MCU TWO-SHOT, JOHN AND ETHEL BESIDE THEIR MAILBOX. JOHN'S DISPLAYING CHECK TO ETHEL. BOTH ARE SMILING THEIR SATISFACTION	But it's their annuity check that gives them solid comfort...freedom ...peace of mind.
86	PHOTO: EXT. REPEAT SHOT 50	Thanks to the security it provides, there's been no need for them to give up their home.
87	PHOTO: EXT. MS, HORTON FRONT YARD, HOUSE IN BACKGROUND. JOHN (ARM ABOUT ETHEL) IS HAPPILY WAVING GOODBYE TO BOB, DOROTHY AND THE GRANDKIDS	It's theirs to enjoy, now more than ever...a gathering-place for friends and family.
88	PHOTO: INT. REPEAT SHOT 58	Since they didn't have ~~time~~ to move in with Bob and Dorothy, the Hortons create no friction in their son's home.
89	PHOTO: EXT. MS, ENTRANCE TO SON'S HOME. BOB AND DOROTHY AND THE GRANDKIDS ARE WELCOMING JOHN AND ETHEL ENTHUSIASTICALLY	Instead, financially secure, they're welcome guests--urged to drop by more often!

'Candles on the Cake' script continued—used by permission of Dick Weston, Rocket Pictures, Inc.

Candles--19

90   PHOTO: EXT.   With money coming in regularly
     REPEAT SHOT 46
                                    there wasn't any need for them to

                                    sell their car.

91   PHOTO: EXT   --When fishing season opens, John
     MS, JOHN AND A COUPLE
     OF FRIENDS IN FISHING   even can afford a motor for his
     GARB IN SAME BOAT AS
     IN SHOT 30. THIS TIME,   boat!
     HOWEVER, THE BOAT HAS
     A SHINY NEW MOTOR AND
     JOHN IS PROUDLY GUNNING
     THE CRAFT AWAY FROM THE
     DOCK

92   PHOTO: EXT.   Those scenic trips--?
     REPEAT SHOT 32

93   PHOTO: EXT.   You bet they'll go--because
     MCU, JOHN AND ETHEL
     BOARDING PLANE   travel's in their budget.

94   PHOTO: EXT.   Each day brings new people to
     MS, MIDDLE-AGED MAN
     INTRODUCING YOUNGER   meet...
     MAN TO JOHN AND ETHEL
     ON DOWNTOWN STREET.
     JOHN IS SHAKING HANDS

95   PHOTO: EXT.   ...the warm glow of continuing
     MS, JOHN AND ETHEL
     LAUGHING AND TALKING   friedships...
     WITH COUPLE OF SIMILAR
     AGE IN BACK YARD OF
     NON-HORTON HOME. MAN
     IS BROILING HAMBURGERS
     OVER OUTDOOR FIREPLACE

'Candles on the Cake' script continued—used by permission of Dick Weston, Rocket Pictures, Inc.

Candles--20

96 PHOTO: INT.   ...community respect on the level
MS, CONFERENCE ROOM IN
SHOT 16. MEN ARE   reserved for the stable and the
STANDING BESIDE CHAIRS,
JOHN THIS TIME AT HEAD solvent.
OF TABLE. SOME OF THE
MEN ARE THE SAME AS
BEFORE, BUT OTHERS HAVE
BEEN REPLACED BY NEW
FACES

97 PHOTO: EXT.   The very same years that have
MCU, POORLY-DRESSED
OLD MAN, DEPRESSED   brought so many men and women
EXPRESSION, SITTING
SLUMPED ON PARK BENCH down to the "old and out of a

             job" category...

98 PHOTO: EXT.   ...have seen John and Ethel firmly
CLOSE MS, PARK ACTIVITY
AREA. JOHN AND ETHEL established as happy, honored
ARE LAUGHING AND
PLAYING SOME GAME IN   senior citizens.
FOREGROUND, WITH GROUP
OF FRIENDS

99 PHOTO: INT.   Well, thanks to John's foresight,
REPEAT SHOT 6
            that's the way it worked out for

            the Hortons.

100 ART: ILLUSTRATION But the self-same need for income
SILHOUETTED FAMILY
GROUP--MAN, WOMAN,   arises in _every_ home--simply
TEEN-AGE BOY AND GIRL,
BOY OF EIGHT OR TEN   because sooner or later earned

            income stops for every man--but

            the _need_ for money goes on the

            same.

'Candles on the Cake' script continued—used by permission of Dick Weston, Rocket Pictures, Inc.

Candles--21

101 ART:(CONT.)   And when that day arrives, as it
    CU, MAN'S HEAD IN
    PROFILE, SILHOUTTED   must, what happens to the bread-
    AS HE PONDERS WITH
    HAND ON CHIN   winner and those dependent on his

                               earning power?

102 ART: (CONT.)   Will the result be loss of income
    SOMBER, DEPRESSED MOOD
    MAN IN SILHOUETTE,   --humiliation--bitterness--regret
    CRINGING FEARFULLY
    AND DOMINATED BY   --charity?
    LOOMING BACKGROUND

103 ART: (CONT.)   Or, will intelligence and
    BRIGHT, OPTIMISTIC
    MOOD MAN IN SILHOUETTE   forethought intervene, to provide
    TOWERING DOMINANT OVER
    SUBORDINATED BACKGROUND   a guaranteed, livable income through

                               all the golden years...

104 ART: (CONT.)   ...a chance for the man of the
    MAN IN SILHOUETTE IN
    LOUNGE CHAIR, FEET ON   house to enjoy to the full the
    FOOTSTOOL, RELAXED
    AND EXPANSIVE   happiness he's earned?

105 ART: (CONT.)   Will he "just scrape by", eking
    SOMBER, DEPRESSED MOOD
    MAN'S SLUMPED FIGURE IN   out a meager, worry-racked
    SILHOUETTE, ISOLATED
    AND FORLORN   existence on crumbs from the

                               table of life...

106 ART: (CONT.)   ...or will there, as long as he
    REPEAT SHOT 4
                               lives, be candles on his birthday

                               cake?

'Candles on the Cake' script continued—used by permission of Dick Weston, Rocket Pictures, Inc.

Candles--22

107 ART: (CONT.)   This is the decision every man
    REPEAT SHOT 101
                                    must make for himself and for

                                    his family.

108 ART: (CONT.)   Which will it be for you and
    REPEAT SHOT 100
    SUPERIMPOSE TITLE: yours?
    "WHICH WILL IT BE FOR
    YOU AND YOURS?"

                                    (MUSIC: UP TO FINALE)

obversely, the fear of insecurity, that lurks in so many of us.

To maximise this appeal, the script was developed within a predetermined pattern of proved effectiveness. Then, every video frame and audio line were scrutinised by technical advisors and staff. Endlessly, it seemed, pictures and narration were changed and juggled to sharpen the effect, drive home the key point.

The key point was that with forethought and proper planning—purchase of retirement annuities—the client may anticipate a happy and secure old age. Without it, he very well may fall victim to disaster

The pattern, in turn, develops this theme in terms of the life of one man. His story is told within the framework of a 100-shot (approximately) show, with every bit as careful attention to detail as any major Hollywood production.

(For a consideration of the principles and techniques of dramatic writing in more detail than is practical here, see my *Techniques of the Selling Writer* and *Film Scriptwriting: A Practical Manual.*)

The first half of the presentation, 62 shots, is a sort of burgeoning horror tale in which, after opening bliss, everything goes wrong. The second replays the man's final days in happier form, on the premise of his having invested in a retirement annuity at the proper time. All of which adds up to a combination of drama and emotional impact that is hard to resist.

'Candles on the Cake' (pp 142–163) demonstrates how tightly the chain of logic of a slide show may be linked together. John Horton takes form as an extension/reflection of every annuity prospect, a mirror of what they see as their own lives and sufferings and virtues. Horton's years of hard work, his devotion to family and friends, his thriftiness, his forbearance and fortitude when things go wrong and his dreams are the bricks with which empathy is built. When trouble strikes, it is in terms of non-melodramatic, down-to-earth problems of the kind that we have all known at one level or another. Each time he tries to fight clear, his way is blocked. His every attempt to find a way out fails.

Heart-wrenching fears come into focus: fears of failing health, of financial need, of insecurity and helplessness; loss of privacy and independence; and becoming a burden on one's loved ones.

If that isn't enough, there are the unhappy examples of Horton's friends: Sam Reddick, Ed Roberts and Lillian Goss. The picture is grim and tragic.

Then the clouds break. Retirement annuities can provide the answers—an extra financial edge that helps one's dreams come true. Respect, security, happiness and stability come with money. So that the prospect will not *just* identify with the man John Horton, shot 100 switches to silhouetted figures into which the client can project himself more clearly. In shot 101, he ponders. The contrast between the two potential fantasy worlds the show presents is brought into vivid focus in shots 102 through 105. The whole situation is left open-ended for the salesman's live closing pitch as the last slide-image fades from the screen.

YMCA HOLIDAY HILLS-- WORK AND PLAY IN THE COUNTRY (Don't Read)

1. Holiday Hills is now available to groups for various activities.

2. Whether you call it a conference

3. A retreat ✓

4. Or a training seminar. You need comfortable surroundings where you can talk, train, plan.

5. The last thing you need is the hassel around mid-town facilities.

6. Holiday Hills provides a relaxed atmosphere in the country

7. With the sophisticated conveniences of the city. Three principal conference areas adjoining each other can accommodate the needs of your group.

8. Whether it is two...

9. Or 400. Donaldson Conference Center designed in colorful, contemporary style provides meeting rooms, a foyer, snack lounge and sleeps 48.

10. Lathrop Center offers an auditorium seating up to 400, attractive comfortable lounges and meeting rooms.

11. The Inn, restored and enlarged from a 19th Century country house has two dining rooms and lounges. Nearby Cottage Row, sleeps 98. All together, these flexibly arranged facilities provide a total of 10 meeting rooms, and 8 attractive lounges which are also useful for group meeting, two large auditoriums and sleeping accommodations.

12. YOUR MEETING ARE HOUSED THE WAY YOU WANT THEM. (Don't Read)

13. Our larger auditorium with stage, multi-purpose lights, public address system and sound proof projection booths is ideal for lectures, movies, and seminars for up to 350 people.

'Holiday Hills' script excerpt used by permission of YMCA of Greater New York

CONCEPT/VISUAL	AUDIO/NARRATION
	YWCA Script (Revised 2/25/79) Page 6
	IV. ISSUES OF THE 28th CONVENTION
SLIDES OF PAST CONVENTIONS END AND A SLIDE WITH 1979, 28th NATIONAL CONVENTION WILL COME UP AND SUPER-IMPOSED WILL BE DALLAS CONVENTION SITE.	Each YWCA member has a commitment born of this legacy. It is a commitment that can only be built upon the present.
	We can't just point to our past accomplishments, there is work to be done now, at this time, in this place.
	As we meet in this 28th National Convention, there are many problems that still exist in the world around us and represent the deep concerns of women everywhere.
SLIDES SHOWING POVERTY, UNEMPLOYMENT, THIRD WORLD PROBLEMS, BATTERED WOMEN, ETC. BEGIN.	We must deal with programs to advance equal rights under the law and in practice.
	We must meet urgent human needs arising from racist practices, from unemployment, hunger, inadequate housing, poverty, and dwindling resources.
	We must expand opportunities for work.
	We must provide leadership in the raising of consciousness about and opening up opportunities for employment of women in non-traditional and traditional jobs.

YWCA script excerpt used by permission of National Board, Young Women's Christian Association of the USA.

CONCEPT/VISUAL	AUDIO/NARRATION
	YWCA Script (Revised 2/25/79) Page 7
SLIDES SHOWING CONCERNS OF YWCA CONTINUE	We must press for quality health care, quality education and economic security.

We must live up to our commitment to involve youth, because teen women empowered with knowledge and skills and resources help us strengthen the YWCA today and tomorrow.

Many YWCAs--in large and small communities-- are dealing with problems related to unemployment, the family, career development, women in crisis and transition, drug abuse, juvenile justice, sexuality education, battered and otherwise abused women, displaced housemakers, and spiritual development, as well as issues that have an impact on the total world. Yet, there is so much to be done. |
| SLIDES SHOWING YWCA IN STRENGTH OF NUMBERS OR MEMBERSHIP | It is essential that the YWCA maintain its capacity to attract new members, and to inspire commitment to the purpose and programs of the Association. The YWCA affords an opportunity for women of all ages, of all racial, religious, and economic background to utilize their special gifts in helping to strengthen the Association. |

YWCA script excerpt continued—used by permission of National Board, Young Women's Christian Association of the USA.

Obviously not all slide presentations are as complex as the two examples above. My friend Leonard Snyder put together a show for the Young Men's Christian Association of Greater New York using only available pictures. The goal was to promote increased use of an Association rural conference facility just outside the metropolitan area. To that end, Snyder arranged the shots in a logical order, combining them with title cards (the 'Don't Read' items in the narration script sample shown here) and live, voice-over audio lines.

The show proved highly successful.

Another case in point is the script for the Young Women's Christian Association's 1979 national convention. It was prepared by a professional unit. Though the narration was completely scripted, the script's visual side carried only general descriptive material such as slides showing poverty, unemployment, third world problems, battered women, etc.

The possibilities of slide shows are virtually limitless, yet they lie well within the reach of every producer, every writer.

Filmstrips and filmscripts

15

A filmstrip is a length of 35mm film on which a series of still photos or graphics are printed in sequential order. Ordinarily including from 20 to 50 frames, it may be either in black-and-white or colour, silent or accompanied by sound. In effect an illustrated lecture, the filmstrip permits a pause of any length for any frame, plus the opportunity to change or expand narration to fit special needs.

Except for the packaging of the pictures and the means of projection, there is very little difference between a filmstrip and a slide show.

In the eyes of the users, however, these differences can be great. The slide show costs more (50 slides run markedly higher than an equivalent length of film), weighs more, occupies more space and is more difficult to handle and ship. The filmstrip, in contrast, weighs next to nothing, can be stored in a can an inch in diameter and an inch-and-a-half high and can be shipped neatly in any film mailing envelope. These are all understandable deciding factors if you are buying 10 000 copies of a given presentation.

The projection equipment, by and large, can be called separate-but-equal, with personal preference playing a large role. As for sound, both slides and filmstrips in most cases use tape cassettes or microgroove or electrical transcription discs.

Where the writer is concerned, however, all this tends to be pretty much extraneous. For him, ever and always, the issue comes back to the same basic principles we have talked about so many times before. They apply, whether he is scripting a slide show or a filmstrip.

To get down to specifics, here are some comments by Rachel Stevenson, Director of Filmstrips, International Film Bureau, Inc. In her *A Check List for Writers and Producers of Educational Filmstrips**, she says:

*Excerpt from A Check List for Writers and Producers of Educational Filmstrips *used by permission of Rachel Stevenson and International Film Bureau, Inc.*

1   How do you choose a subject for an educational filmstrip? Look over a school system's curriculum of study. Choose a subject that will fit into the curriculum. Test your chosen subject by discussing it with educators to see whether it would be helpful.

2   Determine the purpose of your filmstrip and keep this purpose well in mind during production.

3   Before writing the script, work out a theme which will be developed. Outline *how* this theme will be developed.

4   Plan how the visuals can develop the theme.

5   Of course, be sure all facts are accurate.

6   Write with a direct, clear style. Keep in mind the vocabulary of the level of the audience.

7   Avoid just a list of pictures. Have the script with its visuals develop the theme and reach a conclusion.

8   A summary may often be helpful.

9   Use your visuals; let them tell the story. Let the picture speak for itself.

10   The first sentence in a new frame should tie in with or identify with the picture. For instance, if the conspicuous part of the picture is a horse in the foreground, don't talk about unrelated information and mention the horse at the end of the frame; people will wonder why they are looking at a horse.

11   It is very important to have only one idea in a frame with a clear visual to illustrate it.

12   The visual should read from left to right. If necessary change the script so that both the script and visual read from left to right. If there is no printing in the picture, it is sometimes possible to turn the picture over to make it read from left to right with the script.

Although Ms Stevenson's remaining points apply primarily to the work of the producer, they are also the kind of thing a writer may find worth remembering—either because he some day may find himself in the role of producer or because these are issues sufficiently important to the success of a filmstrip that he may want to raise his voice a bit rather than see a job go sour through no fault of his own.

13   Often sound and appropriate music enhance a filmstrip. But never let the sound or music detract from the narration.

14   It is often a delicate matter to keep the sound and music at just the right level. It must never drown out the narration, but if too low it will be lost when played on most school equipment that is not hi-fidelity.

15   Take pains when bringing in the audible bell for manually advancing the filmstrip. Sound appropriate for one frame but not for the following frame should end as the bell (or automatic advance) brings in the next frame. Failure to do this accurately results in a sloppily produced filmstrip.

16   Take pains in recording the bell signal. Keep the volume low enough so as not to be startling, but be sure it can be plainly heard. Nothing exasperates a teacher or

student more than to get the filmstrip behind the audio. Be sure to lower the music if necessary between frames to make the bell audible. Avoid recording the bell on a note of music that is identical with the tone of the bell. It is surprising how often this situation arises.

These are all solid points—practical professional advice with years of experience in the field behind it.

Look at the excerpts from the three IFB scripts to see how all this shapes up in script form.

The title page of 'Chicago Builds and Chicago Burns' which is Part IV of a historical series itself warrants a few comments:

1   This filmstrip is part of a series. Which is to say, the project will bring a larger profit—both to writer and producer—than a one-shot enterprise.

2   The filmstrip is copyrighted, with all rights reserved. This point is too often neglected, to the sorrow/loss of all concerned.

3   Rather than relying just on her own work, Ms Stevenson has involved a technical advisor: educational consultant Sarajane Wells, Education Director of the Chicago Historical Society. In addition to adding authenticity and reducing Ms Stevenson's labours, this no doubt helped to throw the Chicago Historical Society's weight behind the project. My bet is that it also brought extra sales.

4   Ms Stevenson received screen credit for producing and writing. Credit is a fringe benefit every writer should try for. After all, who knows when a potential client will see your strip/script, like it and be influenced to give you a call rather than another person.

5   The line about the source of materials tells us that to a considerable degree, this was a research job: running down precisely the right '... old drawings, engravings, and paintings ...' It also helps to explain the importance and value of having Ms Wells on board as educational consultant.

It is entirely possible that some of the 'present-day colour photographs' were also drawn from the Chicago Historical Society's archives.

6   The Chicago Historical Society gets credit. In the process, Ms Stevenson and International Film Bureau Inc. once more add the imprimatur of authority.

7   Finally, International Film Bureau Inc. establishes its position as the strip's distributor ... both for record and just in case someone might want to order another print.

Where the script proper of 'Chicago Builds and Chicago Burns' is concerned, the description of the visuals is understandably limited in view of the use of 'old drawings, engravings and paintings.' Narration is succinct and to the point. None of these paragraphs is more than 30 seconds long. Most are considerably less.

Note that, in the interest of audience interest, plenty of attention was given to 'colour' detail and incidents, both visually and in narration: barges on the river, railroad construction, Long John Wentworth carrying his shoes, high sidewalks, raising a hotel '. . . eight feet, with 500 men turning 2500 jackscrews . . . furniture, residents and all, without so much as jarring a single chandelier.'

INTERNATIONAL FILM BUREAU INC.
presents

CHICAGO BUILDS AND CHICAGO BURNS

Chicago Series: Part IV

© Copyright 1971 International Film Bureau Inc.
All Rights of Reproduction, Including Television, Reserved.

Educational Consultant

Sarajane Wells

Education Director

Chicago Historical Society

An INTERNATIONAL FILM BUREAU INC.
Production

Produced and Written
by
Rachel Stevenson

This filmstrip is illustrated with
old drawings, engravings, and paintings,
together with present-day color photographs.

Illustrations are reproduced with the kind permission of:

The Chicago Historical Society

Distributed by

INTERNATIONAL FILM BUREAU INC.
Chicago, Illinois

Excerpt from 'Chicago Builds and Chicago Burns' used by permission of Wesley H. Greene, President, International Film Bureau Inc.

CHICAGO BUILDS AND CHICAGO BURNS

History of Chicago Series: Part IV

TITLE	MUSIC
CREDITS	

1. SAND, RIVER FORT

Chicago began with a lake, a river a fort and sand.

2. Barges on River

It grew fast, in 1848 business was good. The opening of the Illinois-Michigan canal brought rows of canal barges lining the Chicago river taking local grain and lumber, and eastern manufactured goods to New Orleans.

3. Railroad (PIONEER)

A few months later Chicago's first railroad began operation. This was the Galena and Chicago Union. The Pioneer locomotive chugged to Oak Park and back on its first run about ten miles.

4. Station

Later when this railroad line became the Chicago and Northwestern System, this was its Chicago station.

5. Railroad construction

More railroads were built. Within three years railroads carried more freight than the river and by 1856

Excerpt from 'Chicago Builds and Chicago Burns' continued—used by permission of Wesley H. Greene, President, International Film Bureau Inc.

(2)

6. Long John Wentworth carrying shoes

When "Long John' Wentworth first came to Chicago from the east in 1836, he found the streets so muddy he chose to forget his dignity and walked barefoot carrying his shoes. He later was twice the mayor of Chicago and twice congressman.

7. High Sidewalks

By the 1850's Chicago still had trouble with its muddy streets, "A city on stilts" it was called by some. Others just plainly called it a "mud hole". To get out of the mud some store owners made their second floor the first, and built the sidewalk at the second level.

8. CU sidewalk

But all the store owners did not do this. The result was a sidewalk that constantly went up and down stairs.

9. Raising Hotel

Chicagoans got busy. They raised the level of some of the downtown streets and actually raised some of the buildings. Through the scheme of George M. Pullman both the Tremont House and the Briggs House (shown here) were raised eight feet with 500 men turning 2,500 jackscrews. Here the entire hotel is being raised... furniture, residents...and all, without so much as jarring a single chandelier.

Excerpt from 'Chicago Builds and Chicago Burns' continued—used by permission of Wesley H. Greene, President, International Film Bureau Inc.

The next example is a filmstrip taken from a children's story, 'When the Monkeys Wore Sombreros,' by Mariana Prieto. Rachel Stevenson and International Film Bureau produced versions in both English and Spanish. The visuals were taken from the book's illustrations by Robert Quackenbush.

Note how the framing of the shots of the various illustrations is specifically described in the English script in order to achieve the most effective filmstrip presentation. Then, since the framing has already been decided, the Spanish script offers simple shot descriptions only.

```
        (TITLES OVER FRONTISPIECE)
          TITLE SLIDE
          (IFB Presents)          MUSIC

          WHEN THE MONKEYS
          WORE SOMBREROS

      CUANDO LOS MONOS USABAN
      SOMBREROS
      (Copyright)
      ───────────────────────────

              CREDIT SLIDES       MUSIC

      Story by Mariana Prieto

      Illustrations by
        Robert Quackenbush
      ───────────────────────────

      Produced for International Film
      Bureau by Rachel Stevenson
      ───────────────────────────
```

1. Wide shot of page 6   Once long ago, in the hills of Mexico, lived

                          two brothers.

2. Same picture but   One brother was named Andres. He was short and
   waist shot
                          round like a broad bean. The other brother

                          was named Francisco. He was long and thin

                          like a string bean.

3. Page 7 part of house, They lived in the country where wheat is grown.
   mother and father

4. Page 8 mother making   Their mother, like all the other women, wove
   hats, father harvesting
   straw   broadbrimmed hats, called sombreros. She wove

                          them from paja stit, or straw. She and their

                          father always took the sombreros to the market

                          to sell.

5. Page 9 the two boys   ..but one day she decided the boys should make
   working
                          the journey instead.

6. Page 10 frame mother, "You are old enough now to take the sombreros to
   boys and father
                          market" she told them. "Your father and I have

                          work to do here."

Excerpt from 'When the Monkeys Wore Sombreros' used by permission of Wesley H. Greene, President, International Film Bureau Inc.

CUANDO LOS MONOS USABAN SOMBREROS

1. Two boys mountains in bg	Había una vez, hace mucho tiempo, dos hermanos, que vivian en las colinas de Mejico.
2. Waist shot of boys	Uno de los hermanosse llamaba Andrés. El era bajito y redondo como una haba lima. El otro hermano se llamaba Francisco. El era alto y delgado como una habichuela.
3. Mother and father at house	Vivian en el campo dondo crece el trigo.
4. Parents making hats	Su mamá, como todas las otras mujeres, tejía combreros de alas anchas. Los hacía de paja. Ella y el padre de los muchachos siempre llevaban los sombreros al mercado para venderlos.
5. Two boys working	Pero un día ella decidío que los muchachos debian de hacer el viaje solos.
6. Mother, boys, father	"Ustedes ya son bastante grandes para llever los sombreros al mercado." Ella les dijo. "Su papá y yo tenemos trabajo que hacer aqui."
7. CU of boy in hat	"¡Bueno!" Andrés dijo. "Yo soy valiente. Yo sé que podemos hacerlo bien." Sus ojos brillaban con certeza.
8. Mother and boys	"Yo no sé mama" dijo Francisco ansiosamento. "El camino es largo y muchas cosas puedon pasar." El mivió sus delgados y largos brazos sin esperanza.
9. Burros	"No seas tonto" dijo Andrés "podemos llegar bien. Si tenemos problemas estoy seguro que encontraremos alguien que nos ayudará."
10. Piles of sombreros	Entonces fueron y cogieron sus pequiños burros. Montaron todos los sombreros encima de los burros.
11. Boy and burro	Cuando los sombreros estaban amarrados on su lugar, los muchachos so subicron y salieron hacia el morcado.

Excerpt from 'When the Monkeys Wore Sombreros' continued—used by permission of Wesley H. Greene, President, International Film Bureau Inc.

'The Dragon's Tears' is an adaptation of a Japanese folk tale for IFB by Rachel Stevenson. Here the point to note is less the one-page script excerpt and more the 'Suggestions to the Teacher' and 'Class Demonstration'. Both are good examples of setting AV materials into broader context.

Observe how specifically the purpose is nailed down, the close attention to audience and the elicitation of teacher reaction.

International Film Bureau Inc. presents

STORIES FOR EARLY READERS

THE DRAGON'S TEARS
        adapted from the original Japanese folk tale by
        Rachel Stevenson

PURPOSE

To assist early readers and slow readers. The filmstrips are furnished
with both captions and a narrated text supplied on either record or
cassette. Special features are the slow advance of the frames, giving
the reader time to become familiar with the picture and text; also a
vocabulary called "Words to Learn" is furnished before the beginning of
eash story.

THE DRAGON'S TEARS

        64 frames captioned identially with the narration $6
        $12.50 with 33 1/3 rpm record
        $14.50 with cassette

SUGGESTIONS TO THE TEACHER

Use the filmstrip as the final part of a unit study.
Precede the filmstrip with:
        Discussion of the geography of Japan; find Japan on a world map;
            relate it to the U.S.
        Discussion of customs of Japan
        Bring Japanese objects to class and discuss the crafts and clothes
            of the Japanese
        Find pictures in magazines that are related to Japan
        Discuss dragons. Let the class make a papier maché dragon. Or let
            the class make the head of a dragon to be worn by one pupil while
            the others line up behind with the hands of each on the shoulders
            of the child ahead. Let them make up a dragon dance. Music at the
            opening and close of the filmstrip may be used.
        Use the filmstrip by first looking at the "Words to Learn" section
        Show the filmstrip using the narration on the record or cassette,
            letting the class follow the captions silently.
        Repeat the filmstrip without the narration, letting the class read
            the captions.
        Repeat the filmstrip without the audio and using manual advance so as
            to discuss various frames.

frames
5 Talk about the Japanese building in the picture
8 and 11 talk about the clothes worn in the picture
13 Why did Jiro cry?
20 Do you think Jiro was right in asking, "How do we know he is mean if
   no one has seen him?"
23 Ask the class to tell what parts of the picture show it is night.
33 Why did the dragon cry?
34 What happened to the dragon to make him useful to everyone in the
   village?

Let one class member try to tell the story in his own words.

CLASS DEMONSTRATION OF JAPANESE STORIES FOR READING SKILLS.

School -- public   Scott School, 6435 Blackstone

Teacher -- Ruth Golb (home) 5813 Blackstone, phone 324-7858

Class -- 3rd and 4th grade combined. Negro children, ~~a~~
         a bright class. 28 boys and girls in the class.

Attention -- during the showing of the filmstrip the class was 100%
         attentive.

   Miss Golf described two ways she uses filmstrips.

   1. She prefers to use it as part of a UNIT. This means for several
      days the children have been learning facts pertaining to the subject
      of the filmstrip. For instance, in the case of the Japanese story
      she would have had one class period discuss the geography of Japan;
      in another she would have discussed clothes and perhaps brought a
      kimono to show the class. She would have talked about customs...etc.

      Then she would show the Japanese filmstrip. After the filmstrip was
      seen she would discuss features of the filmstrip that tied in with
      the previous studies of Japan.

   2. Sinc there had been no UNIT study to precede this showing, the teacher
      asked questions all through the filmstrip.

      She called on pupils by turn to read the caption on the filmstrip
      frame. Then she discussed the art work of the film; the dress; the
      customs; the emotions, etc shown in the story. After the filmstrip
      and when the lights were turned on she had the pupils tell her what
      each liked about the story and she listed these on the blackboard.
      Since there had already been a lot of discussion about the story as
      the filmstrip was being shown; some of the pupils got restless during
      this last discussion.

The story did not seem too young for this age group. The pupils had no
trouble reading the captions but they were not bored with it. I would like
to try the same filmstrip with a class of 1st and 2nd graders.

The teacher seemed to think a list of Discussion Questions and Projects that
could round out a UNIT would be very desirable. I showed her the Questions
and Projects I had listed on the first (now out of print) Chicago and
Illinois brochures. She approved of this and said this was the right idea.

I forgot to mention that Miss Golb had the pupils read the "Note to the
teacher" at the first of the filmstrip...and when each of the words in the
vocabulary came up to the class discussed it.

This field trip was very helpful to me. I believe John Chamberlain enjoyed
seeing how one of our products can be used in a classroom also.

                    RS

*Material related to 'The Dragon's Tears' used by permission of Wesley H.
Greene, President, International Film Bureau Inc.*

THE DRAGON'S TEARS

1. 1 BOY	This is a story about Jiro, a boy who lived far away in Japan.
2. 1 DRAGON	This story is also about a dragon who lived in the hills of Japan.
3. 1 EYES	People said the dragon had eyes like two bright lights.
4. 1 MOUTH	His mouth went from one ear to the other.
5. 2 VILLAGE	No one in the village below the hill had even seen the dragon.
6. 2 FULL FRAME	People said he ate anyone who came near. Even the oldest farmer said this.
7. CU FARMER	He would point to the hills and say, "That is where the mean dragon lives."
8. 3 FULL FRAME	If anything bad happened in the town, people said it was the dragon's fault.
9. 3 BOY AND TOOL	Once Jiro was working in the garden, and he broke a tool.
10.3 FATHER'S HEAD	His father said the dragon made his son break it.
11. 4 FULL FRAME	One night Jiro's mother found her little boy crying.
12. 4 MOTHER	"My little Jiro, why do you cry?" she asked.
13. 4 JIRO	"It is the dragon. I feel sorry for him. No one likes him. He must be lonely."
14. 5 FULL FRAME	Jiro wanted to see the dragon. Often he played the dragon came to visit him.

Excerpt from 'The Dragon's Tears' used by permission of Wesley H. Green, President, International Film Bureau Inc.

In the following pages are three more filmstrip script formats, courtesy of the Postal Service Training and Development Institute. The first, a common type, includes a storyboard frame for each shot on the script's visual side—though it is used more for notes than art in our sample.

The second example shows another common format. Note the shot numbers inserted in the narration as cue indicators.

The third is a more formalised format in which the emphasis is on the integration of the AV unit with its accompanying technical manual.

PRODUCTION NO	**PST&DI SCRIPT**	PAGE NO. 1
TITLE HOW TO ADJUST THE DROPPER JAM DETECTOR SWITCH ACTUATOR		OF 39

SCENE NO A   FR COUNT /

```
    TO BEGIN ...


    (4 steps)
```

ART: Standard Start Title

8 or 10

FPS

SCENE NO B   FR COUNT /

```
  PST&DI

    Presents ...
```

ART TITLE

SCENE NO C   FR COUNT /

```
  HOW TO ADJUST
  THE DROPPER JAM
  DETECTOR SWITCH
  ACTUATOR
```

ART TITLE

Excerpt from filmstrip script used by permission of Postal Service Training and Development Institute.

PRODUCTION NO _____	**PST&DI SCRIPT**	PAGE NO __2__
TITLE _____		OF ____39__

SCENE NO __1__ FR COUNT ____/____

STILL / CLASS
—
ALSO #9 #13

Shoot Several also #9

STILL: Mechanic adjusting
    actuator

This program shows how to adjust the Dropper Jam Detector Switch Actuator of the MPLSM Operator Console. Its an important adjustment; if not done correctly it can delay mail processing or even shut down an entire MPLSM operation.

SCENE NO __2__ FR COUNT ____/____

LIVE / CLASS

live roll 1

Consolside

LIVE: jam/shutdown

The Detector Switch is designed to shut down or MPLSM if a jam occurs when a letter is being dropped into a cast compartment. Its purpose is to prevent damage to the equipment and to the mail.

SCENE NO __3__ FR COUNT ____/____

STILL / QC

Still roll 2

STILL: MS student at QC
    projector

This program is being presented on a variable speed projector. From time to time during the program, we'll be asking you questions. When we do, the sound part of the program will stop, or pause, to give you time to answer the questions on a worksheet. When you have answered question you must push the Proceed button to restart the Program.

Excerpt from filmstrip script continued—used by permission of the US Postal Service Training and Development Institute.

PRODUCTION NO_____	**PST&DI SCRIPT**	PAGE NO.___5___
TITLE_____		OF____39____

SCENE NO **10** FR COUNT _____/_____

[handwritten: PST+DI will provide]

[handwritten margin: TRY]

LIVE: sweeper responding
    to buzzer alarm;
    cannot locate a jam

False jam detection occurs when a device
senses a jam that does not exist. The alarm
sounds, the machine shuts down (?); and mail
processing is delayed. Successive false jam
detections not only delay mail processing, but
they become a nuisance to sweepers, who must
respond each time, only to find no cause.
Remember, if correct adjustments are made,
machinable mail does not normally create
dropper jams.

SCENE NO **11** FR COUNT _____/_____

[handwritten: PST + DI]

LIVE: MPE mechanic removing
    jammed letters (console
    slide) from inserter tube

The second problem that can exist when the
dropper jam detector switch actuator is not
adjusted correctly is even more serious.
When valid dropper jams go undetected, serious
damage can result to both mail and equipment.

SCENE NO **12** FR COUNT _____/_____

[handwritten: Hand only]

[handwritten margin: LIVE / SWEEP SIDE]

STILL: sweeper hitting
    sweepside emergency
    stop button

It's even possible for a badly adjusted
dropper jam detector switch actuator to
shutdown an entire MPLSM operation.

Excerpt from filmstrip script continued—used by permission of the US Postal Service Training and Development Institute.

2

10 Sick bed scene repeat *OK*
"Your problem"

11 Split screen of ill
looking employee and
injured employee "Obtain
medical attention"

12 Picture of supervisor
greeting returning
employee "productive again"

see/77

13 Picture of sick employee
in bed with supervisor
seated next to bed ". . .
but not forgotten"

14 Employee on crutches "Be
concerned"

[10] The answer is yes! The good supervisor
is aware of a definite responsibility to make
sure that all employees who become ill or
injured on the job receive medical treatment
as promptly as possible, and that[12] if they
must take time off due to their job related
illness or injury that their pay check
continues to come in, and that they are
restored to duty as soon as they are
physically able. The good supervisor knows
that no one likes to languise around home
unable to return to work and seemingly
forgotten by the boss.[13] It is known that
an employee resents this because it is felt
that he or she is really not needed at work;
that the employee isn't really important and
essential to moving the mail.

[14]Of course a good supervisor is just as
interested in the health and welfare of an
employee who becomes ill or is injured in a
non-duty status. But in such cases, the
employee has leave benefits available as
well as hospitalization and medical insurance
plan paid in part by the U.S. Postal Service

Excerpt from filmstrip script used by permission of the US Postal Service Training and Development Institute.

SIMM Audio Visual Script

Sequence Identifier	Visual (Art Control Number)	Narrative	Time (Sec)
1A1	SAV-200	This program has been developed for the United States Postal Service to introduce you to a new kind of technical manual, the SIMM manual... SIMM stands for Symbolic Integrated Maintenance Manual (CHANGE TONE)	15
1B1	SAV-201	The quantity of mail has increased steadily every year in the recent past. Mail volume will continue to increase, and so must the efficiency of the U.S. Postal Service. Progress in technology helps the Postal Service to handle this constant increase of mail. (CHANGE TONE)	10

Excerpt from the Simm Audiovisual script used by permission of the US Postal Service Training and Development Institute.

SIMM Audio Visual Script

Sequence Identifier	Visual (Art Control Number)	Narrative	Time (Sec)
1C1	SAV-202	But progress in technology means we have to learn to use increasingly complex machines and devices to perform faster and more efficiently, the operations which used to be done by hand. (CHANGE TONE)	13
1D1	SAV-202 ①	Machines and devices can't work without skilled men and women. They need us to operate and maintain them... Our success depends upon people using the machines efficiently. (CHANGE TONE)	12

Excerpt from the Simm audiovisual script continued—used by permission of the US Postal Service Training and Development Institute.

A side glance at the filmscript

One of the facets of visual presentation ordinarily excluded from what we term AV is film, the motion picture. Similarly, the scripting of film is a separate and complex subject that we hardly have space for here (besides, I have already written a book on the subject—*Film Scriptwriting: A Practical Manual*). However, it would hardly be fair to leave you totally in the dark where this specialised type of script and writing are concerned.

A film is simply a series of still photographs—more than 40000 of them in a half-hour 16mm picture.

These stills are photographed at the rate of 24 per second for sound film or 16 per second for silent. Thanks to a physiological phenomenon termed persistence of vision, the image from one shot lingers in the eye long enough to overlap with the next. Thus the sequence of shots appears to the viewer as continuous action rather than a series of separate photographs.

The writer's role in film is simply to devise and then describe a series of events/things for the cameraman to photograph. When the separate strips of film are pasted ('spliced') together skilfully in accordance with a proper plan, you end up with an entertainment film, or an educational film, or a technical film, or a business film or whatever.

Where you as an AV writer are concerned, the thing to remember is that you already are doing the foundation work of film scriptwriting when you organise your material on a given subject and then select the photographs to convey the idea/information. The only difference is that, in film, this data is communicated in terms of motion.

It follows that a topic that depends to a large degree on motion for meaning is perhaps better treated in film than slide show or filmstrip.

Film also has an advantage, it seems to me, where the interplay of people is concerned. Emotion, particularly, comes through with a sharper edge when we see those involved in action.

(Parenthetically, I must note that this interplay often can be projected equally well via sound. The radio dramas of yore stimulated many of us to peaks of imagination perhaps never before or since attained simply because they allowed us to create characters and settings in our mind's eye. The images we fantasised were infinitely more vivid than any 'seen' actor or set could hope to achieve.)

Let us assume that, as an audiovisual writer, you find yourself confronted with a project that calls for film. Your task is to translate your concept into visual motion. In what format do you write it?

You have two major choices of format. One is the traditional fact film script, the other, the Hollywood or feature film style.

The excerpt from the 'Facer Canceler' film script illustrates the format for a fact film script. It is, of course, the two-column script we have met before. The visuals are on the left and narration/dialogue on the right.

Note that though each shot describes action, a single frame could be picked out and used as a unit in a slide show or filmstrip.

Also, on page 3 of the script, note that the shots specified reflect: movement; the changing of image size (LS, CU) to give the audience the visual information it needs; and, the necessity of changing from one strip of film to another (cutting) as the film progresses.

INTRODUCTION TO THE MARK II FACER CANCELER

Shooting Script

Postal Service Training & Development
Institute, Technical Center
1524 Asp Ave., P.O. Box 1400
Norman, Oklahoma 73069

Specifications:	Script for a 16mm motion picture, color and sound, approximately 24 minutes in length.
Audience:	A. Students beginning the four week training course in maintenance and service of the Mark II Facer Canceler at the Postal Service Training & Development Institute, Norman, Oklahoma.
	B. Persons who are interested in taking the training course and becoming Mark II maintenance mechanics but want to find out more about the job before taking this big step.
Purpose:	To teach a basic understanding of the purpose, operation and maintenance of the Mark II Facer Canceler. Also to show the importance of maintaining this machine in perfect working order and the importance of specialized training for the mechanic.

Excerpt from 'Facer Canceler' film script and related materials used by permission of the US Postal Service Training and Development Institute.

INTRODUCTION TO THE MARK II FACER CANCELER

Fade in:

1. A little girl walks along a sidewalk to an outdoor mail box. She drops a letter in and then returns.

(Music starts full, then fades under the narration.)

(Narrator) A letter to her grandmother and an anxious wait for an answer.

2. A young man approaches and drops a letter into the same mail box.

An important step in his life, his application to enter college.

3. A young woman drops a bundle of wedding invitations into the same mail box

A time she has looked forward to for years, sending out wedding invitations.

4. Inside the same mail box we see the letters which have just been mailed on top of the pile. More letters fall in one at a time.

A letter here, a letter there. No problem for the Postal Service to handle...

5. A mail collector opens the front of the same mail box and removes the letters

... until they begin to multiply into thousands or hundreds of thousands or even millions.

6. He places the mail bag in the truck where it joins a dozen or so other bags. Zoom in until the mail bags fill the frame. Hold while the MAIN TITLE fades in, superimposed over the scene.

Then they could very well present a problem.

(Music up full)

7. The same mail truck travels along a city street. The camers is far enough away so that it can follow the truck for about 2 blocks. The SECIND TITLE fades in superimposed.

Excerpt from 'Facer Canceler' film script used by permission of the US Postal Service Training and Development Institute.

14. A Mark II machine in operation.

The Mark II Facer Canceler is in wide use throughout the United States Postal Service.

15. Close up. The camera slowly dollies along the Mark II which is still in operation. First we see the A machine, then the first two stackers, the inverter belt, the B machine and the final three stackers. Mail flows smoothly through the machine and into all five stackers.

It automatically faces and cancels letters and cards up to one quarter inch thick, taking care of two of the three required steps. And it handles them at a rate of six hundred per minute.

(Sound effect of machine)

16. LS - The entire Mark II machine in operation. Show both A and B machines clearly. Slow zoom in to the A machine.

The Mark II Facer Conceler is a tandem unit, that is two machines, very similar, working together. Letters are automatically fed one at a time into the A machine.

17. CU - Letters are feeding into the A machine. The operator's hand reaches in and picks up a letter showing the stamp at the bottom. The letter is then returned to the feed belt.

About half of the letters are upside down, the stamp is at the bottom. The A machine will detect these stamps at the bottom, cancel them ...

18. CU - Letters come out of the A machine and are sorted by the gate flags. Zoom back to include the lead and trail stackers.

... and send the letters into the proper stackers.

19. CU - Letters are feeding into the A machine. Hand is holding a letter with the stamp at the top, then returns it to the feed belt.

If the letter is right side up, with the stamp at the top, it will pass on through the A machine.

Excerpt from 'Facer Canceler' film script used by permission of the US Postal Service Training and Development Institute.

The excerpt from 'The Shape of Things to Come' illustrates the feature film format. This uses a one-column script, set up in accordance with a pattern the entertainment film industry has evolved through the years. This format is seldom used for fact films but the writer, novelist Robert L. Duncan (remember *The Q Document, Dragons at the Gate?*) spent years on the Coast and so, out of habit and personal preference, uses the Hollywood style.

In this approach, each change of locale constitutes a new sequence. The camera crew is informed of the conditions of work for each via unnumbered labels: EXT. (for *exterior*)—POSTAL TRAINING CENTER—DAY; INT. (*interior*)—STATION WAGON—DAY, etc. Each shot within the sequences is numbered, with the action and any other pertinent data described. Narration/dialogue is indented, with the speaker labelled.

Again, as in our previous example, emphasis is on action, controlling what the viewer sees and continuing the flow of the pictures.

This is by no means all there is to film scriptwriting but at least it does not leave you totally in the dark should you some day find yourself faced with a script assignment.

THE SHAPE OF THINGS TO COME

FADE IN

EXT. POSTAL TRAINING CENTER _ DAY

1. MED. FULL SHOT

Of an airport limousine pulling to a stop in front of the
building and men getting out, carrying suitcases. The third
man off is ROGER, late thirties, representative of the men
arriving to take this course, a very clean cut individual.

2. CLOSER ANGLE - ROGER

As he carries his suitcase to the sidewalk, stops, looks up
at the tower with the flags flying.

                    NARRATOR
              So here you are...ready to prepare
              yourself for a new assignment.

3. ROGER'S POV - THE TOWER

                    NARRATOR
              ... a training course which is going
              to make you an expert.

4. CLOSE SHOT - ROGER

As he turns and looks across the street.

                    NARRATOR
              You're already familiar with the self
              service postal centers.   They come in
              all shapes and sizes...

5. ROGER'S POV - SELF SERVICE POSTAL CENTER

The one on Asp Street

                    NARRATOR
              And you're going to be seeing a lot
              more of them in the years to come...

                                        CUT TO:

6. MONTAGE - SELF SERVICE CENTERS

SHOTS of the centers in post offices, shopping center parking
lots, bank parking lots, etc. The angles here should be
dramatic, a series of contrasting shapes. (To include
shot of mail pickup at a center)

                                        Continued:

*Excerpt from 'The Shape of Things to Come' film script used by permission
of the US Postal Service Training and Development Institute.*

```
12. CONTINUED:                                                3.

                              NARRATOR
                    Or consider the problem Mrs. Chylinski
                    faced yesterday afternoon...

    INT. STATION WAGON - DAY

13. CLOSE ON MRS. CHYLINSKI

    Her patience is beginning to wear thin as she peers through
    the windshield.

                              NARRATOR
                    She has to mail a birthday present to
                    a cousin in Mexico City and she doesn't
                    know how to go about it.

14. MRS. CHYLINSKI'S POV - THROUGH THE WINDSHIELD

    A car pulls out of a parking space but another car pulls
    in before she can get to it.

15. BACK TO MRS. CHYLINSKI

    An exasperated expression.

                              NARRATOR
                    No place to park...no place to leave
                    the kids even if she could find a space.
                    She has a problem.

    EXT. POST OFFICE - DAY

16. PANNING with the station wagon as it goes past the post
    office and around a corner, out of view.

                                                  DISSOLVE TO:

17. EXT. JEWELRY SHOP - DAY

    It's a small shop in a shopping center.  CHARLIE SMITH,
    middle-aged, comes out of the shop carrying an assortment
    of packages wrapped for mailing.  As he closes the door,
    he drops a couple of the packages, takes great care to
    pick them up without dropping the rest.

                              NARRATOR
                    Charlie Smith had a problem too...how
                    to mail an assortment of merchandise during
                    a twenty minute break.  Not enough  time to
                    make it to the post office...and yet everything
                    has to be insured...

                                                  DISSOLVE TO:
```

*Excerpt from 'The Shape of Things to Come' film script used by permission
of the US Postal Service Training and Development Institute.*

16   Writing for in-house video

One of audiovisual's fastest-growing subdivisions is in-house video: non-broadcast television, designed for closed-circuit viewing within a given company or other unit. While relatively few full-time writing jobs in this area are as yet available, it is entirely possible that you may find yourself scripting for it, either on a free-lance basis or as part of a public relations or advertising job.

A typical operation may use outside material, purchased as desired, in-house productions or a combination of both. Some in-house shows may be produced live or they may be recorded via film or videotape. Production itself is no different than for any other AV purpose.

Where skills are concerned, in-house video requires none not already set forth in this book.

The script format is ordinarily the same two-column proposition we have met before: visuals to the left, audio to the right. Beyond this, however, and regardless of what anyone may tell you, rigidity is *not* the name of the game.

Specifically, do not worry about whether your area of expertise is film or videotape. Whichever style you use, you will still be understood and the producer/director can make any necessary adjustments.

Further, it is a thorough waste of time to try to tailor your handling too closely to one form or the other because *you seldom know for sure which will be used when production time rolls around.*

'Some of the books make a big thing of film versus tape,' says Bruce Hinson, 'but out in the field I never met anyone who pays much attention to it. You work with whatever comes handy and worry about the details later.'

Bruce Hinson directs the Broadcast News Sequence at the University of Oklahoma's School of Journalism. Co-author of the standard text, *Television Newsfilm Techniques*, for the Radio Television News Directors Association, he has served as coordinator of the National Television

Newsfilm Competition and as assignment editor for the annual National Press Photographers–Department of Defense Television Newsfilm Workshop. In commercial television he spent ten years with major stations.

To illustrate his point of view, Hinson has contributed three typical news script samples. In each case the story is appropriately 'slugged' (labelled) and the length of time it will run stated. It is in the 'Type' space and the video column, however, that the issue comes into focus.

The first story, 'Crosstown construction', is 'VR/SIL', ie the action in the video column is videotape recorded without sound.

The second, 'McClennan on liquor by drink,' is 'VR/SOT', ie action videotape recorded with sound on tape, with live introduction and conclusion.

The third example, 'Garbage collection,' features 'VR/SIL/CART,' ie action videotape recorded without sound but with a cassette tape-recorded cartridge carrying Toby Smith's comments, to be played behind associated video shots where lip-sync is not needed.

Note that in each case of these three examples the video descriptions (LS, MS, CU, cutaway, etc.) would have been equally understandable to someone shooting film instead of tape.

STORY: Crosstown construction	TIME: 27
TYPE: VR/SIL	WRITER: Edwards
CAMERA: Jones EDITOR: Hitchcock	DATE: 9/6/77

VIDEO	AUDIO
VR/SIL	
:00 (LS,MS, road, work cress, trucks)	Construction is still ahead of schedule on the Interstate Crosstown Expressway. Good weather and on-time supplies have permitted a 15 per cent gain in the work accomplished.
:11 (MS heavy machinery)	Heavy machinery still blocks half of the downtown route, but project engineers say all of the
:16 (MS unpaved ramp roads)	worst hazards should be eliminated well before winter complicates the problem.
:20 (LS, from bridge, traffic jam)	Officially, the detours and traffic jams will last until the end of August next year, but frustrated motorists can always hope.
	-0-

'Crosstown construction' by permission of Bruce Hinson.

VIDEO	AUDIO

STORY: McClennan on liquor by drink   TIME: 57

TYPE: VR/SOT   WRITER: Raine

CAMERA: Hall   EDITOR: Daniels   DATE: 9/8/77

VIDEO	AUDIO
LIVE	Oklahoma dry leader Ross McClennan says his organization will fight...and defeat... any proposal for liquor by the drink.
VR/SOT	
:00 (Interview shots, McC. and reporter)	McClennan heads Sooner Alcohol Narcotics Education. In past votes on liquor by the drink, SANE has been the most vocal... and apparently effective...opponent of the proposition.
:09 (CU cutaway of mike in hand)	He outlines the current campaign strategy.
:11 (CU McClennan)	(SOUND UP, SOT :37) (IN CUE: "...We will point out evils...) (OUT CUE: "...over my dead body.") (TAPE ENDS)
LIVE	Dry leader Ross McClennan on liquor by the drink.
	-0-

'McClennan on liquor by drink' by permission of Bruce Hinson.

STORY:	Garbage Collection		TIME: 52
TYPE:	VR/SIL/CART		WRITER: Ash
CAMERA:	Bribiesca	EDITOR: Jones	DATE: 9/8/77

VIDEO	AUDIO
LIVE	Norman residents will have to carry their own garbage...a short distance...or pay more for the service.
VR/SIL	
:00 (LS, MS Garbage crew at work)	Beginning October first, city customers have a choice. They can agree to place their garbage cans at the curb for twice a week pickup...and pay the current rates, or they may receive side-of-the-house pickups for an additional three dollars a month.
:13 (MS, man walks to back of truck, dumps barrel)	Toby Smith, head of the sanitation department, explains the new procedure.
:17 (LS, truck moves to next house)	(CART, SOUND UP: 24) (IN CUE: "Increasing costs have made...") (OUT CUE: "...smelling up the streets")
:41 (LS, MS, garage crew at work)	Smith says the city council adopted the option plan to prevent large-scale protests over a blanket price increase. -0-

'Garbage collection' by permission of Bruce Hinson.

The techniques involved in these scripts are similiar to those used in in-house television. As a case in point, consider the work of the in-house unit at the huge Baptist Medical Center in Oklahoma City, OK. The Center operates two channels: one for patients, emphasising health topics; and another for staff, centred on the continuing professional training of hospital personnel. The Center also publishes a monthly newsletter designed to help orient viewers to the availability of television production and the potential of such productions in a hospital situation.

The newsletter shows the programme's scope: 12 hours per day of programming for patients plus selective programming for staff—an enormous task for any in-house team.

JANUARY

HELLO, I'M NEW.
I'LL BE AROUND EVERY MONTH.

TNT is a newsletter to inform Supervisors, Department Heads and the Executive Staff about the medical center's television service, BMCO-TV. You will be informed about new and existing health education programs available for check-out for staff information and training or seen on channel 6 in patient rooms. TNT will also inform you of the various services and capabilities of our TV studio and how to use them. The television service is still relatively new and we want you to know how it can help you and our patients. We will appreciate your assistance in passing TNT information along to your staff and patients.

IN CASE YOU DIDN'T KNOW

Two TV channels go throughout the hospital from the studio, which is located in the Southeast corner of the first floor.

Channel 6 can be viewed on all patient room TV's. Channel 6 is "on the air" from 7 AM to 7 PM with 9 hours of health education programs. Three hours of entertainment are interspersed between the medical subjects.

Channel 2 can be viewed at 20 monitoring stations, most of them classrooms, in all parts of the hospital.

If you would like to see a videotape just call the studio and tell them the desired subject and time. If the TV receiver isn't working properly or you don't know how to turn it on or adjust it call Bio-Med, 3052.

WHY TV?

You may wonder why the medical center has a TV studio. A couple of videotapes are available which will explain both the value of television in communication and how to use our studio. The studio is here to help you be a better supervisor, teacher, nurse, housekeeper, engineer ... whatever. Videotaping a lecture given frequently can conserve valuable time and improve the effectiveness of the message.

Our portable equipment can go wherever you conduct an orientation, lecture, equipment familiarization, etc., and videotape it on the spot. Or it can be done in the studio, whichever you prefer. The portable camera can go to other locations and obtain pictures of things you refer to but couldn't show in a normal sit down lecture situation. Then the studio crew will dress up the program, edit out sections you want deleted, even rearrange the order of your comments if desired, do a custom made open and close and you've got yourself a permanent training tool ... free! Just call the studio, 3138, and we'll work out the details.

BMCO 6 Television News Time *newsletter used by permission of Baptist Medical Center.*

CHANNEL 6 LOOKING GOOD!!

A new program schedule is playing over channel 6. Virtually every patient education program in our library is being used. Hour programming blocks are given to different subjects such as diabetes, newborn, the human heart, etc.

HELP!

Perhaps there is a particular medical program you would like to see on channel 2 or channel 6. We are very interested in your suggestions.

Please pass along any comments which you hear concerning channel 6 programs, especially those coming from patients.

BMCO-TV PROGRAMS

The following programs are available to play over channel 2:

BMC Time Card Procedure
Proper Use of Centrex System
Use of Charge Card Machine
Death and Dying
Male Catherization
Splint Application

More programs will be listed in future TNT's.

NEW PROGRAMS

"The Sexes" and "The Magic Senses" are our latest purchased videotapes now playing on channel 6. Both were recently run over the commercial network. The programs are 45 minutes in length and contain excellent medical education material.

NEW TV SCHEDULE FOR CHANNEL 6

Monday-Wednesday-Friday-Sunday

7:00	Good Morning BMCO
	Frontier of Health Care
	Daily Devotion
7:30	Hospital Care
8:00	Patient Orientation
8:30	Self Motivation
9:00	Entertainment
10:00	The Human Body
	Breast Self Exam
11:00	Newborn
12:00	Entertainment
12:30	Patient Orientation
1:00	General Health
1:30	Fighting Cancer Together
2:00	General Health
3:00	Entertainment
4:00	Patient Orientation
4:30	Surgery
5:00	Diabetes
6:00	Patient Request
6:30	Patient Orientation

Tuesday-Thursday-Saturday

7:00	Good Morning BMCO
	Frontier of Health Care
	Daily Devotion
7:30	Hospital Care
8:00	Patient Orientation
8:30	Self Motivation
9:00	Entertainment
10:00	The Human Body
	Breast Self Exam
11:00	The Human Heart
12:00	Entertainment
12:30	Patient Orientation
1:00	General Health
1:30	Fighting Cancer Together
2:00	The Human Body
3:00	Entertainment
4:00	Patient Orientation
4:30	Surgery
5:00	General Health
6:00	Patient Request
6:30	Patient Orientation

BMCO 6 Television News Time *newsletter used by permission of Baptist Medical Center.*

When the Medical Center's unit first began operations, about 60 per cent of the programmes were purchased from outside. Now, more and more major in-house productions are being completed and added to the Center's library.

What problems—especially writing problems—are encountered in such an operation? Three major issues come into focus in the course of discussion with Chris Steves, television production supervisor, and his assistant, Chris Hewes:

1 Working with non-professionals.
2 Getting approvals.
3 Working after the fact.

Thus, each programme allegedly starts from an outline which is often a less-than-completely-developed synopsis prepared by staff members of the Center department on which the particular programme will focus.

The scripts developed from these outlines may be of almost any type. Many productions use straight voice-over narration illustrated by video-tape and slides; others have limited lip-sync footage, and still others offer lip-sync dialogue plus voice over narrations in full-scale dramatic or semi-dramatic presentations.

Note particularly the frequent lack of detail—or even general direction—on the video side of these scripts. Often, the action is next to unpredictable. It cannot be controlled, let alone pre-scripted meaningfully.

Indeed, a good many programmes are—of necessity, must be—essentially non-scripted. This is the case in every in-house operation. Always, there are a certain number of 'talking head' jobs which are, in effect, lectures, instructions or pep talks delivered by a superior to subordinates or colleagues. The man knows what he wants to say. The task of the cameraman is simply to shoot the talk. A script would only get in the way.

The same thing holds true of 'record footage' of industrial procedures, coverage of an operation for the benefit of interested doctors or coaching shots of a soccer game.

It is at the outline stage that the writer's problems in working with non-professionals first arise. Despite the all-pervasiveness of commercial television, many non-pros simply do not realise: the necessity for pre-planning; the amount of time it takes; and, the limitations of the medium and/or a particular facility.

This is where the writer comes in. Through his skills as an interviewer and researcher, he gathers information that is not in the original outline and then incorporates it to develop the subject in a logical fashion. If, in the process, he can also work in colour, humour, or excitement, so much the better.

The approval issue comes into focus in the note at the top of the first page of the *Your Day in Surgery* script: 'This version of the script has been approved by Surgery Dept., A. Shaff, J. Moeller, H. Wilson, & Dr Coker.'

BAPTIST MEDICAL CENTER **OF OKLAHOMA** **TELEVISION & AUDIO VISUAL** **SERVICES** **949-3138**	**NAME** _____ **DEPARTMENT** Cardiac Rehab. **TITLE** Athletic Injuries associated with exercise **LENGTH** 1-2 hours **DATE** 7/26/78

VIDEO	AUDIO

	I. Injuries of the foot, ankle, calf, knee.
	
	II. Low back pain.
	
	III. Soft tissue injuries
	
	    A. Strains, sprains and muscle pulls
	
	    B. Tendonitis
	
	    C. Hematomas and contusions
	
	    D. Nerve injuries
	
	IV. Equipment - Shoes, braces, splints
	
	V. Physical assessment of the participant
	
	VI. Primary prevention of orthopedic
	
	    injuries
	
	    A. Exercises to avoid aggrivation of
	
	    pre-existing problems
	
	    B. First eschealon treatment of injuries

Programme outline used by permission of the Baptist Medical Center.

BAPTIST MEDICAL CENTER
OF OKLAHOMA

TELEVISION & AUDIO VISUAL
SERVICES
949-3138

NAME _____

DEPARTMENT _____

TITLE _____

LENGTH _____ DATE _____

VIDEO	AUDIO
	(This version of the script has been approved by Surgery Dept, A Shaff, J Moeller, H Wilson) "YOUR DAY IN SURGERY"
MONTAGE OF SHOTS DEPICTING A SURGICAL OPERATION IN PROGRESS, INCLUDING SHOTS OF EACH MEMBER OF THE TEAM	If you're here for surgery, we want your stay to be as pleasant as possible. That's why we'd like to answer some questions and let you know what to expect.
MCU OF DOOR OF SURGICAL SUITE FROM OUTSIDE, LOOKING INTO IT THRU WINDOW. NARRATOR, WEARING SURGERY GARB, INCLUDING FACE MASK, APPROACHES DOOR AND EXITS SUITE. STANDS TO ONE SIDE OF WINDOW, PULLS DOWN FACE MASK AND SPEAKS TO CAMERA	All these operating room professionals-- (NARRATOR MOTIONS BACK TO OPERATING ROOM DOOR) your surgeon, other attending physicians, anesthesiologist, circulating and scrub nurses; along with recovery room personnel and the nursing team on your patient care unit--are dedicated to you. They're here to make YOUR DAY IN SURGERY a success with as little discomfort as possible.
ROLL TITLE NARRATOR V.O. FROM THIS POINT	Surgery is a unique experience for each individual. It is the process of correcting diseases, injuries or deformities of the body by repairing, rebuilding, replacing or removing the part that isn't functioning properly. Your doctor has chosen ~~this~~ BAPTIST medical center for your surgery because he is confident the high standards for personnel, equipment and procedures here will result in the very best care for you.

'Your Day in the Surgery' used by permission of the Baptist Medical Center.

| BAPTIST MEDICAL CENTER OF OKLAHOMA | NAME _____ |
| TELEVISION & AUDIO VISUAL SERVICES 949-3138 | DEPARTMENT _____ TITLE _____ LENGTH _____ DATE _____ |

VIDEO	AUDIO
	Shortly after you check into your room, a member of the nursing team on your patient care unit will visit you to record vital signs, take a urine specimen and make a general assessment of your condition. At this time you will be asked to fill out a pre-anesthetic evaluation check list, which will help your anesthesiologist determine which anesthetic is best for you. Thereafter, the various members of your nursing team will be attending to your pre- and post-operative needs.
	A laboratory assistant will draw blood for routine tests. Blood typing is done at the discretion of your physician along with other tests such as X-rays or electro-cardiograms, to measure your heartbeat. Results are entered on your medical record.
	Before your operation, your surgeon will visit you. He may have been referred by your personal physician. The surgeon may order additional tests which will be used for consultation regarding your operation. If you have any questions about the surgery, don't hesitate to ask him.

'Your Day in the Surgery' continued—used by permission of the Baptist Medical Center.

BAPTIST MEDICAL CENTER OF OKLAHOMA	NAME _____
um	DEPARTMENT _____
TELEVISION & AUDIO VISUAL SERVICES	TITLE _____
949-3138	LENGTH _____ DATE _____

VIDEO	AUDIO
*	Donor: Hi _____, how's the lab work these days? Lab Tech: It's great, _____. Lately I've been recruiting donors for the hospital's blood drive. The Oklahoma Blood Institute has brought some of their staff and mobile units here to collect blood. You <u>are</u> planning to give blood during the drive, aren't you? Donor: Oh, I don't know _____, I'm really going to be busy this month. I'm playing in a golf tournament and I've got some other things going. I may skip it this time. Lab Tech: This time? Have you ever given blood before? Donor: Well...er a no. Lab Tech: Oh, that's it. _____ giving blood is a simple, painless procedure. It takes about a half hour. 30 minutes of time not spent flirting with the nurses--for the good of humanity.

Blood donor script used by permission of the Baptist Medical Center.

BAPTIST MEDICAL CENTER OF OKLAHOMA	NAME _____
UM	DEPARTMENT _____
TELEVISION & AUDIO VISUAL SERVICES 949-3138	TITLE _____
	LENGTH _____ DATE _____

VIDEO	AUDIO
	Donor: What do you mean? Aren't there going to be any nurses in there?
	Lab Tech: Excuse me. I stand corrected.
	Donor: Is the blood in really short supply?
	Lab Tech: It always is, and if you'll excuse a really dumb way of putting it: blood is the "life blood" of Baptist Medical Center. No part of the human body can live without it, and this hospital can't function without it either. Baptist Medical Center used over 13,000 units in 1978. We seriously need donations from all who can give. Why don't you give right now and I'll coach you through it.
	Donor: Right now?
	Lab Tech: Right now.
	Donor: 30 minutes?
	Lab Tech: Maximum. And in a matter of 24 short hours your body will have replaced the pint of blood you gave, and you'll be better than new.

Blood donor script continued—used by permission of the Baptist Medical Center.

BAPTIST MEDICAL CENTER **OF OKLAHOMA** **TELEVISION & AUDIO VISUAL** **SERVICES** 949-3138	**NAME** _____ **DEPARTMENT** _____ **TITLE** _____ **LENGTH** _____ **DATE** _____

VIDEO	AUDIO

	Donor: Okay, lead the way.
	
	    As a blood donor, you are a very special visitor to the Oklahoma Blood Institute. The Insitute's first consideration is to protect your health as a donor, while making sure your blood donation will be suitable for the patient. To assure that this will always happen, the donor must go through a "mini physical" and "medical history" procedure.
	    Greeted as a donor, you will be asked to register and be questioned about past donations. This will determine if the necessary 56 days have elapsed since your last donation.
	    When your turn is reached, you will be escorted to the medical history area where your blood pressure, pulse and temperature will be taken. The nurse will take a small amount of blood from a finger stick to insure your hemoglobin or "iron" level is sufficient to give.
	    Next, a series of medical questions will

Blood donor script continued—used by permission of the Baptist Medical Center.

BAPTIST MEDICAL CENTER OF OKLAHOMA	NAME _____	
	DEPARTMENT _____	
TELEVISION & AUDIO VISUAL SERVICES 949-3138	TITLE _____	
	LENGTH _____ DATE _____	

VIDEO	AUDIO
	be asked concerning your health and past physical condition. Any doubts whatsoever about any question should prompt you to ask for a repeat of the question or a clarification of the queston.
	Nurse: Have you had surgery within the last 6 months?
	Donor: No
	Nurse: Have you ever had hepatitis?
	Donor: No mam.
	Nurse: Okay, thank you. Will you please read this...
	After passing the "mini exam" you will be handed a brochure to read about the Oklahoma Blood Institute and the process of giving a blood donation. The Oklahoma Blood Institute was chartered as a non-profit, regional blood center in 1976. It was founded by the Oklahoma County Medical Society, whose members were seeking a non-profit, volunteer, available.

Blood donor script continued—used by permission of the Baptist Medical center.

Physicians frequently are extremely busy, meticulously precise, inordinately jealous of their prerogatives and, to a high degree, individual in their thinking. To win their endorsement of a piece of work which will perhaps be scrutinised by hundreds of their colleagues or thousands of lay people calls for both painstaking writing and diplomacy of a superior order. That Steves and Hewes succeed in getting such OKs consistently says a great deal for their own tact and adroitness.

When at last the production begins the non-pro offers more hazards—this time as a performer. He is stiff in his actions, unable to deliver lines realistically and has the tendency to stare into the camera. Much of the burden of coping with this falls on the writer. He has no choice but to tailor his script to the limitations of his cast.

New frustrations come with the end of shooting. Because much production has to be done catch-as-catch-can and snatch-and-grab (like newsfilm), action may run short or long, footage shot wild has to be edited to make sense and bobbles and oversights must be covered.

The writer, in turn, must piece and patch as necessary. He may have to cut what he earlier was convinced were essential lines or write extra paragraphs so that echoing silences will not drag on too long.

In the course of it all (and in between the moments when he wavers indecisive, trying to choose between hanging himself and slashing his wrists), he quite possibly may discover that he is also enjoying himself beyond his fondest expectations. He may even be writing a few prize-winning scripts.

One of the fringe benefits of in-house work is that every once in awhile you may find your assignments lapping over into the commercial broadcast field. While this may prove a mixed blessing, you should be prepared for it and know in advance that you can meet the challenge. Imagination is really the only springboard you need, as witness our 'Norman Commercial' sample.

NORMAN COMMERCIAL NO. 2: CYMBALS

PRODUCTION NOTE: SOUND WILL PROVIDE
OUR CONTINUITY IN THIS SPOT. EACH
KEY SOUND THEREFORE SHOULD BLEND INTO
THE NEXT, WITH NARRATION OVER.

'Norman Commercial: Cymbals.'

Cymbals--1

FADE IN:

CU, head-on, of cymbal-player with cymbals poised to strike. Face intent as if awaiting his cue from the (unseen) conductor, player holds for the count of two or three, then clashes cymbals.	SYMPHONIC MUSIC IN AND UP. SOUND: TREMENDOUS CLASH OF CYMBALS
MS, orchestra (audience POV). Conductor faces audience and bows. At his signal, orchestra rises and takes bow also.	SOUND: APPLAUSE IN AND UP, THEN DOWN AS UNSEEN NARRATOR'S VOICE COMES IN OVER.
SLOW DISSOLVE TO:	NAR. (CRISPLY): And so, ladies and gentlemen, with that tremendous crash of sound, we end this concert here at Norman, Oklahoma. --Now, another and far different Norman sound; for at the University, today, your children and mine are learning to take their places in an atomic world.
CU, whatever it is that's bleeping.	SOUND: RHYTHMIC BLEEPING.

'Norman Commercial: Cymbals' continued.

Cymbals--2

MCU establishing the bleeping
object against laboratory
background. Two white-coated
technicians are actively at
work on the gadget.

MCU two-shot or three-shot   SOUND: LAUGHTER AND HAPPY SHOUTS
children laughing. Background OF CHILDREN.
is school playground.

MS, group of laughing   NAR.: Another sound so typical
children at play on school   of Norman...the carefree sound
playground.   of happy children.

MCU, spectacular football   SOUND: ROAR OF CROWD.
play.

MS, cheering crowd.   NAR.: Grown-ups have fun here,
                                    too, in this town where more and
                                    more people like to live. And
                                    that gives us other sounds--
MCU, moving van pulling up   the sound of people moving in...
to attractive residence

                                    SOUND: HONKING HORN.

'Norman Commercial: Cymbals' continued.

Cymbals--3

NAR.: ...the sound of new homes,
going up...

MCU, new home being framed,   SOUND: BANGING OF HAMMERS.
several carpenters hammering
in foreground.

NAR.: ...the sound of cars
singing down the road to Norman!

MS, car approaching at high   SOUND: CAR APPROACHING.
speed on particularly
attractive stretch of
highway. Camera blur pans
(from its position low to   NAR.: Expand your family's
left side of road) to follow   horizons, in Norman! Come visit
action as car passes, then   us, next time you're out for a
comes into focus on billboard   drive. See for yourself why
advertising Norman. We hold   Norman's rightly called the city
to cover narration, then   designed for better living...for
                                   you!

        FADE OUT

SYMPHONIC MUSIC IN AND UP AS IN
OPENING.

The End

'Norman Commercial: Cymbals' continued.

Scripting programmed instruction   17

'The mechanism of cognitive learning is fairly well understood,' observes Loyd G. Dorsett, president of Dorsett Educational Systems, Inc. 'Some sort of stimulus is presented, a response is elicited, and then immediately reinforced by confirmation or correction.

'Historically, tutors have performed such a function, but today the employment of individual tutors for every student is clearly unfeasible. On the other hand, the teaching methods most commonly defended as economically efficient—group instruction—fail to employ those principles of learning which we know are most effective.'

It is in an effort to utilise these principles more effectively that the process known as programmed instruction has been developed. Since the process also opens up a whole new field—a large and profitable one, at that—to AV writers, it makes the subject well worth attention here.

Broadly speaking, programmed instruction involves using some sort of workbook or 'teaching machine' to break down a given unit of information (programme, module, lesson) into a series of logically arranged sub-units. Topics may range from resistor colour coding to evaluating employee performance, behavioural disorders to Ohm's Law. Each sub-unit presents a necessary fragment of information to the student and poses what amounts to a simple question regarding it or a previously presented fragment.

If the student answers this question correctly (via multiple choice, fill-in-the-blanks, 'branching' etc), he is immediately made aware of that fact and so can move on to the next fragment/question. If he fails to do so, the machine may respond in any one of a variety of ways. The net result is that the student is made aware of his error, so that he may correct his mistake both in terms of answer and of thinking.

By the time the student has successfully completed the entire unit, he is deemed to have learned the things he needs to know about the subject and so is ready to move on to the next module. The whole process is taken at his own speed and with minimal intervention or assistance by a live teacher.

I concede in advance that this description is over-simplified and I have no illusions but that experts will scream at its inadequacies. For our purposes here, however, and on a practical level, you will find it covers most of the ground most of the time. And this in spite of the fact that dozens—hundreds—of programming units have been devised by such prestigious organisations as McGraw-Hill, Prentice-Hall, Encyclopedia Britannica Films, Thompson Ramo Wooldridge, Harcourt, Brace, and TMI Grolier.

The important issue, for us, is that all this programming is based on the work of writers who organise the material logically and present it clearly and effectively.

Further, once you get the idea behind the system and understand the principles involved, you too can script educational modules, adapting to whatever device you are dealing with with a minimum of pain, strain and struggle.

To help you attain this laudable goal, I am reprinting here major excerpts from Dorsett Educational Systems' *Manual for Audiovisual-Response Program Writing,** plus illustrative examples from one of their actual programmes.

Dorsett offers a variety of material and features individualised instruction, audiovisual presentation and discriminated response. It uses a teaching machine which makes synchronised use of both filmstrips and audio cassettes. Its virtues where we are concerned is that it is neither the simplest nor most complex of the mechanical/electronic educational units; it is, consequently, a good entry-point to the field.

... A typical Dorsett program includes color filmstrips, response-coded cassette tapes or records, diagnostic pretests, criterion item post-tests, printed practice/ reference folders or reading panels, instructor manuals, and answer keys. Filmstrips consist of between 40 and 64 frames, and the tapes run 12 to 30 minutes, including stops for response. We expect that during a 50 minute study period a student will usually go through two programs; ie review a program studied previously and study a new program. He or she will also take pre- and post-tests. Thus students who learn rapidly would complete one new program per hour, while slower students might require two hours.

General Writing Considerations

The major portion of time in initial development of a program is spent writing and editing the script, ... The program writer must outline the recommended scope and

**Excerpts from* Manual for Audiovisual-Response Program Writing, *script excerpts and visual materials in this chapter used by permission of Loyd G. Dorsett, President, Dorsett Educational Systems, Inc.*

content of each program before actual script writing begins. Once this planning is done, the program writer must develop both an audio script and sketches for suggested visual frames. The audio script for a single frame contains an average of 20 to 40 words. The visual frames contain necessary illustrations, key words or computations drawn from the audio presentation. From 12 to 24 of the visual frames in each program will call for students to make a response, usually choosing among three possible answers, before they can proceed with the program. On especially difficult frames, the student may be requested to push the center button to proceed after studying the material.

In writing a program script, the learning objectives and the target population must, of course, be kept in mind. But there are two additional areas of concern in the preparation of audio script materials: style of presentation and questioning techniques.

Each program usually contains from 12 to 60 teaching points. These provide a basis for writing the material and a structure for logical development of the topic. The audio script is conversational in style and consists of an average of 50 words per frame, with a maximum of 100 words. Too much audio script per frame results in reduction of the student's attention span and the ability to cover the material adequately in the words on the visual. Frames of over 100 words may be split into two frames for increased effectiveness. This method is particularly important with technical materials.

Obviously, basic rules of grammar, variety and continuity apply in script writing, as they do in other forms of verbal communication. Repetitive vocabulary and sentence structure and numerous subjunctive clauses should be avoided, since they cause the student to lose the teaching point. Humor may be employed at rare intervals, but should be quite dry and not broad, and passing topical allusions should generally be avoided. Also important is to make sure that symbols or ideographs presented in the visual frames are characterized verbally as well. If a new statement or formula is being introduced on the visual frame, it is more effective to read the whole formula on the audio, and not just to refer to it as having been shown on the visual frame.

A similar rule applies to questioning. In designing the 12 to 24 'response frames' in each program, the writer should avoid the 'complete-the-sentence' or 'blank pause' procedure, which calls for the narrator to say a few words and then pause for the student to fill in the blank by pressing the button below the proper word or words. Although this technique is theoretically possible, it is in practice somewhat awkward for AV teaching machine programs.

A variety of questioning techniques should be used both in the script and in the visuals. Reinforcement rather than sheer repetition is the goal and the challenge of audio-visual questioning techniques, and it is important to avoid monotony.

Questions may, of course, be asked at the end of a frame about material covered in that frame. Care should be taken, however, to word the question so that it is not an exact duplication of the text.

Another method is delayed questioning. This technique involves the presentation of several frames of information followed by one or more separate question/response/drill frames. Separate question frames generally should be restricted to accumulated information, reviews, or highly structured material such as computations. Otherwise, they serve simply to extend the number of frames without presenting additional information, thus restricting the amount of new information that can be presented in a standard 40 frame program.

'Splitting' and 'leapfrogging' are similar questioning methods. The former may be employed by providing information on one frame and a question on the next frame after new but related material has been presented. In 'leapfrogging' a frame or two is skipped before posing the question.

The reason for asking these questions is, of course, to supply the student with the reinforcement necessary to cause learning. Correct student activity is needed before reinforcement may occur, and it is the task of the programer to provide prompting that will cause the student to respond correctly sooner and more often. But activity and reinforcement lose their effectiveness in learning when the activity is merely reflexive. The programer, then, must steer a careful course between excessive prompting and insufficient prompting. Excessive prompting causes routine, thoughtless response and weak reinforcement. Insufficient prompting may result in errors, causing partial learning of the errors and requiring a difficult extinction process, or it may result in correct responses for an incorrect reason, which will make the concept difficult to generalize later.

The distinction between the design of 'response elicitors' used in the course of instruction within the program and the questions designed for use as criterion items is important. Because it is undesirable to cause a student to make unnecessary errors when he is introduced to new material while working through a program, responses are prompted to the level required by students who are just encountering new material. In general, we believe that less experienced AVTM programers should tend toward rather full prompting, if it can be done without seeming purile, since from the student's viewpoint the material is new and difficult. There is a tendency for most teachers and writers to expect more rapid insight than can be reliably achieved in a self-instructional system by an average student.

Later, when the behavior is sufficiently fixed in the mind of the student, criterion items may be presented which require finer discrimination, and which would have offered considerable opportunity for distracting errors by students who had not adequately learned the material. In fact, a distinction may be made between pre-test and post-test (criterion) design for this reason, but it is usually convenient to use pre-tests and post-tests interchangeably.

Rewards or reinforcement comments (ie 'right,' 'yes,' 'correct,' 'good') should follow most of the student's responses to questions presented during the program. To avoid confusion, the comment 'right' is used only for responses which occur on the right hand 'C' button. The programer should try to avoid allowing the comments to become stereotyped and should use explanations wherever necessary. When the answer is embarrassingly obvious, the comment 'yes, of course' may be substituted or the script may simply carry on in a conversational manner.

Usually, script writers design visual frames at the same time that they write the audio script for that frame. Some programers, however, prefer to write an entire program, or even a series of programs, before sketching the visual frames. Whatever the technique, the purpose is the same—to highlight the substance of the audio portion verbally or pictorially, or to present a response-type frame. A completed program includes 16 to 20 response frames and 15 to 20 'illustrated' frames. This means that about half the visual frames will be entirely verbal, so it is essential that they be visually interesting. Unless the audio script is quite brief, a dozen words or so, the verbal frame should have a reasonable number of words— perhaps 10 to 25 words on the visual to accompany 50 words on the audio. Different type styles, labels and color inserts or panels provide visual variety and sustain student interest during the half-minute or so that the narration consumes.

Of the 20 or so illustrated frames, several may be simple line diagrams, some may be clip line art, and others may be technical drawings or original art. These frames, too, should contain some verbal material above or to the right of the illustration. Illustrated response frames should have the question and answers below the picture.

In general, verbal material presented on a visual frame should not be in the form of a complete sentence, but should contain highlighted words and phrases used to emphasize the content of the audio script. A complete statement in the visual frame which is essentially the same as the audio script is redundant, tends to compete with it for attention and distracts the student's thoughts. Short statements with an operative verb from the audio script are most effective. The question (stem) in the visual frame should be extremely abbreviated, and hardly needs to stand alone. It is merely a reminder of the question asked audibly.

In writing scripts and designing visual frames, all of these techniques are useful. Perhaps the most helpful guideline, however, is that once complete, both the audio script and the visual frames should have instructional impact. Much of the impact and cost-effectiveness of audio-visual teaching lies in its recognition of the fact that some students learn better aurally than visually, and vice-versa. In terms of content, the script and the visual should each be capable of providing some coherent instruction by themselves. It is obvious, however, that maximum effectiveness is achieved only when the audio modality is effectively integrated with the visual presentation and response reinforcement.

As a crutch, some speakers and writers first outline the material to be presented, present it, then review it at the end. In producing audio-visual teaching programs, we believe it is more effective and interesting to start instruction at once, so Frame 1, after the title frame, usually starts in immediately with instruction both on the visual and in the audio. Some AV programs present a sequence of review frames at the end. This may be useful drill for some purposes; it is generally suggested that each frame be lean and meaty and students who need drill should repeat the entire program. In general, the material moves so rapidly that several repetitions of the program will still result in reduced study time compared with conventional instruction. We find that this repeated study of attractive, colorful, well-programed, individualized audiovisual-response material is quite acceptable to students. This convenient selective repetition, perhaps even of only a few frames, at the control of the student, is an effective branching procedure.

Writing the program and sketching the visuals, of course, only begins the process necessary to produce an audio-visual teaching program. The programing Flow Chart included with this manual shows that about 20 hours per program, or 320 hours per series of 16 programs go into research, writing and first revision. This amounts to about 30 minutes per frame. These figures are based on program averages for a 16-program series on a subject which is relatively familiar to the writer. Isolated programs or unfamiliar subjects may require more time. It is expected that about 12 hours per program or about 200 hours per series is required to review and check art, to proof final art against audio and write progress tests. This amounts to about 32 hours per program for an experienced writer for all activities.

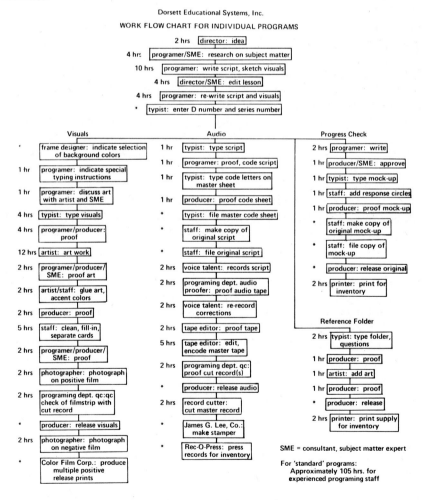

Dorsett Educational Systems, Inc.

WORK FLOW CHART FOR INDIVIDUAL PROGRAMS

2 hrs	director: idea
4 hrs	programer/SME: research on subject matter
10 hrs	programer: write script, sketch visuals
4 hrs	director/SME: edit lesson
4 hrs	programer: re-write script and visuals
*	typist: enter D number and series number

Visuals

*	frame designer: indicate selection of background colors
1 hr	programer: indicate special typing instructions
1 hr	programer: discuss art with artist and SME
4 hrs	typist: type visuals
4 hrs	programer/producer: proof
12 hrs	artist: art work
2 hrs	programer/producer/SME: proof art
2 hrs	artist/staff: glue art, accent colors
2 hrs	producer: proof
5 hrs	staff: clean, fill-in, separate cards
2 hrs	programer/producer/SME: proof
2 hrs	photographer: photograph on positive film
2 hrs	programing dept. qc:qc check of filmstrip with cut record
*	producer: release visuals
2 hrs	photographer: photograph on negative film
*	Color Film Corp.: produce multiple positive release prints

Audio

1 hr	typist: type script
1 hr	programer: proof, code script
1 hr	typist: type code letters on master sheet
1 hr	producer: proof code sheet
*	typist: file master code sheet
*	staff: make copy of original script
*	staff: file original script
2 hrs	voice talent: records script
2 hrs	programing dept. audio proofer: proof audio tape
2 hrs	voice talent: re-record corrections
2 hrs	tape editor: proof tape
5 hrs	tape editor: edit, encode master tape
2 hrs	programing dept. qc: proof cut record(s)
*	producer: release audio
2 hrs	record cutter: cut master record
*	James G. Lee, Co.: make stamper
*	Rec-O-Press: press records for inventory

Progress Check

2 hrs	programer: write
1 hr	producer/SME: approve
1 hr	typist: type mock-up
1 hr	staff: add response circles
1 hr	producer: proof mock-up
*	staff: make copy of original mock-up
*	staff: file copy of mock-up
*	producer: release original
2 hrs	printer: print for inventory

Reference Folder

2 hrs	typist: type folder, questions
1 hr	producer: proof
1 hr	artist: add art
1 hr	producer: proof
*	producer: release
2 hrs	printer: print supply for inventory

SME = consultant, subject matter expert

For 'standard' programs:
Approximately 105 hrs. for experienced programing staff

It is hard to imagine a more useful set of guidelines. While other firms may follow somewhat different rules, shifting gears to fit their patterns certainly is not beyond the skill of a competent professional AV writer.

How these rules work out in practice is illustrated in this step-by-step look at the way one unit—on terms used in meat packing processes, of all things—developed. The preliminary guide sheet for the programme is shown on p.226. The unit taken is Program No. 7 in an overall course in meat inspection. Look at the outline of the course on p.227, the writer's first draft of the unit's visuals on p.228, and the revision and polishing that follow p.229. Note that in many instances a question—the answer for which is on the preceding card—is appended to the text.

After the script has been written, a sketch is worked up by the art department to indicate what goes on each visual card. Not all the verbal text is necessarily used on the card. For key frames, a picture may be included. Ordinarily the writer will suggest an idea he/she feels will help to get across the written and audio information. Often drawing from the clip art file, the artist selects a proper picture and, if necessary, reduces it to a size that will fit the card. (See p.230.)

These sketches of course are preliminary only. When the time to prepare the final version comes, an appropriate colour card is selected and the text typed on it with a standard machine using a white ribbon.

If there is a picture, a hard copy is made and colour (usually water colour) added. The painted picture is then cut and glued to the typed visual, with a series of checks to insure accuracy and neatness before photographing for the filmstrip (pp.231–234).

Finally, a reference folder (p.235) carrying the complete text for the audio track is prepared. Note that not all audio material is included on the cards. Frame 1, for example, has no card text but the sound cassette carries a paragraph. Similarly, audio text is markedly abridged on Cards 2 and 3.

The main difficulty writers encounter in preparing material for programmed instructional units is centred on their tendency to introduce—without being aware of it—extraneous information which confuses the student or distracts his attention from the task at hand.

Take, for example, a lesson on verb forms for non-English speakers. The goal is to teach the difference between the form used with the singular *he* and that used with the plural *they*. The one point which we wish to get across is that *s* is added when the subject is *he*. An example might be:

Singular	*Plural*
He talk*s*.	They talk.
He speak*s*.	They speak.
He cook*s*.	They cook.

What you have taught here is the point you intended: after a singular subject, the verb ends in *s*.

GUIDELINES FOR GLOSSARY SCRIPTS

MEAT AND POULTRY SERIES

DIFFERENT LIMITS : 40 frames to a program. Average of 30 words per frame. 1200 words total- shorter than usual. 8 minutes running time. Range of words : 15 - 45. Most frames should be in the 20 - 40 word range. All frames should have some inform- ation as well as a question, but not less than 32 frames will be question frames . Only 8 non-question frames . Refer to the dictionary and encyclopedia and other material from the D of A for help in fleshing out your program. Be sure to do more than merely copy down the definitions from the D of A Glossary.

SEQUENCING : Most of the question frames will not be separated from " discussion frames " by more than 1 or 2 frames and will often follow immediately after the discussion frame. No two non - question frames in series (except perhaps # 1 and 2).

Terms to be defined should be sequenced in accordance with some interesting rational arrangement instead of mere alphabetic order. The script should explicitly state or explain the rationale at the beginning of the program. Preliminary analysis of terms needs to be made to determine grouping and sequence of terms.

STYLE : Conversational, discursive style will be used, which for some text will require change of wording from the Glossary.

Intransitive verbs will always be used to begin a definition : eg, " Salami is ....". Vary these verbs from time to time.

OTHER REMARKS : Other sources of information personal and otherwise may be used. Their correctness may be checked by referring the material to the MPI in Denton. They will read our scripts in advance of production.

L. G. D.

8 - 16 - 78

Preliminary guide sheet for a programme on meat packing processes.

Program Series Description Sheet

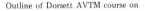

Outline of Dorsett AVTM course on

MEAT INSPECTION

1. Basic Terminology - convenient introduction to the whole series, stressing Latin and Greek roots, prefixes, and suffixes.

2. Anatomy - the rest of the series is based on this program, which presents basic knowledge of animal anatomy in simplified form.

3. Varieties of Sausage - review of twenty kinds of sausage, from bratwurst to mortadella. Each type is described and shown in a photo.

4. Meat Cuts - more basic information, this time about 20 kinds of meat cuts presented in order of their carcass anatomy.

5. Meat Packing Substances - a miscellaneous array of certain important substances widely used in the packing industry.

6. Meat Packing Conditions - 20 terms connected with various conditions found in packing plants. Includes such terms as aerobic, aqueous, chronic, etc.

7. Meat Packing Processes - important set of terms found in the slaughtering process, presented in narrative form.

8. Meat Packing Terms - broad array of general terms, ranging from cold spot to apron.

9. Meat Packing Mechanisms - deals with twenty common machines and devices used in modern packing plants. Detailed illustrations.

10. Animal Diseases - probably the most 'difficult' program in the series, since it describes almost twenty common diseases of cattle, sheep, and pigs, and includes medical slides and pictures.

11. Miscellaneous Terms - as its name implies, this program presents a number of terms which do not readily fit into any of the other categories, but are still worth knowing.

12. Weight Conversions - simple problems in the calculation and conversion of weights. Deals with ounces to pounds, pounds to ounces, and kilograms to pounds.

13. Volume and Capacity - presents formulas and problems for the calculation of volumes of cubes, rectangular boxes, cylinders, and cones.

14. A Review of Fractions - practical refresher course on doing problems with all kinds of fractions -- proper, improper, decimal, and percentages.

15. Fahrenheit and Celsius - helpful program on learning to convert from one temperature scale to the other, and back again. Nontechnical, informal style makes material painless to learn.

16. The Metric System - presents general information about the system, then offers series of problems which will help trainee acquire real mastery of basic units and concepts.

This series of 16 programs is designed to provide meat inspection trainees with help in developing their technical vocabularies, as well as refreshing their skills in dealing with a variety of calculation problems and methods. The series is not intended to take the place of regular instruction in the subject. It is divided into two parts --- eleven programs on vocabulary items, followed by five programs on calculation problems and methods.

Dorsett Educational Systems, Inc. P.O. Box 1226, Norman, Oklahoma 73070   405-288-2300

Outline of course on meat inspection.

MEAT PACKING PROCESSES (1)

1. Before 1850, and the development of refrigeration, packing houses operated only in the winter and were often built directly adjacent to ice houses. Men cut the ice from rivers and lakes all winter and stored it in icehouses for use in warm weather. (ent.)

2. During the cattle run days market centres were usually in big cities. More recently what were once big city markers are becoming involved in the prepared foods industry and the production of the many varieties of processed meat products, as packing houses, themselves, are being built in towns closer to the farms and ranches where livestock are raised. (ent.)

3. Processed meats may come from almost any edible part of domestic animals. Many edible organs, and lesser parts of meat cuts go into these products. The removal of viscera, or internal organs, from an animal is called evisceration. Where are most processed meat products made?

Small towns   Big cities *   On farms

INSERT
This process
is called
rendering

4. Some meat cuts are so impregnated with fats and oils that they must be heated until solid tissues seperate, and fats and oils become liquified. What is the removal of internal organs called?

culling   edifying   evisceration

Part of the first draft of the visuals for the meat packing processes programme.

MEAT PACKING PROCESSES

1. Before 1850, and the development of refrigeration, packing houses operated only in the winter and were often built directly adjacent to ice houses. Men cut ice from rivers and lakes all winter and stored it in icehouses for use in warm weather. (ent.)

2. During the cattle run days market centers were usually in big cities. More recently what were big city markets are becoming involved in the prepared foods industry and the production of the many varieties of processed meat products, as packing houses themselves, are being built in towns closer to the farms and ranches where livestock are raised. (ent.)

3. Processed meats may come from almost any edible part of domestic animals. Many edible organs and lesser parts of meat cuts go into these products. The removal of viscera, or internal organs, from an animal is called evisceration. Where are most processed meat products made?

   small towns   big cities*   on farms

4. Some meat cuts are so impregnated with fats and oils that they must be heated until solid tissues separate and fats and oils become liquified. This process is called rendering. What is the removal of internal organs called?

   culling   edifying   evisceration*

5. Right. When a product is designated as "inedible" or condemned, precautions are taken to "denature" it. This means chemicals are poured over it which give it a distinctive color and unpleasant odor so it cannot be mistaken as edible. By what means does rendering break down fats and oils?

   (chemicals   heat*   compression)

6. To achieve various flavors in meat it is sometimes put through one or several curing methods. Curing meat also retards bacterial action which partially preserves a product. Salt is the primary curing agent. Other additives may include: sugar, vinegar, and spices. When a condemned product is given a distinctive color and odor, what does it do to the product?

   (denature it*   coalesce it   coagulate it)

Revised draft of visuals.

MEAT PACKING PROCESSES

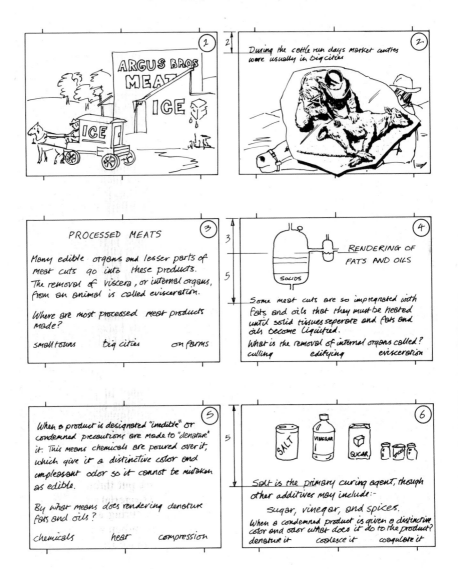

Rough visuals of the cards with drawings and text.

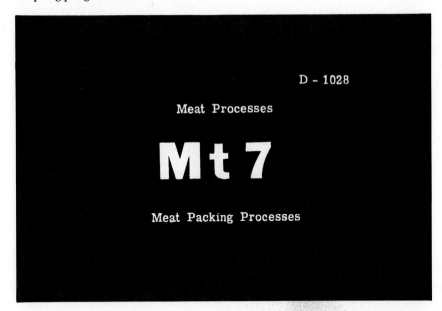

The final cards for the programme.

2

During the cattle run days
market centers were usually
in big cities.

3

PROCESSED MEATS

Many edible organs and lesser
parts of meat cuts go into these
products. The removal of viscera,
or internal organs, from an
animal is called evisceration.

Where are most processed
meat products   made ?

small towns   big cities   on farms

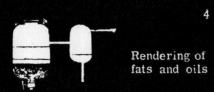

4

Rendering of
fats and oils

Some meat cuts are so impregnated
with fats and oils that they must be
heated until solid tissues separate.

What is the removal of
internal organs called ?

culling   edifying   evisceration

5

When a product is designated "inedible"
or condemned, precautions are made
to "denature" it. This means chemicals
are poured over it which give it a
distinctive color and unpleasant odor
so it cannot be mistaken as edible.

By what means does rendering
break down fats and oils ?

chemicals   heat   compression

6

Salt is the primary curing agent though other additives may include: sugar, vinegar, and spices.

When a condemned product is given a distinctive color and odor what does it do to a product?

denature it   coalesce it   coagulate it

7

Meat may be submerged in liquid cure, may be dry-salt cured just on the surface, or internally injected with a curing solution.

Why is meat cured?

for flavor   to preserve   both

Whether you realise it or not, however, you may also have drilled it into the student that this rule is true only for verbs that end in *k*! Faced with the verb *swim*, the student may be unsure.

Now, suppose you give the verb *watch* for the student to work with. The singular form is watch*es*. For you, the lesson is: watch out! You have not prepared the student for the *es* ending, which is a change from the point we are making. In programmed instruction, this is a separate issue and should be treated in another module.

The same holds true for the example 'He cries.' You *must* prepare your pupil for the change from *cry*, which ends in *y*, to *cries*, which ends in *ies*, when the subject is *he*.

Beware of *she* or *it*. You dare not assume that the student knows that they use the same verb form as *he*.

Meat Processes   Reference Folder   Mt 7
Meat Packing Processes

1. Before 1850, and the development of refrigeration, packing houses operated only in the winter and were often built directly adjacent to ice houses. Men cut ice from rivers and lakes all winter and stored it in icehouses for use in warm weather.

2. During the cattle run days market centers were usually in big cities. More recently what were big city markets are becoming involved in the prepared foods industry and the production of the many varieties of processed meat products, as packing houses themselves, are being built in towns closer to the farms and ranches where livestock are raised.

3. Processed meats may come from almost any edible part of domestic animals. Many edible organs and lesser parts of meat cuts go into these products. The removal of viscera, or internal organs, from an animal is called evisceration. Where are most processed meat products made? (small towns) (big cities) (on farms)

4. Some meat cuts are so impregnated with fats and oils that they must be heated until solid tissues separate and fats and oils become liquified. This process is called rendering. What is the removal of internal organs called? (culling) (edifying) (evisceration)

5. Right. When part or all of a meat product is designated "inedible" or condemned, precautions are generally made to "denature" it. One method of denaturing is to pour chemicals over it which give it a distinctive color and unpleasant odor so it cannot be mistaken as edible. By what means does rendering denature fats and oils? (chemicals) (heat) (compression)

6. To achieve various flavors in meat it is sometimes put through one or several curing methods. Curing meat also retards bacterial action which partially preserves a product. Salt is the primary curing agent, though other additives may include sugar, vinegar, and spices. When chemical or physical changes are made in a product to alter its original state so that it will not be used as edible product, what does it do to the product? (denature it) (coalesce it) (coagulate it)

The reference folder which carries all the text for the audio track.

18   Farther fields

Back at the beginning of Chapter 1, I made reference to a vehicle/ multimedia centre called a drug-mobile, designed by my friend Richard Thorp. A modified mobile home with a 30 foot rear projection screen, it featured twelve 35mm slide projectors, three film units and stereo audio track with control track; all were pre-programmed through a digital programmer and decoder. Needless to say, it was a spectacular operation.

This is indicative of the way much audiovisual is going these days. Writers and producers are experimenting endlessly, vying with each other in their efforts to produce those fantastic effects that have come to be known as multimedia.

Definitions of multimedia vary. Some of those found in the more academic works are so involved, not to mention fatuous, that they are hard to make sense of at all.

My own tendency is to categorise the term as a convenient waste-basket used to describe the combining of various audiovisual techniques in order to capture/increase viewer attention and drive home a programme's message. Thus, a presentation might use sound, light, slides and film; or simulation on a level that includes sight, sound, movement and odour; or a combining of film, living actors and moving stages. Every world fair and major international industrial/cultural exposition extends the boundaries farther.

No one knows where it will all end. Indeed, no one *can* know. Each new technical development, each step forward in such fields as film, optics, miniaturisation, computer graphics and the like cannot but lead to new efforts, new evolutions and amplifications in AV approach.

How effective multimedia is depends on the individual show. I have a sneaking suspicion, however, that often it offers more flash than fundamentals; that the audience departs dazzled rather than enlightened. A screen on which six images are projected simultaneously, while multiple speakers blare contrapuntal cacophanies, may hypnotise viewers but it

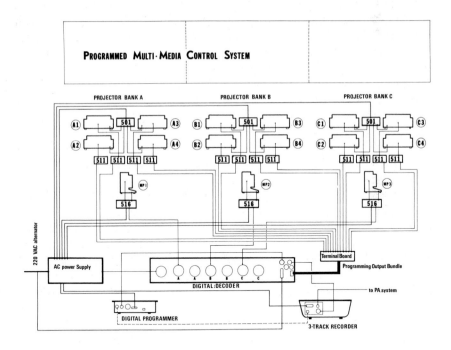

Drug-Mobile diagrams courtesy of Richard L. Thorp.

does not necessarily sell the product. Often it confuses more than it convinces.

This is not to deny that some such efforts work out beautifully nor to argue that you should forego experimenting with the methodology. It might be wise, though, to bear in mind that audio that does not make a point is merely noise and pointless video comes out as little more than glare.

What really counts is the fact that AV today is a field virtually without limits—or at least with only such limits as the imagination of the conceptualiser/writer may impose.

Consider, for example, an innovative Postal Service training programme called the Management Action Series. Designed to present management trainees with the sort of 'real life' dilemmas that they will face on the job, it combines location-filmed incidents with videotaped studio segments. More than two hours of filmed/taped incidents are included in each unit, in fragments running from 90 seconds to 3½ minutes. Student response involves taking whatever action is necessary to handle the imaginary situation, from filling out accident reports to counselling employees, developing training plans to analysing crisis causes. It is simulation on a grand scale.

Contrast this with the 'Great Map' AV presentation at Oklahoma City's National Cowboy Hall of Fame and Western Heritage Center. Here coloured lights flash on and off on a giant (32 × 48 foot) relief map of the United States in coordination with a tape recording that outlines the nation's growth in terms of pioneer trails, extension of railroads, and establishment and expansion of settlements. Supplementing this presentation is a printed brochure (remember Chapter 11, Setting It in Context?) that describes how the map came into being and reprints the tape's narration.

As yet, no standard format has evolved for scripting a multimedia project. As is so often the case in AV, you are on your own.

The only issue in such scripting, actually, is intelligibility. However you decide to tackle the problem, just be sure the people to whom you are going to present your work can understand what you are talking about.

To that end, use any or all of the techniques offered in this book plus whatever innovations of your own divising as strike you as potentially effective. Sometimes, you may decide that a particularly detailed production script may do the job; at other times, a storyboard or perhaps even some sort of graph or flow chart may be better.

At no time, however, should you forget the possibility that your best bet may be a clever treatment that captures the essence of your project *without* production details. Often it is simply too much to expect that your sponsor will be able to follow a complicated shot list. It may be better to limit yourself to something like 'Simultaneously we see stills of what is going on

INTRODUCTION

The Great Map was of prime importance in the mind of Dean Krakel, Managing Director of the Hall, during the early planning stages of the Hall's exhibit and program development.

Museums throughout the country were visited during the search for a map that would suggest the one the Director had in mind, but it was up to Chief Curator Juan Menchaca and his staff to interpret the idea, plan and construct our map. Many years' experience in the design and construction of museum exhibits and dioramas enabled Juan to develop the special material and processes used in modeling the thirty-two by forty-eight foot relief map of the United States. The concept is unique. The map is not a flat representation with raised features, but is tilted toward the viewers and curved to suggest the curvature of the earth's surface.

A tape recording is coordinated with multi-colored lights to show in historical sequence the development of settlements, trails, and railroads across the county.

For the first-time visitor especially, the map lecture is a helpful introduction to the history of the West and the scope of the exhibits in the Cowboy Hall of Fame.
- - - Compiled and written by Kathrine Binkley.

BACKGROUND AND MAP LECTURE

Welcome to the National Cowboy Hall of Fame and Western Heritage Center. This Center is a national memorial recognized by an act of Congress on August 5th, 1957. This building is dedicated to the courageous men and women who pioneered the vast and rich empire known as the American West. It is a living lesson in initiative and free enterprise which has given our generation and many generations yet unborn the richest heritage ever given a free people. We also honor the men and women who continue to make outstanding contributions to western life, which includes the cowboys, stockmen, and ranchers.

The idea for a center dedicated to the heroes of the West was conceived by Chester A. Reynolds, a manufacturer from Kansas City, Missouri, while visiting the Will Rogers Memorial in Claremore. He thought we should have a shrine to honor not only one but many outstanding men of the West. He personally visited the governors of the 17 states represented here to interest them in his idea. Funds have been provided by popular subscriptions from more than forty thousand people of the 17 states, including some twenty-five thousand school children. No government funds are involved.

Oklahoma City was selected from more than one hundred sites. A branch of one of the old cattle trails, the Chisholm Trail, ran very near the foot of Persimmon Hill, on which the building is located.

Great Map material used by permission of National Cowboy Hall of Fame and Western Heritage Center.

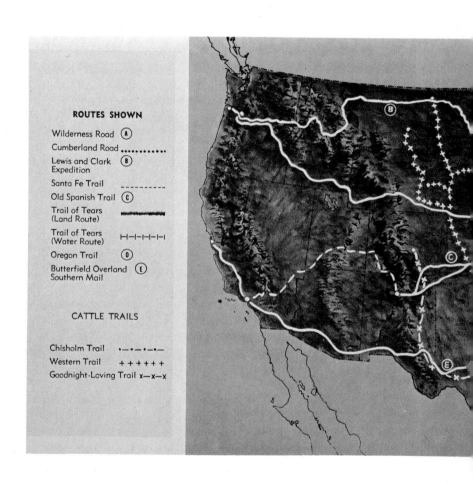

Great Map material used by permission of National Cowboy Hall of Fame and Western Heritage Center.

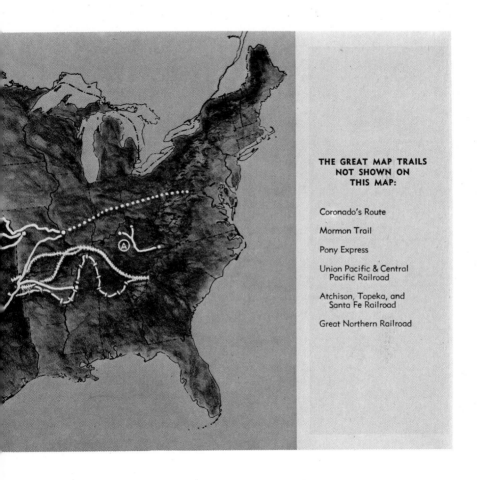

THE GREAT MAP TRAILS
NOT SHOWN ON
THIS MAP:

Coronado's Route

Mormon Trail

Pony Express

Union Pacific & Central
Pacific Railroad

Atchison, Topeka, and
Santa Fe Railroad

Great Northern Railroad

Great Map material used by permission of National Cowboy Hall of Fame and Western Heritage Center.

The architecture competition of the building design was won by Jack Begrow and Jack Brown, who designed the Center with the idea of the early days of the West in mind. When you look at the ceilings you are reminded of the tents used by the pioneers. If you drive by at night, it looks as if there are tents used by the pioneers around a campfire because a glow of light radiates from the center of the building. The water and fountains are a symbol of the importance of water to the early settlers.

The exhibition hall is one of the largest in the United States with windows extending from the ceiling to the floor to convey the feeling of the wide open spaces of the West.

The lights on the map show some of the early settlements and trails which led to the conquest of the West. You will see lights designating the capitals of the seventeen western states supporting this Center. These are: Phoenix, Arizona; Sacramento, California; Denver, Colorado; Boise, Idaho; Topeka, Kansas; Helena, Montana; Lincoln, Nebraska; Carson City, Nevada; Bismarck, North Dakota; Santa Fe, New Mexico; Oklahoma City, Oklahoma; Salem, Oregon; Pierre, South Dakota; Austin, Texas; Salt Lake City, Utah; Olympia, Washington; and Cheyenne, Wyoming.

In the early 1500's the Spaniards arrived in the New World seeking gold. They established forts along the lower eastern coast. One of the lights is St. Augustine, Florida, oldest city in the United States. The top white light off the eastern coast is an English colony, the lost colony of Roanoke. It consisted of about 221 men, women and children. Three years after its founding, when supplies arrived from England in 1591, all that remained was the word "Croatoan" carved on a tree. No trace of the settlers was found.

Years before these ill-fated English people had arrived, Mexico had become a Spanish colony and exploring parties had been sent northward. One of these leaders, Francisco Vasquez de Coronado, left Mexico City in 1540 and starting at Compostela, traveled north along the coast through the states of Sinaloa and Sonora, and into our present state of New Mexico. He was looking for the legendary Cibola, one of the Seven Cities of Gold. Disappointed in finding only Zuni Indian pueblos, he continued to the north and east as far as our present state of Kansas, where he hoped to find the gold he was seeking in Quivira. Again disappointed, he returned to New Mexico by a slightly different route.

On the East Coast the French, Dutch, and English were arriving. The French were seeking one thing — furs. The top green lights are Montreal, Three Rivers, and Quebec on the St. Lawrence River. Below are the Dutch in the Hudson River Valley settlements, and in Virginia, Jamestown is being settled by the English.

The English began to arrive in great numbers and carved their homes and settlements out of the wilderness. Eventually there were thirteen English colonies along the Eastern seaboard.

Great Map material used by permission of National Cowboy Hall of Fame and Western Heritage Center.

in each of the sports activity areas: bowling, tennis, swimming, diving, riding, racquet ball . . . perhaps with a full-screen comedy topper of a turtle race, ping-pong, or a skate-boarder falling into the pool.' The details you can save for the producer.

For a sample of how one relatively uncomplicated multimedia show was handled, four pages from a three-screen script for a programme designed to help train charity solicitors are shown on pp.244–247. Using simple cartoon figures, voice-over dialogue and discussion during the 'Stop Tape' periods, it achieved maximum results with a minimum budget.

Whatever your project, know that in the last analysis you and your imagination are in command. In multimedia, as everywhere else in AV, you start with a topic, an audience and a purpose; you work up an idea, concept and key point, and search out a logical approach and a means of presentation. All these factors are then incorporated in the proposal, treatment or production script.

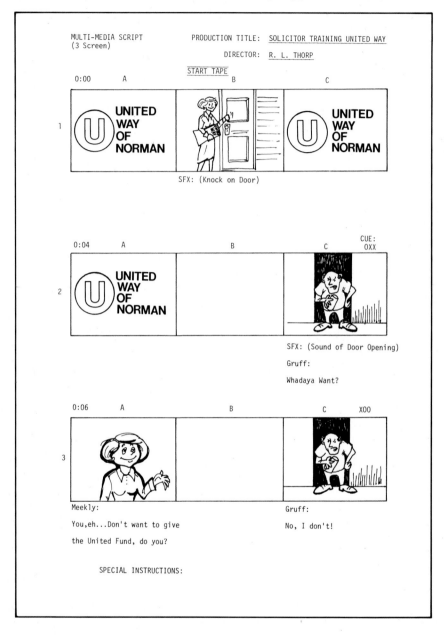

Excerpt from United Fund multimedia script used courtesy of Richard L. Thorp.

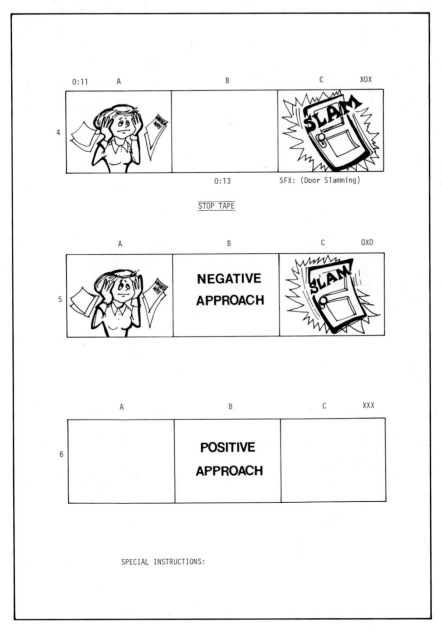

Excerpt from United Fund multimedia script continued—used courtesy of Richard L. Thorp.

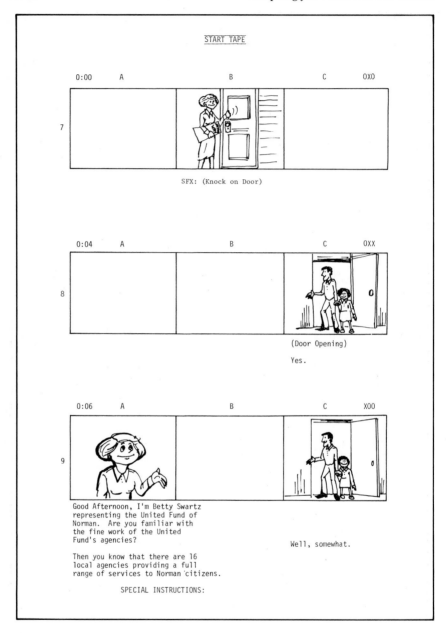

Excerpt from United Fund multimedia script continued—used courtesy of Richard L. Thorp.

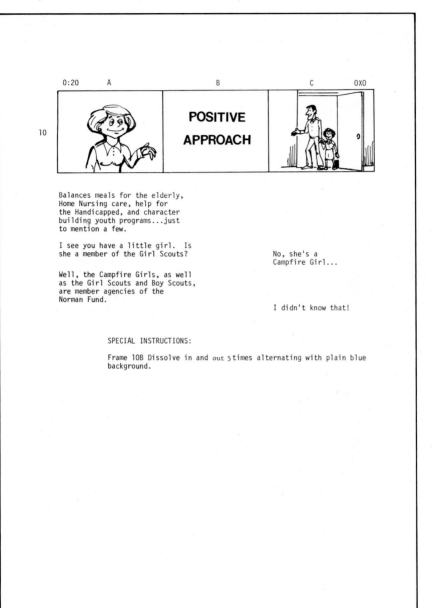

Balances meals for the elderly,
Home Nursing care, help for
the Handicapped, and character
building youth programs...just
to mention a few.

I see you have a little girl. Is
she a member of the Girl Scouts?

No, she's a
Campfire Girl...

Well, the Campfire Girls, as well
as the Girl Scouts and Boy Scouts,
are member agencies of the
Norman Fund.

I didn't know that!

SPECIAL INSTRUCTIONS:

Frame 10B Dissolve in and out 5 times alternating with plain blue
background.

*Excerpt from United Fund multimedia script continued—used courtesy of
Richard L. Thorp.*

Afterword

It is, of course, the best job in the world.
And the worst.
The easiest.
And the hardest.
The most satisfying.
And the most frustrating.

Naturally, what I am talking about is audiovisual scripting. But not *just* scripting, for what I say applies equally to almost any creative activity.

Most work today involves your time, your muscle and maybe even your brain. AV scripting takes vision also.

Do I need to tell you that this moves AV scripting over to the unique side of life's ledger? Vision is neither common nor does it always come easily. It brings with it the gnawing anguish of ideas that refuse to surface when you need them, and ideas that do surface but then are rejected by your colleagues and/or clients.

That kind of thing can be hard to take. Many find it too painful to endure.

On the other hand, if you spark to the excitement that ideas bring; if you enjoy the stimulus of vision, of seeing things not as they are but as they might be; if you thrill to the challenge of finding new ways to catch interest, reach viewers, then maybe scripting *is* the kind of calling you are cut out for.

To put it another way, if what you want is work without strains and stresses, something you can leave behind when you walk out of the shop, scripting is not for you. Whereas, if, on occasion, you lose track of hours because your work is your fun also; if 'mounting, goal-oriented inner tension' sometimes counts for more with you than mindlessness or a cushy spot, then consider scripting.

Scripting is a field in which your success, your failure, your pleasure and your fulfilment *all* depend on you. Nowhere are you more in command of your own destiny.

I hope you like that idea. And that you have the intelligence and imagination and backbone to stick with it. This is a weird and wonderful game you are sitting in on—poker with everything wild. The sky is no limit.

Further reading

Bibliographies in this field tend to scare me. Too many go in for pages of citations from scholarly journals and assorted esoterica.

Here is the other, practical side of the coin: a selection of works I've found useful and which, I hope, you will also.

Brown, Lewis, Harcleroad. *AV Instruction Media and Methods*, 3rd ed. McGraw-Hill, 1969.

Eastman Kodak Co. *Basic Titling and Animation for Motion Pictures*, 2nd ed. (1970) and *Basic Production Techniques for Motion Pictures* (1971).

Edmonds, R. *Scriptwriting for the Audio-Visual Media.* Teachers College Press, 1978.

Gillis, D. *The Art of Media Instruction.* Crescendo Book Publications, 1973.

Halas, J. (ed.) *Visual Scripting.* Focal Press, 1976.

Herman, L. *Educational Films: Writing, Directing, and Producing for Classroom, Television, and Industry.* Crown, 1965.

Hilliard, R. L. *Writing for Television and Radio*, 3rd ed. Hastings House, 1976.

Kemp, J. *Planning and Producing Audiovisual Materials*, 3rd ed. Crowell, 1975.

Lee & Misiorowski. *Script Models: A Handbook for the Media Writer.* Hastings House, 1978.

Lewin, F. *The Soundtrack in Nontheatrical Motion Pictures.* Society of Motion Picture and Television Engineers, 1959.

Madsen, R. *Animated Film: Concepts, Methods, Uses.* Interland, 1969.

Parker, N. S. *Audiovisual Script Writing.* Rutgers University Press, 1968.

Smith, R. W. *Technical Writing.* Barnes & Noble, 1963.

Stork, L. *Industrial and Business Films.* Phoenix House, 1962.

Swain, D. V. *Techniques of the Selling Writer.* University of Oklahoma Press, 1974. *Film Scriptwriting: A Practical Manual.* Hastings House, 1976.

AV idiom

It's hard to know where to start or stop on a glossary of this sort. A majority of terms obviously are lifted from other fields or appear in any good dictionary so, in the end, selection must of necessity be arbitrary.

It should also be pointed out that usage varies from area to area and shop to shop. Often, therefore, your best guide is the phraseology you encounter on the job.

On the other hand, I know from experience that it does help to have at least a minimal technical vocabulary to fall back on. To that end, I hope this brief listing helps.

adaptation. Presentation in one medium of work originally designed for another, as in the case of a film developed from a novel.

angle. Positioning of camera in relation to subject: high angle, low angle, 45° angle, etc.

animation. Simulation of life or movement in inanimate objects/drawings by cinematic means.

aspect ratio. The ratio of a picture's width to its height. In film, this ordinarily is four to three.

audio. The sound portion of an AV programme. It includes narration, music, sound effects and dialogue.

background (BG). Sound, setting or action subordinate to a given scene's foreground/dominant elements.

busy. Setting or action which, through inclusion of unnecessary detail, distracts from the desired impression.

cartridge projector. A slide projector whose storage unit keeps the slides in proper order for programmed projection.

close-up (CU). A picture that emphasises a particular feature of a subject by showing it in disproportionately large size.

commentary. The voice-over spoken remarks/explanation that often accompanies a programme's visual presentation.

continuity. The sequence of events to be presented in a programme. The smooth linking of one event or picture to another.

credits. Titles which name the people who worked on a programme.

cue. A signal to begin some specified fragment of a programme—a movement, a speech, a strain of music, or the like.

director. The person who supervises a programme's production, translating the script into audiovisual form.

dissolver. A unit that cross-fades projection from one slide projector to another in multimedia productions.

establishing shot. A shot that makes clear the relationship of one element in a picture to another. Ordinarily, this means that it takes in all or a considerable portion of the setting in a long shot.

filmstrip. Still photographs and/or graphics presented on a strip of 35mm film, with or without accompanying sound.

format. Established pattern for presentation of a particular type of script or AV programme.

frame. One of the individual still photos which, collectively, comprises a motion picture.

IN, UP, DOWN, OUT, etc. Terms used to describe introduction, conclusion and handling of volume of a programme's sound elements.

layout. Visual presentation for planning purposes of a proposed display.

lead-in. A programme's visual or aural introduction to a particular subject or aspect of a subject.

lighting set-up. Arrangement of camera, lights, etc. for a given picture or pictures.

location. A natural setting (as contrasted with a sound stage) where a programme, in whole or in part, is to be shot.

long shot. A picture that relates a subject to its background, as in an establishing shot.

loop. Film packaged in a cartridge for special projects, end spliced to beginning to permit continuing repetition.

medium shot. A picture dominated by a particular subject (person, house, car, etc.) with only incidental background.

miniature (model). A small-scale simulation of a set or object.

montage. Assortment of photos or artwork items arranged on a display surface for visual interest. In film, fast cuts and optical effects combined to build emotion or provided time/space transitions.

multimedia programme. One that combines a variety of audio and video techniques (frequently including split screen work, multiple sound tracks, etc.) in a pattern designed to seize audience attention.

narrator, narration. The person who delivers the voice-over comments which accompany a programme's visual presentation. The commentary which he/she delivers.

off screen (OS). Action or sound closely related to a picture but not included in it, as when an unseen character cries 'Help!'

optical effect. Changes in a film's pictorial image (fades, dissolves, wipes, etc.) which are created in the laboratory rather than the camera or editing room.

orientation shot. Another name for an establishing shot.

overlay. Acetate cover sheet that adds words or pictorial elements to an existing picture.

point or view (POV). A picture from the position held by a particular character.

poop sheet. Written record identifying shots, people, etc. in a photo or film shot.

producer. The person who supervises/coordinates a programme's overall production.

production script. The script from which a programme is actually produced; another term for shooting script.

proposal. Summary of proposed AV project, presented as interestingly/persuasively as possible.

shooting script. A script that describes each picture to be included in a given programme.

shot. A single picture. In film, those pictures recorded by a motion picture camera in a single run.

shot list. Another term for shooting script.

slide show. Series of 35mm slides arranged in predetermined order and (ordinarily) presented with interpretive voice-over commentary.

sound effects (FX, SFX). Any non-voice or music sound (wind howling, engines roaring, knock at door) included in a programme.

sound on film (SOF). Film with a sound track.

Special effects. Photographic effects obtainable only under controlled conditions and through use of specialised techniques.

splice. Physical joining of two pieces of tape or film.

split screen. Different pictures shown on portions of a single screen at the same time.

sponsor. The person/group/organisation for whom an AV programme is produced; generally, whoever puts up the money.

sting. A sudden, emphatic sound, often musical, used to punctuate an AV presentation.

stock shot. Picture taken from existing sources rather than shot specifically for a given programme.

storyboard. A plan/outline of a programme set forth in sketches of still photos.

superimposition. One photographic image placed on top of another in order to create a new effect.

synchronisation. Precise matching of sound to action, as when voice fits lip movements exactly.

target audience. The group to which an AV or other presentation is intended to appeal.

teaching machine. A device for presenting a sequence of informational items to students in such a manner as to make possible mastery of the subject with minimal waste motion.

time-lapse photography. Exposure of single frames of film at set intervals so that projection time is compressed, making it possible to see flowers grow or the like.

titles. Screened words which provide information about a programme.

treatment. Summary of a proposed project's contents, elaborating on the project proposal and 'selling' it to the client.

two-shot (three-shot, etc.). Shot that includes two (three, etc.) people, often in conversation.

variable-speed projector. A specialised unit that can project material at assorted speeds, ranging from single frame to full sound speed. often used as teaching device, with the student controlling progression of the material.

video. The visual/pictorial aspect of an AV programme.

videotape. Magnetic tape which records both sound and picture.

voice-over (VO). Spoken lines from an unseen source which accompany a programme's visuals.

VTR. Videotape recording.

wild. Video shot or audio recording recorded independently of each other, with no attempt to synchronise.

Index